The Global Politics of Globalization

Are we moving inexorably towards a 'new empire' or is global civil society transforming global politics into a 'new cosmopolis'?

In *The Global Politics of Globalization*, the alternatives of 'Empire' and 'Cosmopolis' are counter-poised as representative of two antithetical conceptions and practices of world order, both historically and in the present era, and each expresses an alternative idea of human unity and community. Today global politics is embroiled in a clash of globalizations, a clash between these two opposed forms of world order. The contributions in the debate range from deep historical reflections on world civilizations, critique of neoliberal economics and imperialism, new thinking on the ideals and practices of (global) citizenship, the philosophical basis for cosmopolitan politics, and the emergence of new forms of global social forces and movements.

This book brings together a very distinguished set of contributors to explore and debate the relationship between globalization processes and world order in light of recent controversies over the return of 'empire'.

This book was previously published as a special issue of *Globalizations*.

Barry K. Gills is Professor of Global Politics at the School of Geography, Politics and Sociology at Newcastle University.

Rethinking Globalizations
Edited by Barry Gills, Newcastle University, UK

This series is designed to break new ground in the literature on globalization and its academic and popular understanding. Rather than perpetuating or simply reacting to the economic understanding of globalization, this series seeks to capture the term and broaden its eaning to encompass a wide range of issues and disciplines and convey a sense of alternative possibilities for the future.

1. Whither Globalization?
The Vortex of Knowledge and Globalization
James H. Mittelman

2. Globalization and Global History
Edited by Barry K. Gills, William R. Thompson

3. Rethinking Civilization
Communication and terror in the global village
Majid Tehranian

4. Globalisation and Contestation
The New Great Counter-Movement
Ronaldo Munck

5. Global Activism
Ruth Reitan

6. Globalization, the City and Civil Society in Pacific Asia
Edited by Mike Douglass, K.C. Ho and Giok Ling Ooi

7. Challenging Euro-America's Politics of Identity
The Return of the Native
Jorge Luis Andrade Fernandes

8. The Global Politics of Globalization
"Empire" vs "Cosmopolis"
Edited by Barry K. Gills

9. The Globalization of Environmental Crisis
Edited by Jan Oosthoek and Barry K. Gills

The Global Politics of Globalization

"Empire" vs "Cosmopolis"

Edited by Barry K. Gills

Routledge
Taylor & Francis Group

LONDON AND NEW YORK

First published 2008 by Routledge
2 Park Square, Milton Park, Abingdon, Oxon, OX14 4RN

Simultaneously published in the USA and Canada
by Routledge
270 Madison Avenue, New York, NY 10016

Routledge is an imprint of the Taylor & Francis Group, an informa business

Transferred to Digital Printing 2009

© 2008 Edited by Barry K Gills

Typeset in Times Roman by Techset Composition, Salisbury, UK

British Library Cataloguing in Publication Data
A catalogue record for this book is available from the British Library

Library of Congress Cataloging in Publication Data

ISBN 10: 0-415-42518-2 (hbk)
ISBN 10: 0-415-49503-2 (pbk)

ISBN 13: 978-0-415-42518-6 (hbk)
ISBN 13: 978-0-415-49503-5 (pbk)

Contents

In Memoriam: Andre Gunder Frank
(24 February 1929 to 23 April 2005)

'Prophet in the Wilderness'

Andre Gunder Frank, perhaps the most prolific and controversial development economist and sociologist of the post-war era, best known as the author of 'Dependency' theory, died on Saturday in Luxembourg, age 76, after a long battle against cancer. His opus includes some 40 books and nearly a thousand articles and other pieces, in numerous languages, spanning 50 years of global political and economic development. His life and work was full of movement, argument and counter-argument. Always ahead of his time, his achievement was to repeatedly stand tradition and received theory on their head in field after field (especially economics, development studies, sociology and history) and issue after issue. Decades later, many of his ideas have now been generally accepted, as events proved his analysis and predictions accurate: the stubborn persistence of Third World poverty and 'underdevelopment' despite foreign investment and because of unmanageable debt-servicing imposed by foreign creditors; the failure of 'really existing capitalism' in much of the Third World as well as the failure of 'really existing socialism' in the former 'Second World' (including China) and their re-integration to global capitalism and subsequent partial 'Third-Worldization'; the reappearance of persistent structural economic crisis and imbalance in the West (including Japan and the US) and in global capitalism as a whole and the ineffectiveness of Keynesian and fiscal stimulatory means to redress this; the polarizing and fragmenting consequences of 'globalization', rendering nation states largely incapable of offering real solutions and giving rise to new social movements on a global scale which now carry forward the hope for progressive change, and at the same time to new rightist, nationalist, ethnic and religious fundamentalist movements that may eventually undermine the democratic culture needed by the former; and finally, a profound rejection of traditional 'Eurocentric' theories and understandings of global development and world history in favour of an alternative 'humanocentric' world-historical perspective, which views the 'rise of the West' to global dominance as occurring very 'late' and likely to be temporary, and in fact already passing into 'history'.

He was born Andreas Frank, in Berlin, the son of a pacifist novelist who took him into exile at age 4 to escape Hitler's Germany. The 'Gunder' was added by his high school team mates as a cruel jibe about his slowness on the track field, by comparison with a then famous Swedish runner, Gundar Haag. (As Gunder later explained, 'Unfortunately, I did not know how the name was spelled'.) His youthful experiences in Hollywood, USA exposed him to his father's circle, which included Thomas Mann and Greta Garbo. He became a Keynesian while studying economics at Swarthmore College, but by the end of his PhD at the University of Chicago (begun in 1950) he had rebelled against his monetarist tutor Milton Friedman and against all development thinking of US origin, which he saw as 'part of the problem' rather than the solution. His rejection of mainstream economics, in favour of an 'equity before efficiency' approach focussed on the importance of social and political factors, turned him into a maverick who spent the next 50 years energetically and cogently challenging established wisdom and policy on 'development' around the world. His early work established the concept of 'general productivity' (later known as 'total productivity') and its centrality to measuring 'Human Capital and Economic Growth' (1960). It was his 1967 publication of the essay 'Sociology of Development and Underdevelopment of Sociology' (rejected by a dozen journals) and his first book, *Capitalism and Underdevelopment in Latin America* (also 1967) that catapulted him to international fame, laying the basis for what was to be known as Dependency theory, and its later spin-off, World System theory.

The decisive turning point in his career came when he visited Cuba in 1960 (Che Guevara wrote to Frank asking for help in transforming Cuba's dependent economy) and Ghana and Guinea in Africa. He spent the rest of the 1960s living and working in Latin America, mainly in Brazil, Mexico and Chile, analysing their underdevelopment. The Peruvian theorist Anibal Quijano introduced Gunder to his wife of 30 years, Marta Fuentes, a Chilean who shared his passion for social justice and dedication to 'change the world'. His students at the University of Brasilia included Theotonio Dos Santos and Ruy Mauro Marini, both of whom later became Dependency theorists in their own right. Frank's trenchant analysis of underdevelopment in Brazil, Mexico and Latin America argued directly against not only Keynesian and Monetarist economics and 'Modernization' theory, but also against orthodox Marxism and communist party theory and policy, as well as criticizing the 'indigenous' structural reformism of Fernando Henrique Cardoso (once welcomed by Frank at Santiago airport as he fled from the military coup in Brazil in 1964 and later President of Brazil in the 1990s) and Raul Prebisch of CEPAL/ECLA, and the US-sponsored 'Alliance for Progress'. His unrelenting attacks on the inefficacy of existing policies and reformist ideas, and his preference for political revolution (as in Cuba) and socialism earned him a persona non grata status in the US for 15 years.

He and Marta lived in Santiago, Chile, during the Allende years, where his ideas were coming into favour. Allende, then President of the Senate, met Gunder at the airport to prevent him being instantly deported. Thereafter, their home became a centre of refuge and discussion for intellectuals from across Latin America, until the military coup by General Pinochet on 11 September 1973 abruptly ended the socialist experiment, democracy and the lives of countless friends. It was another decisive turning point in Frank's life and career. While Chile became a monetarist 'heaven' run by Milton Friedman's 'Chicago Boys', Frank became (again) a political exile, this time back to Europe (arriving back in Berlin exactly 40 years after fleeing Hitler's regime) and dedicated the next 20 years to analysing the global crisis and the rampant failures of neo-liberalism and 'Reaganomics'. It was in this period that he moved beyond Dependency theory, saying that while dependency itself was alive and kicking in the world, its usefulness as a guide to political action had come and gone ('Dependence is Dead! Long Live Dependence and the Class Struggle', 1972). His subsequent work turned increasingly to analysis of the 'global crisis of capital accumulation', in both historical and contemporary perspective. His thinking ran parallel to that of others working in the same track, including his long time friend Samir Amin (whom he met in Paris during the 'events' of 1968), Giovanni Arrighi (who first introduced the 'world system' approach to Frank), and Immanuel Wallerstein. In the 1970s, they together developed the analysis known as 'World-Systems theory'.

Frank's copious work on 'the crisis' chronicled the disastrous onset of 'market ideology' and the return of 'efficiency before equity' in theory and policy. He predicted (in 1974) that the Third World's response to the global crisis would be predicated upon increasing exports to world markets and that this transition to export-led growth would be organized under authoritarian regimes (including in East Asia as well as Latin America), while it would inevitably lead to a deeper global depression and the amassing of gigantic unsustainable debts – that is, to the Debt Crisis and 'vastly increased foreign dependence'. In the end, Frank felt that 'development' itself had 'all but disappeared' from discussion, replaced by 'only economic or debt crisis management'. He continued to analyse the tendencies of globalization, including the replacement of productive investment by financial speculation and the consequent increase in imbalances between regions and countries of the world economic system. He argued that increasing marketization and privatization as responses to the crisis would only further exacerbate underlying poverty, inequality and marginalization, leading to tremendous pressures on democratic political culture and to the inexorable rise of both new progressive and reactionary social movements to fill the void left by the nation state's incapacity and unwillingness to deliver real change.

The final phase of his life and work saw him returning to world development as the main subject of analysis, but this time across all of world history. Working with a co-author (Frank and Gills, 1993) he offered an alternative to Eurocentrism which placed the contemporary crisis and globalization in a much longer historical perspective based on the long cycles of world system development going back not only centuries but even millennia. This work led him to conclude, in his final radical rejection of received theories, that we should be brave enough to reject 'capitalism' itself as a 'scientific' concept, as well as 'feudalism' and even 'socialism' as separate 'modes of production' nor should we any longer look for any real historical 'transitions' between them. He argued that 'too many big patterns in world history appear to transcend or persist despite all apparent alterations in the mode of production'. His final position therefore encapsulated a lifetime of movement and critique, including of his own previous positions. In his penultimate and perhaps best work, *ReOrient* (1998), and in the unfinished sequel, *ReOrient the 19th Century*, he explored the historical method in new directions, again challenging received theory about the 'rise of the West' and the supposed role played by the market and 'free' trade as opposed to coercion and imperialism. His final analysis of global development included the idea that it is the system as a whole that is the inescapable framework of both analysis and practice and that any 'de-linking' from it at 'local' or national level is unrealistic, nor will global development ever be 'uniform' across the world. He felt that shifts in (temporary) competitive advantage (not always achieved by non-coercive or 'market' means alone) and the presence or absence of 'hegemonic power' were historically persistent patterns that in a sense define the long-term development of the world system. However, he always embodied the idea of both 'the pessimism of the intellect' as well as the 'optimism of the will' and so left a final admonition: the real 'global majority', the disadvantaged of the world, should and would act to protect their lives and interests and to improve social existence. He believed to the end that change for the better remains possible.

As a person, Gunder Frank was principled and uncompromising, yet always willing to listen to the evidence and an opposing argument, and even to accept that he was wrong and to change his views. Above all, he was always courageous and never afraid to be unpopular. He gave people the answers they needed to hear not the answers they wanted to hear, even if they didn't always want to hear them. He could be difficult at times but his life was always about heart, and he was deeply caring and humane and had many long-time friends. Within 24 hours of his death, his family received a thousand email and other messages of condolence and support from around the globe. He was above all a generous man, both to his friends and to his critics. He was combative intellectually and thrived upon this approach, but he also possessed a wonderful dry sense of humour, that endeared him to all who knew him well. His attitude to life can perhaps be summed up in his phrase, said to his third and final wife, Alison: 'Only two people in this world are always right – the Dalai Lama [whom he met and liked, but didn't always agree with] and me', followed by 'and only two people in this world know how to load a dishwasher – the Dalai Lama and me!' Gunder Frank is survived by his two sons, Paul and Miguel and three grandchildren. He was still working until two weeks prior to his death in hospital in Luxembourg on Saturday, 23 April 2005.

Barry K. Gills
Newcastle upon Tyne

'Empire' versus 'Cosmopolis': The Clash of Globalizations

BARRY K. GILLS

'How can there be laughter, how can there be pleasure, when the whole world is burning? When you are in deep darkness, will you not ask for a lamp?'
Siddhartha Gautama, (the Buddha) from The Dhammapada, translated by Juan Mascaro.

'Pillagers of the world, they have exhausted the land by their indiscriminate plunder... A rich enemy excites their cupidity, a poor one, their lust for power. East and West alike have failed to satisfy them. To robbery, butchery, and rapine, they give the lying name of 'government' ('imperium'); they create a desolation and call it peace.'
Tacitus, Agricola (from the speech of the Briton chieftain Calgacus to his army before the battle of Mons Graupius, 84 AD, translated by H. Mattingly and S.A. Handford)

'The cloud-capped towers, the gorgeous palaces, the solemn temples, the great globe itself, yea, all which it inherit, shall dissolve, and like this insubstantial pageant faded, leave not a rack behind.'
William Shakespeare, The Tempest, Act IV, Scene I

The Clash of Globalizations

For a brief moment, in recent memory, globalization was a term that meant we were fast arriving at an end of history in which the final outcome was already predetermined by the laws of market economics, liberal democracy, and technological progress. There were no real choices, only the laws of history. Now we have awoken, as if from a slumber, to find once again that life and history are never quite so simple, and to realise that we can never abdicate from our responsibility to make difficult moral and political decisions or confront the perils and opportunities of our own times and common destiny.

In our present state of heightened intellectual and political awareness of the dilemmas of globalization and of its uncertainties as opposed to supposed certainties, we come face to face with old enemies and old friends, now in the guise of archetypal forms, which we will name 'Empire' and 'Cosmopolis'. These words represent two antithetical conceptions and practices of world-consciousness and world order, though both express an ideal of human

unity and community. Far from being new and recent phenomena, these concepts convey a sense of perennial historical tension, deeply embedded in history and the human psyche. As archetypes, they both constitute and reveal the deep structure beneath apparent events. Their power to inform and motivate both what we know and how we act is thus far greater than we may readily admit. Each represents a very different understanding of the nature and future of globalization.

I will argue that the contest between these concepts, and the forms of consciousness and action they animate, is at the very heart of the globalization debate. Moreover, this clash of globalizations, between Empire and Cosmopolis, is in my view the underlying defining element of the politics of the post Cold War era. It is no exaggeration to conclude that the future of humanity depends upon our serious reflection on this contest and the actions we take as a consequence of this reflection. The historic contestation between Empire and Cosmopolis is a titanic struggle for the 'soul' of humanity itself. At stake are the defining aspects and experiences of global civilization, both now and for generations to come. Thus, this struggle is of concern to all, not merely to a few.

Globalization, both as a concept and a research agenda, and the emerging field of global history to which it is related, is inextricably linked to the idea of humanity as a whole, and not confined to any national, ethnic, religious or cultural fragment of it. In this sense, the debate about globalization and its historical direction and ethical content is about our understanding of the world as a single place and a single community. This kind of knowledge construction self-consciously engages with normative and moral issues, with a critical analysis of the past, present and future, and more so than any simplistic, narrow or economistic conceptions of globalization would permit.[1]

On the one hand, we are witnessing a renewed impetus to the formation of world-consciousness, as globalizing processes bring humanity into intensified physical and communicative proximity. These same processes, and contending globalizations, are rapidly and profoundly altering the social relations and social networks that compose the very basis of the human community, whether locally or globally constituted, and the two are increasingly intertwined. It may even be the case that this new experience of global community is having the effect of renewing the desire for perfection in the social universe; a deep human need that has animated so much social activity throughout the centuries. Cosmopolis has historically tended to be perhaps more 'imaginary' or utopian than Empire. Nevertheless, the impetus to Cosmopolis has made itself felt in repeated aspirations for a universal state, universal peace, a universal church or faith, and a perfect justice and social order – as pursued by so many millenarian and other radical and revolutionary social movements throughout history, including in the present era. Thus, we can identify the possibility of a receding Empire and a resurgent Cosmopolis, where the latter re-emerges as a potent force of the human imagination and a guide to a new global politics of hope and genuine progress.

On the other hand, we simultaneously face a powerful danger. This danger takes the form of the temptation either to wilfully or unwittingly turn away from the opportunity to achieve greater human unity, and succumb to sharpened separation, alienation, and inevitably, conflict. Our existing international order, and its principles of sovereignty, has the inclination to encourage these negative tendencies, thus preventing any radical transformation of world order to a fundamentally new, more inclusive and more just form of governance.

To my mind, this is the central issue of globalization: whether humanity will embrace and enact the politics of Cosmopolis, based on ideas and practices that assign the highest value to collective responsibility for the welfare, happiness and dignity of all human beings, no matter where they may live; or whether, by will or accident, we will find ourselves caught indefinitely in the snares of Empire, engulfed by the naked pursuit of power and wealth, and surrounded by the sheer magnitude of exploitation, injustice and continued human suffering on global scale. The present rekindling of ancient enmities in many parts of the world, and of new and old rivalries, will, if unchecked, inevitably lead to a new era of global conflicts, unleashing a spiral of violence and counter-violence, fear and securitization. Empire thrives in such an environment of the politics of fear. Yet there are signs that Empire may be fundamentally weakening rather than strengthening.

It is our first premise that globalization is not leading inexorably to a pre-determined historical outcome. Neither Empire nor Cosmopolis are yet the assured end state, nor should either be understood simply as stages or phases in a linear conception of world history. These processes need to be understood as remaining historically open and undetermined, and subject to our collective will. The clash of globalizations is nevertheless certainly occurring, and the historical tension between these forms, which express radically different visions of humanity and global governance, is intensifying moment by moment. The 'outcome' of contemporary history still stands in the balance. The on-going intellectual and political debates and the myriad social struggles generated by the effects of our present form of world order (in which Empire and global capitalism take centre stage) lead us to confront the choice between Empire and Cosmopolis with renewed seriousness and historical urgency.

Finally, we should be aware that this clash of globalizations takes place both in the realm of 'mythos', where appeal to emotion and abstract symbolism is most potent, and in the realm of 'praxis', where theory becomes practical, willed social action. Of these two, 'mythos' is the more dangerous and we must beware of the manipulation that resides in the political use of mythos, whereby we are mislead by those who deploy rhetoric specifically designed to this purpose, as a deliberate form of deception and mobilisation. It is as old as history itself that political leadership and the state will seek to disguise their real intentions and present their actions in the guise of the supposed innate truth and justice of their cause. The present era is no exception, though we should not be so easily fooled this time around. Let us remember, however, that Empire is unlikely to call itself by that name or to reveal to us freely its true intentions, nor does it ever relinquish power easily.

Towards a 'New' Empire?

Rather than being new, it is more accurate to view Empire as an historical constant, having played a role in history for centuries and even millennia. Empire remains present in the contemporary era, despite formal decolonisation and systematic denial by its perpetrators. There is at present a lamentable but telling tendency, increasingly popular among some fashionable intellectual and political circles, to rehabilitate Empire. Not only do some authors recognise the role of Empire in shaping our present historical system, but they paint this contribution (in both past and present) as being very positive indeed.[2] This return to nineteenth century themes of the 'civilizing mission' is of course a revisionist history born out of the immediate context of the return of explicit imperialist practices in the early 21st century. It is also symptomatic of the idea that Empire may be the preferred solution to mounting 'disorder', i.e. the means to preserve the global status quo and see off challengers. As such, it is a warning of the potential for yet more Empire to come. We should duly take note.

Much ink has already been spilt recently debating whether we are, in the present moment, entering a new empire or a new imperialism.[3] In my view, this debate, though important and topical, sometimes misses the greater truth, which is that we have long been living with Empire and there is no sudden break with this tradition at present. On the contrary, hundreds of millions of people have been living during the past several decades in historical structures of power, domination and exploitation that they, and we, recognise as imperial. The real question therefore is not whether Empire is suddenly emerging or being born anew, but whether in fact Empire is changing and, if it is, what should or can we do about this change? In the classical theories of imperialism, Empire is fundamentally about two things: the concentration of power; and the concentration of wealth. The two are of course not mutually exclusive but complementary and reinforcing. For the past two centuries the processes of concentration of power and wealth (in this epoch linked to the global expansion of capitalism) have, by intention, primarily benefited that part of the world and those social forces we call 'The West' (though Japan long ago joined this global condominium, making the common geographical reference somewhat misleading, and today China and others in 'the East' ardently wish to be admitted to the club). It is the global dominance of this power bloc over 'the Rest' that still today centrally defines the character of Empire on global scale, and which remains most resistant to any radical transformation. We have experienced shifts within the centre of this global oligarchic power structure but not a fundamental break with the structure itself. The preservation of this structure is presented by the mainstream media and politicians as common sense, yet this disguises the fact that no real global consensus exists to legitimate this highly unequal power structure. No one, however, can fully disguise the fact that the structure as we know it is coming under increasing pressure, especially from 'below'.

In so far as the question of whether a 'new' Empire and particularly an American Empire is presently emerging, I prefer to turn this question around, and ask instead whether the (American/Global) Empire is already past its apogee, and is in fact at the beginning of a protracted decline phase. It is, nevertheless, still too early to decisively decide this debate, though we can be confident that it will become increasingly pertinent and topical as events and structures unfold and reveal their historical logic. Unexpected events may yet accelerate our perception that change in the global status quo is already more advanced than we thought.[4] There is already good and mounting evidence to suggest that the foundations of American global power, while still formidable, are not invulnerable, that they are subject to challenge, and may in fact be seriously weakening, though slowly and with as yet unpredictable long term consequences.[5] Such a downward spiral of power by one state would be consistent with history, in that no hegemony, much less global dominion, lasts forever. However, while American financial and economic power is clearly showing signs of vulnerability, its military and political power are in a quite different modality. If indeed the economic underpinnings of American hegemony are eroding, then the recourse to greater use of coercive methods of exercising control could be a direct result of this decline. The increase in the rhetoric and practice of militarization and securitization in US policy may reflect an internal perception by those now holding power that time and history are not on their side and that they must act quickly to reassert and extend control, before it becomes too late. Yet, the trend of increasing national assertiveness, accompanied by re-invigorated nationalism, is not exclusive to the US. Unfortunately, it extends to many more states, especially among the aspirant great powers of an anticipated post-hegemonic period (for example, Russia, China, India and Japan). If this trend gathers momentum, then it could become truly dangerous.[6] Those powers, peoples and social forces that have been most disadvantaged, excluded, suppressed or exploited in the passing hegemonic order will very likely be the most active during the coming hegemonic transition. If this is indeed a fairly accurate picture of the real tendencies in world order, i.e. not for the appearance of a 'new' American or Global Empire, but rather the onset of the period of gradual decline, then we must ask a further central question: how can we respond to this decline in ways that do not make the situation worse for us all, but lead away from Empire altogether and towards global Cosmopolis in its place? Can we find responses that do not lead to renewed power rivalries and conflicts but rather to increased collaboration in pursuit of common interests and goals? Can we turn this conjuncture in world history into an opportunity to build Cosmopolis? If not only the American, but also the Global Empire of the established powers and social forces is showing signs of change, how can we influence the global situation to move towards a post-imperial order? Is there a real chance for radical transformation of world order? This seems to me to be more hopeful and positive as a guide for both analysis and action in the future than asking whether a new Empire is upon us. The real question is clearly what to do about the existing imperial or hegemonic order, whether designated as American or Global, as its foundations seem about to start crumbling.

Moving Beyond Empire: Towards Cosmopolis

Imperialists have sought to glorify and ennoble their actions throughout the ages, as so many monuments, ruins and texts still testify. But is Empire truly good?[7] Perhaps what is good might persist, but empires come and go with the tides of history. Their glory is always fleeting in the long run, and their fate reminds us of the vanity of the quest for unbridled power, wealth or privilege. By contrast to the empires of history, the institutions that last longest seem to be based on principles that represent quite a different aspect of the human psyche, i.e. our spiritual side and our quest for harmony, moral order and community, as so many extant but very ancient world religions and cultures still attest. Historically the attempts to build a world community via religion or faith have been more successful than the myriad but always fleeting efforts at material Empire. This should tell us something very important about the contest of Empire versus Cosmopolis.

One thing should by now be very clear to all, that the present form of world order and the present global status quo cannot provide real stability, security or welfare for the global majority. It is to Cosmopolis that we must look for a source of inspiration to guide practice in search of those deeper values that do persist. Cosmopolis is not a dream, or a mere vision of utopia. Rather, like its dyadic antithesis Empire, it is a constant in world history. This should give us confidence for the future.

Let me say that it is my own position that Empire can never truly be 'good'. Some empires may be less evil than others, or do less harm than others, but none of them are actually good on their own merits. We can no more politically justify the existence of great power for a few at the expense of the powerlessness or subjugation of the many, than we can morally justify the co-existence in the world of great wealth and privilege alongside great poverty, deprivation and bitter suffering. We need to move to a new global covenant, as some have recently been arguing,[8] but any such covenant should be based on a clear rejection of the fundamental bases of Empire, which include the acceptance of the co-existence of great wealth and poverty in the world, alongside great power for a few and domination for the many. The real global power structure must be transformed; merely changing the leadership within Empire would not lead us far towards Cosmopolis, and the process of reconstructing Empire could be bloody and chaotic. Perhaps the final argument against Empire (and thus for Cosmopolis) rests on taking account of the damage and costs it inflicts not only on others but on the perpetrators themselves. In relatively recent world history, both the German and Japanese peoples suffered terribly in the final debacle of their own imperialist adventures. In the post war world the Soviet peoples suffered in a different manner, while the citizens of America, and of the West more generally, today suffer negative consequences of the reigning structure of global wealth and power. It is undeniable that Empire changes the societies that practice it, and certainly not all for the better. Historically, Empire has often if not always come at a high cost even to those who are supposedly meant to benefit by it. This price may be economic, for example in higher taxes to support the imperial machinery; environmental, in the form of lost natural habitat and other forms of degradation and pollution; or political, in the form of deep compromises made with the state in regard to personal or collective liberty. Indeed, the original liberal, Adam Smith, was against imperialism and colonialism for precisely such reasons. Today there is also the so-called 'blowback' of the consequences of covert intervention.[9] Other detrimental effects of empire can take the form of imported social ills or vices (such as the drugs trade; sexual trafficking, etc.) or the long term ill effects of experience in imperial wars on the soldiers and families who have to bear the direct cost of these enterprises.

Where does this leave us then, in choosing between Empire and Cosmopolis? The answer is all too obvious. If we seek to pursue the interests of the global majority, as opposed to the interests of a few, a special class, then we can only choose to reject or resist Empire. This means embracing Cosmopolis and making every effort possible to build an entirely new world order, one that transcends the unequal structures and gross injustices inherited from the previous imperial order. Cosmopolis represents the hopes for and vision of a new post-imperial world order. To be successful, it must be built on the principles of equality and justice among and between nations, not only in terms of political power and representation but also in terms of the fair distribution of the world's wealth, the world's health and welfare, and the use and preservation of the world's natural and environmental resources.

Empire and neoliberalism may seek to destroy democracy in all but name, and the responses of the dominant elite to the present crisis may tend to be politically shallow, coercive and manipulative, but the door to reform and even to radical transformation is not closed, but open. The crisis tendencies of the present order are indeed intensifying, including in the global economic system as well as the political order. Decades of neoliberal economic policies, unilaterally imposed by the rich developed countries upon the poor developing countries, combined with the continued and devastating effects of unmanageable debt burdens, have rendered many national governments increasingly incapable of delivering real change to their people. In the rich countries, politics has increasingly become a matter of monotone management and cynical manipulation rather than genuine and pluralistic democracy and representation. Geopolitically, the fissures in the pax Americana are obvious for all to see, and the spectre of increased violence lays heavily over the world. It is precisely because there is a crisis rather than a triumph of democracy worldwide, which runs parallel to the expansion of neoliberal global capitalism and the intensification of militarization and securitization, that the focus for change has been shifting to social movements (new and old) that seek to transnationalize their struggle and address the fundamental causes of this global malaise. Indeed, it is the paradox of neoliberal globalization that the stronger it seems to become, the more it actually stimulates the growth of popular movements of resistance and transformation.[10] The more the dominant elite attempt to forge a permanent conservative hegemony, the more popular forces the world over respond by attempting to form countervailing power and reclaim democratic culture. What we are in fact witnessing is a uniquely important historical moment in which we can reconstruct global solidarities and movements for change. These movements will form a new global democratic culture and be the agents that could construct a new global order. These movements continue to form and to evolve, but it is vital that they practice inclusion and mass participation as well as internationalism if they are to be successful in the long term. Moreover, it is already clear that the obstacles are formidable, not least the real danger of re-authoritarianization. Moreover, these movements must overcome divisions of the past and resist fragmentation, while linking at all times the local level with the regional and global, a task which requires great energy, commitment and resources. Nevertheless, there is no alternative to globalizing these struggles for reform and radical transformation. Nor is there any choice other than to collectively re-examine, re-imagine and eventually re-invent all the basic concepts of politics and political theory, including: authority, power, empowerment, legitimacy, state, civil society and, above all, democracy and the new 'global democracy'. All the old categories must be questioned and new solutions must be found to old problems.

The focus now must be on harnessing all of this creative political energy into strategic action. The debate about what organizational forms this should take is central, but so is the articulation of a programme of action. It is clear already that no single overarching ideology can possibly emerge to politically unify the many strands of the 'movement of movements' into a single 'world party' or its equivalent, and diversity is the defining characteristic of the present popular politics.[11] However, it is also clear that although the debate on reform versus radical transformative strategies will persist and is important, there is no critical need to abandon one in favour of the other, and both will inevitably be pursued. Moreover, a new form of 'unity' is emerging, exemplified in the succession of World Social Forum gatherings in Porto Alegre and Mumbai, which have combined extraordinarily diverse groups under the common banner of 'Another World is Possible'. However, even that forum must take account of lessons learned so far and move on to the next stage, or risk missing the historical moment's best opportunity.[12]

Finally, therefore, the matrix of change, which we hope will lead us beyond Empire and towards Cosmopolis, will involve a combination of institutional and parliamentary reforms and radical transformatory ideas and innovations. They will be aimed at strengthening democratic global governance and undermining or acting outside the entrenched oligarchic establishment.[13] The general contours and outline of this combination are already beginning to be articulated. The ideas already being discussed include: introducing global taxation (for example on arms sales, financial transfers, airline fuel, carbon emissions and other pollution, transnational shipping) to fund genuine development around the world and perhaps to sustain other global democratic institutions or a reformed United Nations system; introducing a global parliament or popular assembly and the use of global referenda; strengthening the international court system, particularly the International Court of Justice and the International Criminal Court, and thus strengthening the rule of law internationally; overhauling the present UN system and its key institutions (including the General Assembly, the IMF and the World Bank to name but a few) and make them both more autonomous and more inclusive and representative of the global majority rather than dominated by the most powerful states as at present; introduce a global debt arbitration system based on the goal of eliminating the debt crisis in the shortest possible time; introducing a Global Truth Commission to investigate abuses of human rights, crimes against humanity and other breaches of the peace and legal order around the world; strengthening the democratic character of parliaments throughout the world by increasing their international or transnational linkages and functions; increasing the inclusiveness and representativeness of all major institutions that form part of the global governance structure by directly empowering agents of global civil society.[14]

In conclusion, the democratization of globalization, and the globalization of democracy, depend upon the social forces who will in the future respond to the decline of Empire by actively building an alternative Cosmopolis. The hopes of humanity to democratize global institutions, and bring into reality a truly just and democratic world order rest upon their shoulders.

Notes

1 The relationship between globalization and global history and the questions it raises for knowledge construction and world politics are addressed in Barry K. Gills and William R. Thompson, 'Globalizations, Global Histories, and Globalities', in Barry K. Gills and William R. Thompson, Eds, Globalization and Global History, London: Routledge, 2005, forthcoming.

2 For example, the historian Niall Fergusson has written two volumes to illustrate the thesis of the positive impact of imperialism: Empire: How Britain Made the Modern World; and Colossus: The Rise and Fall of the American Empire. The economist Deepak Lal has produced a work entitled In Praise of Empires, Palgrave, 2005, in which he addresses the relationship between globalization and empire and argues that the US could bring untold benefits to the entire world if only it would cast off the idea 'that empires are bad things per se' (Andrew Roberts in The Sunday Telegraph).

3 See for example the collection edited by Leo Panitch and Colin Leys, entitled The New Imperial Challenge, Socialist Register 2004, Merlin Press, 2003, and particularly the article by David Harvey 'The 'New' Imperialism: Accumulation by Dispossession', pp. 63–87. See also David Harvey, The New Imperialism, Oxford: Oxford University Press, 2003. For another example of this genre see the special issue of Monthly Review entitled 'Imperialism Now', July-August 2003, Monthly Review Press, and particularly the lead essay by one of the journal's editors, John Bellamy Foster, 'The New Age of Imperialism', pp. 1–14. See also: Gore Vidal, Imperial America, Temple Lodge Publishing, 2004; and Noam Chomsky, Hegemony or Survival: America's Quest for Global Dominance, Penguin, 2004, in which he discusses 'imperial grand strategy' in the present context. For a review of Michael Mann's Incoherent Empire, New York and London: Verso, 2003 as well as the recent works on empire by Chalmers Johnson (2004), David Harvey (2003), and Emmanuel Todd (2003) see the article by Ganesh K. Trichur on 'the new imperial conjuncture' in this volume.

4 Such a sudden change of perception could come in one of several ways: for example a sudden shift in the value of the dollar following a significant change in the purchase of US treasury bonds, especially by East Asian countries; the onset of another major regional or global financial crisis or a serious global economic downturn; further acts of extreme violence perpetrated by terrorist cells within the territory of the United States itself; the outbreak of a major regional conflict between great powers; a sudden and catastrophic epidemic spreading around the world with millions of deaths; an environmental catastrophe deemed to be the direct result of climate change and global warming.

5 One of the most important studies in this regard is that by Emmanuel Todd, After the Empire: The Breakdown of the American Order, London: Constable and Robinson, 2004. He is the author of the extremely prescient study La Chute finale, Paris: Seuil, 1976. Translated as The Final Fall: An Essay on the Decomposition of the Soviet Sphere, New York: Karz, 1979, in which he predicted the decline and fall of the USSR. His new research on the US argues that far from being at its apogee of power, the US has already started its decline and therefore the urgent question for the world is how to manage this period to limit the damage. For an earlier and very interesting work on the coming hegemonic transition, understood in historical context, see Giovanni Arrighi and Beverly J. Silver, Chaos and Governance in the Modern World System, Minneapolis and London: University of Minnesota Press, 1999, particularly the Conclusion and its analysis of the global financial expansion of the 1980s and 1990s and its anticipated consequences for world order.

6 For studies that point to the dangers of increased competition, rivalry and conflict in the international order see: Michael T. Klare, Resource Wars: The New Landscape of Global Conflict, New York: Henry Holt and Company, 2001; Robert Harvey, Global Disorder: How to Avoid a Fourth World War, London: Robinson, 2003. See also the paper by Heikki Patomaki in this volume.

7 We have heard much rhetoric about 'evil Empire'. But what if all Empire is more evil than good? The selfjustification for Empire rests on a tautology. It goes like this: our present world order is 'good' (for us); therefore anything that contributed to bringing it about is by definition good (i.e. Empire); since we are intrinsically good, and it was/and is we who built Empire (past and present), then it follows that not only is this world order good but we also are good for having built such a world. This reasoning is convenient, but deeply flawed. Let us apply this reasoning to an individual person. Can one say one is virtuous by making a comparison to a much more evil person, or even to the worst of men or women? Does doing so render our claim to be virtuous the truth about ourselves, or is it merely a self-serving and probably selfdeceptive moral justification? Yes, by comparison to the worst of men, perhaps I can say that I am virtuous or 'good', and yet this in no way confirms the reality of my own virtue, which must always be a quality in itself. This logic in turn leads to a trap of self-righteousness, which so many imperialists (as well as persons) have fallen into willy-nilly. The trap works like this: to the extent that one believes absolutely in one's own virtue and goodness, i.e.

in one's own righteousness, is the extent to which one may also fall into the trap of believing that 'I am good, therefore anything that I do is for the good, therefore I can do no wrong'. As a consequence, anything I may do is (self) justified, regardless of the harm or suffering I may inflict on others. This is so because I do not take account of the real effects of my actions and may even be blind to them. I only take account of my intentions, which are by definition 'good', regardless of the real consequences. At its worst extreme, this attitude allows one to commit almost any crime, no matter how heinous, and still believe one has done no wrong, or even that one has done 'good'. Unfortunately, the present political climate of the global 'war on terror' is redolent with such 'moral' undertones on both sides of the conflict. Indeed some have argued that the antagonists in this conflict constitute mirror images of one another in some respects. For an example, see Tariq Ali's recent book, published by Verso, The Clash of Fundamentalisms.

8   David Held, for example, has called for a new global covenant, which we may link to his ideas on cosmopolitan democracy and global social democracy.

9   Chalmers Johnson advanced the thesis of 'blowback' upon American society and interests prior to the events of 9/11 (in the book by the same title) and has more recently continued this theme of analysis in The Sorrows of Empire: Militarism, Secrecy, and the End of the Republic, New York: Henry Holt and Company, 2004. The term blowback was based on the CIA's own word for the unanticipated consequences of unacknowledged actions (by the US) in other people's countries; i.e. covert actions and other forms of secret intervention or subversion.

10 For more on this thesis see Barry K. Gills (ed.) Globalization and the Politics of Resistance, London: Palgrave, 2001.

11 See for example: Paul Kingsnorth, One No, Many Yeses: A Journey to the Heart of the Global Resistance Movement, The Free Press, 2003; and David Held and Antony McGrew, Globalization/Anti-Globalization, Polity, 2002. See also the papers by Scott Byrd and Ray Kiely in this volume.

12 Immanuel Wallerstein made this comment, having attended the Mumbai WSF in 2004. The WSF in Porto Alegre in early 2005 was meant to place less emphasis on the plenary system and more on mass participation and focussed strategic discussion, following Mumbai's lead, where mass movements and trade unions played a very central visible role. For an in-depth analysis of the WSF and its potential see Teivo Teivainen, Democracy Unbound: The World Social Forum and the Dilemmas of Global Democracy, Routledge, series on Rethinking Globalizations, Series editor: Barry K. Gills, forthcoming.

13 Lecture by Jan Aart Scholte, 'Towards Global Democracy?' delivered at the University of Newcastle upon Tyne, in the 'Globalizations' lecture series, 14 March 2005.

14 Most of this list is taken from Heikki Patomaki and Teivo Teivainen, A Possible World: Democratic Transformation of Global Institutions, London: Zed Books, 2004. See also an earlier version by the same authors, Global Democracy Initiatives: The Art of the Possible, NIGD Working Paper 2/2002, Network Institute for Global Democratization, Helsinki, Finland and Notingham Trent University, UK. See also: 'Reforms of the System of International Institutions to make Another World Possible', London Declaration, 1 April 2004 of the World Campaign for In-Depth Reform of the System of International Institutions, www.reformcampaign.net, supported by a coalition of institutions in Catalonia, Spain. Susan George has a recent work entitled Another World is Possible If... which addresses the strategic issues of the movements.

Empire or Cosmopolis? Civilization at the Crossroads

FRED DALLMAYR

Not long ago, Saddam Hussein—the former president (or dictator) of Iraq—was captured by Western troops who quickly proceeded to display him, shackled and disheveled, to an avid world press. This display of the former ruler, one observer commented, resembles 'pretty much what the Roman Emperors used to do to defeated barbarian kings' (Boyle, 2003, p. 2; also see 2004). The observer was not a simple man in the street, but a distinguished expert in the history and governing norms of international law—norms which had been briskly brushed aside in the war against Iraq (which, in the end, showed itself as a war of conquest). According to general agreement, it is the adherence to ethical and legal norms which distinguishes a 'civilization' from primitive, lawless, or barbaric forms of life. Thus, the legal expert's statement contained a double indictment. On the one hand, his comment disclosed a dark spot in the Roman imperial edifice: the fact that, in its treatment of alien rulers and peoples, Rome was itself near-barbaric and certainly not as civilized as it claimed to be. More important is the second point: that things have remained 'pretty much' the same since the time of the Caesars—and this despite two thousand years of 'Christian civilization' (which, at its inception, was meant to transform and perhaps replace the Roman Empire). This realization casts a melancholy pall on hopes expressed by Immanuel Kant that the progressive improvement of humankind is not just a dream or 'empty chimera' (Kant, 1970; regarding the recent escalation of global violence and its relation to 'civilization' cf, e.g., Drury, 2004). It also lends credence to Mahatma Gandhi's quip about Western culture or civilization: 'It *would be* a good idea'.

The issue I want to address in the following pages concerns the future of this so-called 'civilization'. Basically, as it seems to me, the events in Iraq throw into relief a dramatic crossroads facing the world: the crossroads between empire and global cooperation, between world dictatorship and an interdependent community of peoples (which can loosely be called 'cosmopolis'). A major factor triggering this crossroads is the twilight besetting the so-called 'Westphalian system', that is, the traditional system of inter-state relations dating back to the Peace of Westphalia. Twilight prevails in this domain because of the unresolved status of that system: the fact that some of its central ingredients are neither defunct nor fully intact. On the one hand, contrary to some premature prognoses, the Westphalian principle of state sovereignty continues to be eagerly championed, especially by powerful nation-states; on the other hand, given the relentless growth of global markets and communication networks (what is often termed 'globalization'), no state—no matter how self-contained—can fully escape the inroads of global interdependence. It is precisely this ambivalence, this juncture of radical state autonomy and globalization, which gives rise to opposing tendencies: on the one side, the ambitions of empire where globalization is subjected to global sovereignty (a global Leviathan); on the other side, a democratic cosmopolis achieved through the subordination of sovereignty to global interdependence. The following discussion seeks to explore this contemporary crossroads and its divergent paths, mainly with an emphasis on normative and philosophical considerations. I proceed in three steps. While the opening section examines the nature or character of the emerging global empire, the ensuing sections concentrate on normative assessments: rehearsing first arguments which traditionally have been, and continue to be, offered in defense of empire, in order finally to present counter-views of champions of an alternative (cosmopolitan) path or vision.

Globalizing Leviathan

In assessing the nature of 'empire', especially in the contemporary context, one needs to recall the hybrid character of the global arena: the odd collusion of sovereignty and interdependence. To some extent, or to a lesser degree, a similar hybridity can also be found in earlier periods. However, what lends to the present situation its dramatic novelty is the juncture of unparalleled superpower autonomy and the global reach of that power's effects. The novelty of this global reach can easily lead analysts to dubious conjectures or conclusions: especially the conjecture of an entirely unheard-of and amorphous imperial structure, an edifice without center and periphery, without obedience and command. Thus, under the combined influence of 'postmodern' rhetoric and functionalist theories of social complexity, some recent analysts have depicted the emerging empire as a system of intricately interlocking subsystems, of markets and communications networks, of 'micro-powers' and 'virtualities'—without any trace of a sovereign Leviathan (for recent assessments of the global arena in terms of functional networks compare, e.g., Keane, 2003; Sassen, 2002; to some extent, traces of functionalist and postmodern imagination are also evident in Hardt & Negri, 2000; for extensive comments on the latter book see Passavant & Dean, 2004). What is correct in this conjecture is the fact that Leviathan no longer monopolizes the scene but shares the global arena with a vast array of public, non-public, and often unaccountable institutions and agencies. To this extent, the Indian novelist Arundhati Roy is undoubtedly on target when, in pondering the nature of empire, she urges us to consider not only the American superpower but also 'the World Bank, the International Monetary Fund, the World Trade Organization (WTO), and multinational corporations'. As she concludes: '*All* this is Empire' (Roy, 2003, pp. 103, 107).

Yet, the complexity of the imperial structure does not tempt the novelist for a moment into political naiveté. In fact, the quoted passage is instantly followed by the observation that the vast 'confederacy' of imperial networks has also vastly increased the distance 'between those who make the decisions and those who have to suffer them'. With this insight Roy is in concurrence with American 'realists' and 'neo-realists' (for whom, no doubt, the distance is an occasion for rejoicing). As one such realist observer recently remarked, without embarrassment or subterfuge: 'The military, economic, and political power of the United States makes the rest of the world look Lilliputian' (Weiner, 2002, p. A11). To be sure, the emergence of the new, America-centered empire is not the discovery of American realists or neo-realists; it was predicted and analyzed more than a decade ago by one of the country's leading cultural critics: Edward Said. Reflecting on 'American ascendancy' in his book *Culture and Imperialism*, Said noted at the time that 'imperialism did not end, did not suddenly become "past" once decolonization had set in motion the dismantling of the classical empires'; on the contrary, the rise of the United States 'as the last superpower suggests that a new set of force lines will structure the [entire] world' (Said, 1993, p. 282; cf. Aronowitz & Gautney, 2003; Johnson, 2000). Couched in polemical language, Said's prediction of an emerging new imperialism could be, and was often, dismissed as the rambling of a literary academic out of tune with the complexities of international politics. Even today, the notion of an America-centered empire tends to be denied by well-meaning liberals fondly attached to the old constitutional republic. However, how can nostalgia blind us to obvious facts? Listen to the comments of Michael Ignatieff, a writer not suspected of critical or subversive tendencies, who depicts the United States as

> the only nation that polices the world through five global military commands; maintains more than a million men and women at arms in four continents; deploys carrier battle groups on watch in every ocean; guarantees the survival of countries from Israel to South Korea; drives the wheels of global trade and commerce; and fills the hearts and minds of an entire planet with its dreams and desires. (Ignatieff, 2002, p. 22)

What these lines reveal is the presence of an immense superpower, a giant super-Leviathan extending its influence into every corner of the earth. This is precisely what the term 'empire' signifies. In a nutshell, empire means the extension of political and military power beyond the scope of the metropolitan homeland, that is, the wielding of dominion over foreign territories inhabited by non-citizen populations. As one will note, it is not geographical size per se that is decisive. Thus, although composed of fifty states, the domestic United States is not an empire, because all the (adult) inhabitants of the homeland are at least in principle entitled to political participation.[1] The crucial criterion of empire is rather rule over non-citizen, that is, over alien populations not entitled to participate in the shaping of metropolitan policies. This indicates that 'empire' cannot be democratic as an empire (no matter what its domestic practices may be). Simply put: empire and democracy are contradictory terms—an aspect too readily ignored by champions of *pax Americana*. Thus, when Walter Russell Mead (2002, p. 10) observes that America is 'the sole global power' relying on a 'global consensus' and that it 'dominates to an unprecedented degree' the 'first truly global civilization', he glosses over (or fails to notice) the incoherence of his concepts—because global superpower collides with global consensus just as full-scale domination militates against global civilization. The same slide or slippage is favored even by distinguished international experts. Thus, in examining 'key factors' in contemporary international politics, Zbigniew Brzezinski (2000, p. 149) singles out two: 'the primacy of American global power' and 'the global appeal of democracy'—but without worrying in the least about their incongruence or about the impact of the latter appeal on the former primacy.

By extending its reach to foreign lands, imperial superpower elides the nexus of civil mutuality and reciprocity. Basically, in setting aside democratic rules of active participation and representation, imperial rule over non-citizen populations amounts to a relation of command and obedience—which, at its core, is a relation of fear. In his recent study of the new imperialism, Benjamin Barber very correctly emphasizes this component of fear, by speaking candidly about 'fear's empire' or the empire of fear. In his presentation, fear operates in two directions. On the one hand, by amassing an immense arsenal of sophisticated weaponry, the superpower instills fear, and in fact seeks to strike 'terror', into the hearts of its adversaries and would-be competitors. On the other hand, being deprived of representation or an active voice, subordinated populations are likely to feel frustrated and hence may resort to violent retaliation or acts of 'terrorism'—thereby enmeshing themselves in unending 'terror wars'. Locked into the cycle of fearful enmity, terror and counter-terror reinforce each other over time, progressively eroding all residues of civility both at home and abroad. In Barber's words: the empire of fear in the end becomes 'a realm without citizens, a domain of spectators, of subjects and victims whose passivity means helplessness and whose helplessness defines and sharpens fear' (Barber, 2003, p. 216; regarding the rampant erosion of civility, dramatically illustrated by torture videos, see Brooks, 2004; Sontag, 2004). His analysis vividly underscores the parallels between empire and the Hobbesian image of Leviathan. As will be recalled, Hobbes' image of domestic peace was profiled against a condition of anarchic warfare, a condition governed or 'terrorized' by the fear of violent death. Seeking to escape from this terror, people launch into the construction of a commonwealth only to find themselves at the mercy of a fear-inspiring potentate whose edicts can nullify the hoped-for personal safety.[2]

During recent years, the fear factor has been vastly intensified on all sides. Partly in response to the attacks of September 11, the superpower has unleashed the 'war against terrorism' and then the unprovoked war in the Near East. It also has unilaterally abrogated international disarmament agreements and embarked, again unilaterally, on the development of new strategic weapons, including 'smart' nuclear bombs. Still more provocatively, the United States has announced to the world a global policy agenda with clearly imperialist features—something previous empires were reluctant to do. The agenda is called the 'National Security Strategy of the United States of America' and was formally promulgated on 20 September 2002. The document reflects an ambitious imperial design—whose scope dwarfs the ambitions of all previous empires. A number of features clearly stand out: first, the assertion of America's absolute military supremacy in the world; next, the refusal to allow the emergence of any possible 'peer power' capable of challenging imperial rule; and, finally, the claimed right to resort to war—if necessary in a preventive or preemptive fashion—against any hostile challenges mounted by 'rogue states' or non-state actors. As a presidential letter prefacing the document blandly affirms: 'The United States possesses unprecedented—and unequaled—strength and influence in the world'. To ensure the undisputed maintenance of this supremacy, American forces—the letter adds—must remain strong enough 'to dissuade a military buildup in hopes of surpassing, or equaling, the power of the United States'. In order to forestall any unwelcome surprises, the document finally assigns to America the right to act preventively or preemptively (that is, beyond the traditional confines of self-defense)—a passage which, on some readings, includes a nuclear first-strike capability.[3]

Probably the most disturbing feature of the document is the notion of preventive and/or preemptive warfare. In Benjamin Barber's words, the logic of such warfare 'relies on long-term prediction and a presumed concatenation of events' vastly exceeding the bounds of self-defense: 'By shooting first and asking questions later, it opens the way to tragic miscalculation' and 'sets a disastrous example for other nations claiming their own exceptionalist logic' (Barber, 2003, p. 81). In still more forceful terms, the idea has been criticized by Richard Falk in an essay on 'The New Bush Doctrine'. By allocating to America powers vastly in excess of international agreements, Falk writes, the new doctrine is willing 'to abandon rules of restraint and of law, patiently developed over the course of centuries, rules governing the use of force in relation to territorial states'. By claiming preventive and even preemptive prerogatives, the strategic policy amounts in effect to the proclamation of a global absolutism. This is the case, he adds, because the policy is 'a doctrine without limits, without accountability to the United Nations or international law, without any dependence on a collective judgment of responsible governments and, what is worse, without any convincing demonstration of practical necessity'. For Falk, one of the most problematic aspects of the policy is the fear factor implicit in a global absolutism freed from civic mutuality and accountability. In his words:

> Since the end of the cold war the United States has enjoyed the luxury of being undeterred in world politics. It is this circumstance that makes Bush's 'unilateralism' particularly disturbing to other countries . . . [For] there is every reason for others to fear that, when the United States is undeterred, it will again become subject to the 'Hiroshima temptation' in which it might threaten and use such weapons in the absence of any prospect of retaliation. (Falk, 2002, p. 3; see also Falk, 2003; Prestowitz, 2003)

Surely, it cannot be the objective of a 'civilized' country to dominate other peoples through fear and nuclear blackmail. Neither Falk nor Barber limit their arguments to critical indictment but proceed to offer viable alternative agendas (whose fuller discussion I postpone to a later point). Instead of seeking to impose its will on the world and its peoples, Falk asks that America join the world in tackling the ethical-political challenge of promoting a form of 'humane global governance' compatible with democratic standards, thus laying the groundwork for a well-ordered global regime (or 'cosmopolis') (Falk, 2003, pp. 27, 36). A similar aim is espoused by Benjamin Barber who, in lieu of the policy of preventive and preemptive warfare, advocates the idea of 'preventive democracy', insisting that terrorism can be mitigated or stopped 'only in a world of peaceful democracies' while imperial strategies are 'less than ideal instruments' and in fact are counter-productive for equitable global governance (Barber, 2003, pp. 176, 205).[4]

Apologies for Empire

Let me now turn to normative or evaluative assessments, by asking these questions: What arguments are used, and have been used in the past, in defense of empire? And what arguments can be

marshaled in opposition to empire? As it happens, in the history of the West, imperialist ventures
have invariably been accompanied by ambitious moral and civilizational claims seeking to vin-
dicate these ventures. Differently phrased: despite manifestly brutal and dehumanizing policies,
empire-builders in the West have acted, or pretended to act, with a seemingly good conscience (an
aspect which may distinguish Western imperialists from their non-Western or Asiatic counter-
parts).[5] Sometimes famous thinkers and philosophers have lent their names to this moralizing
subterfuge. Well known (or notorious) is Aristotle's statement, as recorded in his *Politics*:
'Meet it is that barbarians should be governed by the Greeks'. The main justification for this
claim was the Greeks' (supposed) greater rationality and self-control as compared with the barbarians' dissolute and profligate life style (Aristotle, *Politics* 1295b7; see also Barker, 1946,
p. 181). Aristotle's statement furnished welcome support to his Macedonian pupil Alexander
when he embarked on his far-flung military conquests. In due course, Alexander's legacy was
taken over by imperial Rome, which extended its military control into all corners of the (then
known) world. In the works of Roman apologists—especially some Stoics and imperial
jurists—Aristotle's maxim of justified rule was developed into an elaborate system of moral
and legal principles claiming to be anchored in universal human reason and immutable laws of
nature.

Following the fall of Rome, roughly one thousand years elapsed before another European
power resumed Rome's imperial ambitions.[6] At this point, the claim to rule was raised by mon-
archical Spain, which, at that historical juncture, was the dominant hegemon or superpower in
late-medieval and early-modern European politics. What distinguished Spanish imperialism
from earlier precedents were two points: first, the near-global scope of its dominion. Propelled
by the voyages of the 'Age of Discovery', the new empire was able to establish its control over
distant lands, over populations located beyond the 'ocean blue' and wedded to vastly different
cultural traditions. The second distinctive feature was the infusion of Christian religious doctrines into discussions about conquest and about the rightness of imperial-colonial practices.
In large measure, this infusion explains the intensity of claims and counter-claims advanced
during this period and the missionary zeal animating many conquistadors (a zeal not found
among classical precursors).

A high point in the exchange of claims and counter-claims was a disputation held in 1550 in
Valladolid between a prominent defender and an equally prominent critic of empire. The defender was the philosopher-theologian and court historian Ginés de Sepúlveda, a man well trained
both in classical (Aristotelian and Stoic) philosophy and in the Christian scholastic tradition. In
his defense of empire, Sepúlveda mobilized a broad amalgam of past teachings which, with some
ingenuity, could be read as warrants for Spanish imperial rule. In an instructive fashion, the
Mexican philosopher Enrique Dussel has summarized the apologist's arguments into five
major claims. The first claim is the assertion of Spain's superior rationality, maturity, and cultural
sophistication, an assertion buttressed by the maxim that, 'in the nature of things', the higher is
supposed to rule over the lower, reason over passion, form over matter (Dussel, 1996, pp. 52, 60
note 22). Borrowing from Aristotle's teachings (especially his notion of 'natural slavery'), Sepúlveda affirmed it as a general principle that 'the perfect always ought to dominate and rule over the
imperfect, the excellent over its opposite'—a principle which was tailor-made for the cause of
Spanish imperialism. For, when comparing Spaniards with native people in the New World,
the conclusion was evident: 'Being by nature slaves, the barbarians [in the Americas], uncultured
and inhuman [or barely human] as they are', ought to submit to superior rule. For Sepúlveda, this
was not just a matter of brute power, but a dictate of ethics and justice: 'By natural right it is found
to be "just" that matter should submit to form, body to soul, the appetites to reason, animals to

humans, women to men, the imperfect to the perfect, the worse to the better, for the common good of all' (Sepúlveda, 1987, pp. 83, 153).

Once the premises of this thesis were granted, the other claims followed as a matter of course. The second point was the idea that Spanish rule over the barbarians was exercised generously for the latter's benefit, so as to promote the Indians' cultural and spiritual uplift and advancement. In Sepúlveda's own formulation of this version of 'white man's burden': 'What better and more salutary thing could occur to these barbarians than to be governed by the imperial rule of those whose prudence, virtue, and religion will convert the barbarians finally ... into civilized people?' Of course, there were limits to Spanish benevolence—which leads to the third point: the threat of violent coercion and punishment for all those resisting Spain's civilizing mission, a violence proclaimed to be 'just and necessary' by natural right. In Sepúlveda's words again: 'If they [the barbarians] refuse our empire, they can be compelled by arms to accept it—and this will be a just war in accordance with natural right and law'. Whenever the imperial rulers had to resort to such military force or violence—this is the fourth point— they could do so with a perfectly 'good conscience', being justified both by classical metaphy- sics and Christian doctrine: 'For, were we not to do it [i.e. exercise violence and coercion], we would fulfill neither the natural law nor the commandment of Christ' (Sepúlveda, 1987, pp. 133, 135, 137). This point culminated in the fifth and last claim: namely, that imperial violence is actually instigated by the obstinacy and (terroristic) recalcitrance of native populations who merely reap what they sow. In Dussel's poignant expression: The victims of imperialism in the periphery are finally held 'responsible for their own victimization'. In their intricate conca- tenation—he adds—the five claims raised by the Spanish doctor were thoroughly absorbed and reiterated by subsequent imperial elites, from British and French apologists to defenders of *pax Americana* (Dussel, 1996, pp. 52, 60–61, notes 23–25; cf. Said & Hitchens, 1988).

To be sure, despite a certain argumentative continuity, the nature of imperial claims underwent important transformations during subsequent centuries. With the rise of modern science and rational enlightenment, Christian apologetics receded steadily into the background (without being completely erased), making room instead for 'secular' ideas of scientific management and technical-instrumental control. As a corollary, the notion of a Christian empire—partially buttressed by classical 'natural right'—steadily gave way to artificially designed political struc- tures held together by a combination of contractual or market principles, functional networks, and Leviathan-style sovereignty grounded in human will. Initiated and nurtured first in the empires of Britain and France, these modern changes reached their full fruition in the contempor- ary period. The basic challenge facing present-day empire—as it faced previous empires— remains justification or legitimation; and the challenge is greatly complicated by comparison with the situation at Valladolid. Simply put: How can one justify imperial domination over sub- jugated (non-citizen) populations given the retreat of classical metaphysics and Christian theol- ogy, and their replacement by modern science and secular rationality coupled with the spreading of democratic aspirations and the global appeal of human rights? As the available evidence suggests, the solution resides in a combination of diverse (sometimes conflicting) argumentative strategies, chiefly the following: civilizational benevolence or 'developmentalism'; technocratic scientism and economism; 'realist' power politics (relying on thinkers from Machiavelli and Hobbes to Nietzsche and beyond); plus remnants of classical metaphysics and Christian apolo- getics. Joined together, these strands at times coalesce into a heady agenda of global conversion, an agenda pursued with the same missionary zeal exhibited earlier by the conquistadors.

Among the assorted strategies, developmentalism is the most widely preferred claim, due to its deceptively moralizing appeal. In this domain, the legacy of Sepúlveda is very much alive. In a speech delivered to Congress shortly after September 11 and announcing a world-wide 'war on terrorism', the American President declared: 'This is the world's fight. This is civilization's fight. This is the fight of all who believe in progress and pluralism, tolerance and freedom.' With this statement, America proclaimed itself the guardian of 'civilization', and in fact the standard-bearer of a mission to preserve civilization by spreading its benefits world-wide (what the French used to call *'mission civilisatrice'*). In the same speech, the President denounced America's opponents as enemies of genuine (American-style) civilization, as people who 'hate *our* freedoms—*our* freedom of religion, *our* freedom of speech, *our* freedom to vote and assemble and disagree with each other' (Falk, 2003, pp. 57, 74).[7] Following the logic of the 'war on terrorism', opponents of civilization have to be forced militarily to change their ways, unless they can be pressured or converted by other means to submit to the global mission. What is new in this developmental concept by comparison with Sepúlveda is mainly the goal: instead of spreading Christianity to the New World the objective now is to spread 'our freedoms' and 'our culture', that is, the benefits of Western modernity. This kind of developmentalism is a cherished notion not only of politicians but of academic social scientists. According to a prominent American expert, writing during the cold war period, global advancement involves in essence a form of modernization, that is, a process in which 'tradition-bound villages or tribal-based societies are compelled to react to the pressures and demands of the modern, industrialized and urban-centered world'. As he added candidly:

> This process might also be called Westernization, or simply advancement and progress; it might, however, be more accurately termed the diffusion of a world culture—a world culture [or civilization] based on advanced technology and the spirit of science, on a rational view of life, a secular approach to social relations . . . At an ever-accelerating rate, the direction and volume of cross-cultural influences has become nearly a uniform pattern of the Western industrial world imposing its practices, standards, techniques, and values upon the non-Western world. (Pye, 1966, pp. 8–9, 44–45; cf. Eisenstadt, 1966; Dallmayr, 1996, pp. 149–174)

At a closer look, developmentalism actually is a jumble of diverse facets, not all of which share the same moralizing appeal. While some facets—the core of *'mission civilisatrice'*— are purposive or intentional in character, other aspects seem to operate in a more anonymous and quasi-automatic fashion, beyond the range of direct political control. Most prominent among the latter are modern industry, the economy, and advanced technology. In their combination, these features are central components of modern Western society and their evolution seemingly obeys a logic of its own. Yet, despite this appearance, none of these features are free of deliberate impulses; nor are they outside the range of fear's empire. This is clearly evident in the case of the capitalist market economy whose global reach renders it a crucial instrument of developmentalism—but an instrument severely marred by its domineering effects. Falk speaks in this context of 'predatory globalization' and 'predatory capitalism'. As he points out, at least since the fall of the Soviet Union, the energies of governing elites in the United States have been directed toward 'globalizing the world economy', in the direction of a 'predatory globalization' under the auspices of a minimally regulated, neoliberal form of capitalism known as the 'Washington consensus'. The overall effect of this policy has been the tendency 'to widen income gaps between North and South, as well as to ignore persisting poverty and longer-term environmental decay'. As Falk adds, this policy—seemingly self-propelled and self-generating—has more recently been placed more tightly under imperial control. In the aftermath of September 11, he notes, the 'nerve-center of empire-building' has, for the time being, 'decisively shifted back to the state, with the political discourse moving from "globalization", an economistic framing of the new reality, to "war" and "security"' (Falk, 2003, pp. xii–xiii, 32).[8]

A similar role is played by modern science and technology. Although seemingly non-political or extra-political, science and technology have increasingly been placed in the service of political and military-industrial elites—to the point that (in the view of a prominent philosopher) the entire world is being transformed into a giant artifact bent on reducing everything into a mere resource for domineering power (Heidegger, 1977, pp. 283–317). Given steady advances in sophistication, contemporary technology readily lends itself to techniques of social surveillance and control beyond the predictions of George Orwell and the dreams of earlier totalitarian rulers (like Hitler and Stalin). With the extension of surveillance techniques into outer space, human life around the globe is tendentially placed into a grand 'Panopticon' where every move is tracked by a global overseer. Richard Falk paints a grim picture of the evolving scenario. As part of the 'fundamental American project of global domination', he writes, the ongoing 'weaponization of space' yields (or is meant to yield) 'an unlimited capability to destroy at a moment's notice a point of resistance or hostility anywhere on the planet . . . If this project aiming at global domination is consummated, or nearly so, it threatens the entire world with a kind of subjugation, and risks encouraging frightening new cycles of megaterrorism as the only available and credible strategy of resistance' (Falk, 2003, p. xxvii). Undeterred by such prospects, the American Secretary of Defense (Rumsfeld) has already initiated major programs to develop laser and kinetic-kill weapon systems on battle stations in outer space, asserting that America must 'have the means to exert force in, through, and from space' (Carroll, 2001, p. 3).

Clearly, a policy of this nature seems far removed from any kind of developmentalism or *'mission civilisatrice'*. Some defenders of empire—called realists or neo-realists (Falk speaks of 'war thinkers' or 'Pentagon warriors')—completely dismiss the missionary idea, placing themselves squarely on the ground of sheer power politics (or superpower politics). Some even show openly their contempt for ethics and civility. When some European leaders remonstrated against a war launched in violation of global norms, the abovementioned Secretary of Defense ridiculed such moral scruples as signs of weakness and senility, as the whimpers of an 'old Europe' unable to keep up with the strides of a youthful (or better: juvenile) America. Another 'war thinker'—a renowned expert in international politics—ventured into planetary mythology by likening cautious and recalcitrant Europe to a feminine Venus as contrasted with America's mighty-armed and truculent Mars (Kagan, 2003; see also Kagan, 2002; Friedman, 2003). Given their obsession with sheer power, (neo)realist defenders of empire are unlikely to be deeply steeped in philosophy, especially the tradition of political philosophy; nevertheless, remnants of that tradition may on occasion provide welcome support. Thus, Pentagon warriors may find congenial Machiavelli's preference for a politics of fear over a politics of consensus. Likewise, they are bound to relish portions of Thomas Hobbes' *Leviathan*, especially his argument regarding the primacy of the 'sword' over mere words. Among more recent philosophers, some of Nietzsche's teachings are prone to attract the warriors' attention—just as they have attracted the attention of earlier imperialists. Among these teachings, notions like 'grand politics' and 'will to power' inevitably hold great fascination, given their intimation of a global hierarchy or rank order based on command and obedience. With some transatlantic correction, sympathy may also greet Nietzsche's futurist scenario when, in response to external threats, Europe would 'resolve to become menacing too, namely, to acquire *one will* by means of a new caste that would rule Europe—a long, terrible will of its own that would be able to cast its goals millennia hence' (Nietsche, 1966, para. 208).[9]

More philosophically inclined partisans of imperial dreams are unlikely to be satisfied with mere snippets of the intellectual tradition. In their effort to find a deeper warrant for rank order or hierarchy, such partisans often delve into older (pre-modern) philosophical or metaphysical teachings. It is in this context that remnants of classical 'natural right' are retrieved, where natural right means the affirmation of an essential status hierarchy differentiating between higher and lower, superior and inferior, rational and irrational. In large measure, this effort of retrieval is the hallmark of the camp of (so-called) 'neo-conservatives' whose members wield considerable influence both inside and outside the American government today. To be sure, in an age of liberal democracy and civic equality, the defense of rank order must be cautious or circumspect—which explains the frequent resort to verbal subterfuge and camouflage (or what is called 'esoteric' discourse). Politically, this camouflage is paralleled by the tendency of neo-conservatives to rule not directly but quietly and behind the scenes (perhaps in the fashion of Plato's 'nocturnal council'). A main problem encountered by partisans is the remoteness of classical metaphysics: the fact that the assumption of 'natural' rankings is not only rejected by democrats, but no longer fully believable to devotees themselves. It is for this reason that classical nostalgia is often supplemented by a very modernist type of voluntarism: especially by resort to the re-creation and imposition of rank order through a Nietzschean 'will to power'. The end result is a Platonic-Nietzscheanism—incongruous on philosophical grounds, but rendered congruous by its political aims.[10]

As for neo-conservative thinkers, sheer power politics is unsatisfactory also for religious supporters of 'grand politics'. Curiously, our time has seen the recovery not only of classical teachings, but also of Christian politics on a grand scale—in a Protestant variation on Sepúlveda's Catholic discourse. Intermingled with Machiavellian and Nietzschean phrases, religious rhetoric is routinely employed by American politicians and religious leaders alike. Thus, during his election campaign in 2000, candidate Bush called Jesus his 'favorite political philosopher', and on the eve of launching the Iraq war, the same Bush proclaimed the attack to stand in 'the highest moral [and religious] tradition of our country'.[11] Religious sermonizing of this kind is a stock-in-trade of clerical defenders of imperial policies, led by well-known Protestant televangelists. In many ways, Christian televangelists have been the most fervent and virulent missionaries of empire. Joining the 'war on terrorism' (and converting it implicitly into a crusade), several have not hesitated to denounce Islam as an 'evil religion' and its prophet as a vile impostor. Some of them have even proclaimed the terror war as the opening salvo in the final battle between good and evil (Armageddon), a battle to be won by preemptive nuclear strikes (with Christ possibly returning on a mushroom cloud).[12] Even Sepúlveda would have been stunned.

Empire Rebuked

Just as defense of empire can look back to a long intellectual pedigree, opposition to empire can claim its own (more illustrious) lineage extending to the ancients. Emperor Alexander was snubbed by Diogenes, while imperial Rome nurtured in its womb non-imperial thinkers like Seneca as well as recalcitrant religious movements which ultimately could not be absorbed. It is well to remember that Christianity first emerged in the shadow of the Roman Empire, and not as a welcome guest or accomplice. In fact, the birth of Christian religion heralded something vastly different from imperial domination: namely, the promise of a reign of justice, goodness, and genuine peace. Although infiltrated and partly obscured by imperial ambitions, the evolving Christian 'civilization' always preserved a recessed memory of these beginnings, a memory which could be activated (and was activated) at crucial moments of Western history. One such crucial moment was the formation of the Spanish Empire, at the onset of the modern age. At this point, the gospel's non-imperial or anti-imperial promise was invoked powerfully by Bartolemé de las Casas who met and disputed Sepúlveda in Valladolid.

A Dominican friar and at one point bishop of Chiapas, Las Casas had no difficulty in rebutting the arguments of his opponent. For one thing, in contrast to Sepúlveda's mere book learning, Las Casas had first-hand experience of the effects of Spanish rule in the Americas. Having spent many years in the New World, he was intimately acquainted with the atrocities inflicted by so-called 'Christian' armies on the native inhabitants. As he wrote in his 'Very Brief Account of the Destruction of the Indies': 'Among these gentle sheep [the Indians], the Spaniards entered like wolves, tigers, and lions which had been starving for many days, and for forty years they have done nothing else . . . than outrage, slay, afflict, torment, and destroy them' (Sanderlin, 1971, p. 166. Cf. Las Casas, 1992a, p. 11; 1992b, p. 29). And in his posthumous 'History of the Indies' he added bitterly: 'I leave, in the Indies, Jesus Christ our God scourged and afflicted and buffeted and crucified, not once but millions of times, on the part of the Spaniards who ruin and destroy these people and deprive them of the space they require to live' (Las Casas, 1957–58, vol. 2, p. 511; vol. 5, pp. 136–137). In addition to his first-hand experience, Las Casas was also a highly educated scholar, a man steeped in scriptures and classical texts—and apparently better able to understand their meaning than his opponent. Thus, without denying 'natural' rankings and different human aptitudes or talents, he was able to disconnect these rankings from claims to political domination by simply remembering Jesus' words as reported in Mark's gospel: 'Whosoever wishes to be first among you, must first be the servant of all' (Mark 10:44). In a similar manner, he was able to debunk the invocation of classical authorities in support of Spanish rule, by showing the incompatibility of that rule with classical conceptions of politics. For, when properly read (or read 'against the grain'), Aristotle defined politics as a relation between equal citizens and not as a 'household' relationship (with Indians clearly not being part of the Spanish household). Moreover, Aristotle's distinction between just and unjust types of government implied that Spanish despotism, wielded solely for the benefit of Spain, could not claim to be a just regime, as it violated the freedom and equality shared by indigenous peoples.[13]

Among the claims advanced by Sepúlveda in Valladolid, those most readily demolished by Las Casas were the assertions of Spanish superiority and of their moral benevolence displayed in their effort to bring their culture and religion to the Indians ('*mission civilisatrice*'). For how could one attach the moral or 'civilizing' claims to an enterprise carried out with so much violence and brutality? In Las Casas' own life-time, hundreds of thousands, perhaps millions of Indians perished due to Spanish actions. As his 'Very Brief Account' relates: 'Whereas there were more than three million souls whom we saw in Hispaniola, there are today not two hundred of the native population left'. Devastation on such a scale—he rightly complained— left an indelible stain on Western 'civilization' and made a mockery of Christian religion. In terms of his 'History': 'The Spaniards who traverse the land with their violence and wicked example . . . make the name of Christ into a blasphemy' (See Las Casas, 1957–58b, vol. 5, pp. 136–137; 1957–58a, vol. 2, p. 511). Far from educating or 'civilizing' native (or non-European) peoples, the example of the Spanish conquest was likely to have the very opposite effect, by producing stubbornness and violent resistance. Here is a passage from his famous '*Del Único Modo*' ('The Only Method of Attracting All People to the True Faith') which deserves to be quoted in full:

> A rational creature has a natural capacity for being moved, directed and drawn to any good gently, because of his freedom of choice. But if natives find themselves first injured, oppressed, saddened, and afflicted by the miseries of wars, the loss of their children, their goods, and their own liberty . . . how can they be moved voluntarily to listen to what is proposed to them about faith, religion, justice, and truth [we might add today: freedom and democracy]? If it is true that a soft word multiplies friends while 'an ill-tempered man stirs up strife' (Proverbs 15:18), how many enemies will

not such bitter words and deeds make? Therefore, if man ought to be guided and persuaded to good gently and mildly, while warfare compels in a harsh, bitter and violent manner, it is clear that the latter means—unnatural and opposed to the condition of human nature—will produce contrary effects. (Las Casas, 1942, pp. 400–401; for the English translation see Sanderlin, 1971, pp. 162– 163; cf. Las Casas, 1992c, p. 118)

Las Casas has been called the 'protector of the Indians'—and with good reason. Not only was he passionately committed to their well-being and just treatment, but his pleas (at least for a time) exerted a definite influence on imperial and church policies.[14] Beyond the immediate context of the Spanish conquest, his example retains an important lasting significance: by intimating an alternative course for Western civilization (and civilization in general), away from imperialism and 'grand' power politics. In his *The Underside of Modernity*, Enrique Dussel credits Las Casas with having originated an alternative or 'counter-discourse' to the story of European expansionism. This initiative would not have been possible for Las Casas, he writes, 'without [his] having resided in the periphery, without having heard the cries and lamentations, and without having seen the tortures that the Indians suffered at the hands of the colonizing Europeans. That [experience of the] Other is the origin of the European counter-discourse' (Dussel, 1996, p. 136). In a similar vein, Gustavo Gutierrez—a chief spokesman of contemporary 'liberation theology'— acknowledges the continuing importance of Las Casas through the centuries, and especially in our own time. Emphasizing the religious dimension, Gutierrez states that the friar's chief task consisted above all 'in letting it be known in the Indies that there is a God, and that God is the God of Abraham, Isaac, Jacob, and Jesus' who is an enemy of injustice and oppression. Given the persistence of large-scale oppression and injustice in the world—he adds—it is obvious 'why the figure of Las Casas is of such striking universality: here we have someone who, still today, issues a challenge to people at various corners of the planet'. In struggling for an alternative path, his example is 'invested with characteristics of prophetic denunciation that maintain all their validity today' (Gutierrez, 1993, pp. 9–11).

To be sure, as previously indicated, (Western) modernity has introduced many changes, and the strategies of contemporary apologists of empire are no longer quite the same as Sepúlveda's. To this extent, the arguments of Las Casas need to be supplemented and amplified—but surely not discarded. One area where his example remains eminently fruitful relates to the handling of traditional teachings and practices, including the teachings of classical metaphysics and scholastic theology. By proceeding carefully but reading 'against the grain', his example illustrates the possibility of retrieving the best and most promising aspects of older legacies rather than succumbing to their worst and most oppressive features. Aristotle is a case in point. Instead of insisting on invidious rankings and the 'naturalness' of slavery, Las Casas preferred to accentuate the philosopher's contributions to a politics of freedom, equality, and friendship. The same approach guided his treatment of Roman Stoics and scholastic theologians. With some modification, a similar approach can be applied to modern writers or thinkers with whom Las Casas was not or could not be familiar. Thus, in the case of Machiavelli—a favorite author of (neo)realists—a proper reading involves deemphasizing the politics of fear and center-staging the 'republican' Machiavelli, that is, the champion of the Roman republic (vis-à-vis the empire). With regard to Hobbes, a reading faithful to the Spanish friar entails a decentering of the Leviathan coupled with a foregrounding of the consensual and normative dimensions of his work. The task is made particularly easy in the case of Nietzsche—the mentor of many hardline neo-conservatives—because of the sprawling multidimensionality of his work. Thus, as a counterpoint to grand politics and will to power (with their war-mongering implications), Nietzsche himself provides the antidotes of self-overcoming and infinite longing for goodness, for those 'blessed

isles where my friends are dwelling'. Here are some lines from *Zarathustra*, completely unpa-
latable to contemporary realists: 'I am driven out of fatherlands and motherlands. Thus, I now
love only my *children's land*, yet undiscovered, in the farthest sea: for this I bid my sails search
and search' (Kaufmann, 1968, pp. 196–197, 233).

The point where Las Casas' example remains most clearly pertinent today is in the debunking
of imperial benevolence (*mission civilisatrice*)—what more recently is called 'developmentalism'. As he pointedly remarked: How can indigenous or non-Western populations trust the
'good intentions' of colonizers or missionaries, if at the same time their lands are being confis-
cated, their possessions plundered, and their families and compatriots either killed or thrown into
dungeons (or internment camps)? Under such circumstances, civilization itself is turned into a
cloak for violent domination and oppression—an outcome bound to trigger violent resistance as
well as an upsurge of worldwide cynicism. There are obvious lessons here for our own time of
endless 'terror wars'. As Richard Falk remarks, denouncing the deceptive mask of developmental beneficence (evident in such slogans as 'Operation Enduring Freedom'): 'It is difficult for the
international public not to think that power politics alone is what counts, at least for the strongest
and most imperial of sovereign states' (Falk, 2003, p. 11).[15] Most damaging for the credibility of
Western civilization, conceived as a 'Christian civilization', is the complicity of Christian
clerics and televangelists in imperial power politics. Clearly, when Christ is turned into a
stand-in (or 'mascot') for a country's national security policies, something has gone terribly
wrong. When the message of the 'prince of peace' is converted into an agenda for war-mongering and imperial aggrandizement, then—in Las Casas' terms—the name of Christ becomes a
'blasphemy', with the result that religion itself becomes suspect and objectionable in the eyes
well-meaning and peace-loving people. In the words of a prominent contemporary
theologian—still mindful of the friar's legacy—the collusion of God-talk with empire-building
is a 'sin of pride', a failing incompatible with and destructive of genuine faith.[16]

There remains a further lesson from the past. Apart from denouncing the violence of imperial
policies, Las Casas in his writings and actions also intimated another path for the future: the path
of a commonwealth of free and equal peoples based on mutual respect and sympathy. In our
time, his vision has to be expanded and globalized—which brings into view the notion of a
global commonwealth or 'cosmopolis' embracing different cultures and societies and held
together not by a central Leviathan but by lateral connections and bonds of cultural and political
interdependence. Benjamin Barber stresses this vision when he opposes to preventive warfare
the agenda of 'preventive democracy' with global implications. In Barber's presentation, preventive democracy is not a missionary doctrine imposed by an imperial center, but rather a practice nurtured at the grassroots level—that is, at local and national levels—and radiating out from
there to regional and global arenas. A similar view is endorsed by Falk (2003, p. 36) when he
writes that 'we must [first] rescue shipwrecked democracy here at home and find the path that
leads away from American empire-building toward humane global governance'. The alternative
path of cosmopolis is not anti-American or anti-Western, although it is clearly opposed to American imperial ambitions. Actually, given its domestic diversity and multiculturalism, American
society—cleansed of these ambitions—might well serve as a model or prototype for an interdependent and multicultural cosmopolis. In Barber's words:

> A multicultural nation whose majority will soon comprise a host of minorities and whose society
> looks more and more like the world it paradoxically refuses to join can, if it wishes, promote its
> diversity as a model for others. A society of global cities is well suited to global democratic leader-
> ship; tolerance, humility, inventiveness and a belief in self-government . . . are values that others can
> emulate without feeling like they are being colonized. (Barber, 2003, p. 214)[17]

As to the concrete structure of the future cosmopolis, much is left to human ingenuity, prac-tical experimentation, and political prudence and good judgment (*phronesis*). Given the dangers of empire, the structure cannot or is unlikely to be that of a world government or even a world federation. More promising are looser forms of interconnection between nation-states and regions, involving (importantly) not only governments but people as citizens (that is, as potential global or transnational citizens).[18] More crucial than formal structures are the spirit and motiv-ation animating cosmopolitan institutions, that is, the cultivation of global civility, civic engage-ment and responsibility. Here we are back at 'civilization', but now seen as a civilizing or educational effort from the ground up—admittedly a difficult and laborious undertaking. As Joseph Nye has correctly noted, cultivating this kind of civility can require 'years of patient, unspectacular work, including close civilian cooperation with other countries' (Nye, 2002, p. xv; cited in Barber, 2003, pp. 203–204; on 'transnational' citizenship see specially Balibar, 2004). Despite its difficulty, this is the only viable path open and acceptable to people aspiring to the status of 'civilization'. The first thing people embarking on this path have to learn is to forgo the 'power trip': to realize that genuine change does not result from domination, manipulation, or will to power. Basically, a precondition for turning away from empire is another kind of turn-about (*periagogé*): a turning from power lust to ethics and civility, from violence to peace. It is at this point that we encounter again Nietzsche's 'blessed isles', his longing for the 'children's land' unspoiled by adult corruption. In a way it is the same land that is invoked by Arundhati Roy when she writes that we cannot and should not oppose empire with empire. All we can do is 'to lay siege to it, to shame it, to mock it: with our art, our music, our literature, our stubbornness, our joy, our brilliance, our sheer relentlessness—and our ability to tell our own stories' (Roy, 2003, p. 112).

Notes

1   In the same manner, imperial Rome was not an empire over Romans, just as imperial Britain was not an empire for its citizens. This does not mean that imperial rule abroad will not affect domestic politics; in fact, some contamination seems almost inevitable. Referring to Socrates' opposition to Athenian imperial ventures, Dana Villa (2001, p. 34) writes: 'An imperial democracy cannot stay a democracy for long, since the basis of democratic justice—equal shares for all—demands a self-restraint directly at odds with the energies and ambitions of imperialism.'

2   In his Introduction, Barber (2003, p. 15) quotes the maxim from Machiavelli's *The Prince* that 'it is better to be feared than loved'. The maxim also applies to the sovereign in Hobbes' *Leviathan*. The difference, of course, is that for Hobbes the commonwealth is founded on contractual agreement—which makes room for at least a measure of civic mutuality.

3   For the text of the National Security Strategy paper see http://www.whithouse.gov/nsc/nss.html. Regarding nuclear capability see Allen & Gellman (2002).

4   Barber (2003, pp. 209–211) also cites a 'Declaration of Interdependence', sponsored by the 'global citizens campaign' and patterned on the American Declaration of Independence, according to which the 'people of the world' recognize their 'responsibilities to the common goods and liberties of humankind as a whole'.

5   Thus, it is hard to imagine that Genghis Khan or Timur (Tamerlane) would have defended their actions on moral or civilizational grounds. By contrast, there are important Asian rulers denouncing empire on moral grounds: e.g., King Darius of Persia and Emperor Ashoka of India.

6   I bypass here the so-called 'Holy Roman Empire' which, apart from the adventures of the crusades, was not an expansionist 'empire' (in the sense used here); nor was it a centralized or monolithic imperial structure.

7   For the attachment of many American neo-conservatives to '*mission civilisatrice*' or 'white man's burden' see Shavit (2004) As Shavit indicates, the attachment is amplified (and complicated) through borrowings from 'realist' political thinkers like Machiavelli and Thomas Hobbes.

8   In Falk's view, the roots of this empire-building can actually be traced back before September 11. In his words (2003, pp. 31–32): 'Even prior to September 11 there were good reasons to believe that the United States was

seeking to achieve an imperial grip on the *new* geopolitics of globalization: by controlling the technological frontiers of information technology; by shaping the world economy along neoliberal lines as articulated through the medium of such subordinate actors as the IMF, World Bank, and the WTO; by presiding over an innovative "humanitarian" diplomacy of selective intervention; by aspiring to and demonstrating military dominance in "zero casualty warfare" . . .; and by pursuing new generations of nuclear weaponry and quietly moving ahead with plans to militarize space.'

9   As he continues: 'The time for petty politics is over; the twentieth century will bring with it the struggle for world domination, the *compulsion* of grand politics.' For an explicit American defense of world conquest and global domination see Frum & Perle (2003). The point of the above comments is not to reduce Machiavelli, Hobbes or Nietzsche to a narrow power-political reading, but only to note that certain aspects of their works can be and have been used (or abused) for imperial purposes.

10   For probing efforts to discern the combination of Platonic and Nietzschean elements in the neo-conservative (sometimes called 'Straussian') camp see, e.g., Lampert (1996); Drury (1997); Bluhm (2002); Atlas (2003); Lobe (2003); Frachon & Vernet (2003); Muravchik (2003). As in the case of Machiavelli, Hobbes, and Nietzsche, I need to add a disclaimer: the above comments in no way seek to hold Leo Strauss responsible for the policies of his neo-conservative followers. For a thoughtful essay on Nietzsche see Strauss (1983).

11   The statements are reported respectively in: Bush wears religion on his armored sleeve, *The Washington Spectator*, 29(10), 15 May 2003, p. 1; and President's corner, *The Light* (Newsletter of the Interfaith Alliance), Spring 2003, p. 2. In the latter publication, the Rev. Welton Gaddy asks sharply (p. 2): 'How dare any politician, including the president, even implicitly suggest that God is a kind of mascot of the nation?'

12   For derogatory remarks of prominent televangelists on Islam and its prophet see Ahmed (2003). Compare in this context also Blaker (2003), and Qureshi & Sells (2003). One wonders how and to what extent Christian rhetoric is palatable to hardcore Pentagon warriors and Nietzschean-style neo-conservatives. One suspects that hardline neo-conservatism is meant for a restricted circle of experts and 'war thinkers', while gospel-talk is designed to enlist the loyalty of the 'masses'.

13   Invoking the teachings of 'the philosopher' (Aristotle), Las Casas (1957–58a) tried to show that American Indians were not 'barbarians' and hence could not be treated simply as slaves. Moreover, relying both on Aristotle and Cicero, he argued that Indians were rational human beings like Europeans and hence were entitled to freedom and equality. To quote passages from Las Casas: 'As Cicero sets it down in *De Legibus*, Book I, all the races of the world are men, and of all men and of each individual there is but one definition, and this is that they are rational. All have understanding and will and free choice, as all are made in the image and likeness of God . . . And consequently, all have the power and ability or capacity . . . to be instructed, persuaded, and attracted to order and reason and laws and virtue and all goodness . . . They are likewise prudent, and endowed by nature with the three kinds of prudence named by the philosopher [Aristotle]: solitary, economic, and political . . . And in following the rules of natural reason, they have even surpassed by not a little those who were the most prudent of all, such as the Greeks and Romans' (1957–58a, vol. 3, pp. 3–4, 165–166; vol. 4, pp. 433–434; translation taken from Sanderlin, 1971, pp. 115, 143, 200–202).

14   Partly due to the friar's pleas, Emperor Charles V in November 1542 promulgated a series of laws ordering the fair and equal treatment of the Indians and prohibiting their enslavement. Unfortunately, the laws were not fully enforced. In June 1537, Pope Paul III had already issued a bull ('*Sublimis Deus*') ordering that Indians 'are by no means to be deprived of their liberty or their property . . . nor should they be in any way enslaved' (see Hanke, 1965, p. 73; Sanderlin, 1971, pp. 16, 157; also Sullivan, 1995, pp. 248–252).

15   As he adds, pointing to the consequences of the sanctions imposed on Iraq since the Gulf War of 1990 (Falk, 2003, p. xiv): 'According to reliable and objective estimates, these sanctions have by now been responsible for almost a million civilian deaths and widespread societal suffering'—a situation further aggravated by the subsequent Iraq war.

16   Rev. Marty Martin, as reported in *The Washington Spectator*, 29(10), 15 May 2003, p. 3.

17   To be sure, the significance of American multiculturalism is contested. For many neo-conservatives, American multiculturalism is not the harbinger of cosmopolis but a threat to the maintenance of traditional American 'identity' and exceptionalism (see, e.g., Huntington, 2004).

18   The dangers of a unified or homogenized cosmopolis devoid of local and regional arenas of political contestation have been eloquently underscored by Danilo Zolo (especially 1997; 2002). As he writes (2002, pp. ix–x): 'After the hiatus of the Cold War and the formal liberation of the colonized countries of Africa and Asia, the West's ancient mission to control, occupy and "civilize" the non-Western world is returning with full force and can only provoke, as a bloody counterpoint, a "global terrorism" that is ever more ruthless and effective . . . Now more than ever, [Hans] Kelsen's formula "peace through law", looks like an Enlightenment illusion, with its prescriptive optimism and naïve cosmopolitan universalism.'

References

Ahmed, A. S. (2003) The perfect Christmas gift, in *Religion News Service* (Washington, DC: December).

Allen, M. & Gellman, B. (2002) Strike first, and use nuclear weapons if necessary, *Washington Post, National Weekly Edition*, 16–22 December.

Aronowitz, S. & Gautney, H., Eds (2003) *Implicating Empire: Globalization and Resistance in the 21st Century* (New York: Basic Books).

Atlas, J. (2003) A classicist's legacy: new empire builders, *New York Times*, 4 May (Week in Review).

Balibar, E. (2004) *We, The People of Europe? Reflections on Transnational Citizenship* (Princeton: Princeton University Press).

Barber, B. R. (2003) *Fear's Empire: War, Terrorism, and Democracy* (New York: Norton).

Barker, E. (1946) *The Politics of Aristotle* (Oxford: Clarendon Press).

Blaker, K., Ed (2003) *The Fundamentals of Extremism: The Christian Right in America* (New Boston, MI: New Boston Books).

Bluhm, H. (2002) *Die Ordnung der Ordnung: Das politische Philosophieren von Leo Strauss* (Berlin: Akademie Verlag).

Brooks, R. E. (2004) A climate that nurtures torture, *Los Angeles Times*, 9 May.

Boyle, F. A. (2003) professor of international law at the University of Illinois, comment, 17 December. Available at http://www.democracynow.org/article.pl?sid=03/12/17/1611203.

Boyle, F. A. (2004) *Destroying World Order: U.S. Imperialism in the Middle East before and after September 11* (New York: Clarity Press).

Brzezinski, Z. (2000) Epilogue: democracy's uncertain triumph, in: M. F. Plattner and A. Smolar (Eds) *Globalization, Power, and Democracy* (Baltimore, MD: Johns Hopkins University Press), pp. 148–154.

Carroll, E. J., Jr. (2001) Unilateralism amok, *Inforum* (Fourth Freedom Forum), 29 (Fall), pp. 2–3.

Las Casas, B. de (1942) *Del Único Modo de Atraer a Todos los Pueblos a la Verdadera Religión*, Ed. Augustin Millares Carlo (Mexico City: Fondo de Cultura Economica).

Las Casas, B. de (1957–58a) *Historia de las Indias*, in: Juan Perez de Tudela (Ed) *Obras escogidas* (Madrid: Biblioteca de Autores Españoles).

Las Casas, B. de (1957–58b) *Brevissima Relacion*, in: Juan Perez de Tudela(Ed) *Obras escogidas* (Madrid: Biblioteca de Autores Españoles).

Las Casas, B. de (1992a) *A Short Account of the Destruction of the Indies*, Trans. Nigel Griffin (New York: Penguin).

Las Casas, B. de (1992b) *The Devastation of the Indies: A Brief Account*, Trans. Herma Briffault (Baltimore, MD: Johns Hopkins University Press).

Las Casas, B. de (1992c) *The Only Way*, Ed. H. R. Parish, Trans. F. P. Sullivan (New York: Paulist Press).

Dallmayr, F. (1996) Modernization and postmodernization, in: *Beyond Orientalism: Essays on Cross-Cultural Encounter* (Albany, NY: State University of New York Press), pp. 149–174.

Drury, S. B. (1997) *Leo Strauss and the American Right* (New York: St. Martin's Press).

Drury, S. B. (2004) *Terror and Civilization* (New York: Palgrave/Macmillian).

Dussel, E. (1996) *The Underside of Modernity: Apel, Ricoeur, Rorty, Taylor, and the Philosophy of Liberation*, Trans. E. Mendieta (Atlantic Highlands, NJ: Humanities Press).

Eisenstadt, S. N. (1966) *Modernization: Protest and Change* (Englewood Cliffs, NJ: Prenctice-Hall).

Falk, R. (2002) The new Bush doctrine, *The Nation*, 15 July.

Falk, R. (2003) *The Great Terror War* (New York: Olive Branch Press).

Frachon, A. & Vernet, D. (2003) The strategist and the philosopher: Leo Strauss and Albert Wohlstetter, Trans. N. Madarasz, *Counter Punch*, 24 May.

Friedman, T. L. (2003) Ah, those principled Europeans, *New York Times*, 2 February, Sec. 4, p. 15.

Frum, D. & Perle, R. (2003) *An End to Evil: How to Win the War on Terror* (New York: Random House).

Gutierrez, G. (1993) *Las Casas: In Search of the Poor of Jesus Christ*, Trans. Robert R. Barr (Maryknoll, NY: Orbis Books).

Hanke, L. (1965) *The Spanish Struggle for Justice in the Conquest of America* (Boston: Little Brown).

Hardt, M. & Negri, A. (2000) *Empire* (Cambridge, MA: Harvard University Press).

Heidegger, M. (1977) The question concerning technology, in: D. F. Krell (Ed) *Martin Heidegger: Basic Writings* (New York: Harper & Row), pp. 283–317.

Huntington, S. P. (2004) *Who Are We? The Challenges to America's National Identity* (New York: Simon & Schuster).

Ignatieff, M. (2002) The burden, *New York Times Magazine*, 5 January, p. 22.

Johnson, C. (2000) *Blowback: The Costs and Consequences of American Empire* (New York: Henry Holt and Co.).

Kagan, R. (2002) Power and Weakness, *Policy Review*, 113 (June–July), pp. 3–28.

Kagan, R. (2003) *Of Paradise and Power: America and Europe in New World Order* (New York: Alfred A. Knopf).

Kant, I. (1970) Perpetual peace: a philosophical sketch, in: H. Reiss (Ed) *Kant's Political Writings*, Trans. H. B. Nisbet (Cambridge, UK: Cambridge University Press), pp. 93–130.

Kaufmann, W., Ed. (1968) Thus Spoke Zarathustra, in: *The Portable Nietzsche* (New York: Viking Press), pp. 103–439.

Keane, J.(2003) *Global Civil Society* (Cambridge, UK: Cambridge University Press).

Lampert, L. (1996) *Leo Strauss and Nietzsche* (Chicago: University of Chicago Press).

Lobe, J. (2003) Strong must rule the weak, said neo-conservatives' muse, *Inter Press Service*, 8 May.

Mead, W. R. (2002) *American Foreign Policy and How It Changed the World* (New York: Alfred A. Knopf).

Muravchik, J. (2003) The neoconservative cabal, *Commentary*, 1 September.

Nietzsche, F. (1966) *Beyond Good and Evil*, Trans. Walter Kaufmann (New York: Random House).

Nye, J. S., Jr. (2002) *The Paradox of American Power: Why the World's Only Superpower Can't Go it Alone* (New York: Oxford University Press).

Passavant, P. A. & Dean J., Eds (2004) *Empire's New Clothes: Reading Hardt and Negri* (New York: Routledge).

Prestowitz, C. (2003) *Rogue Nation: American Unilateralism and the Failure of Good Intentions* (New York: Basic Books).

Pye, L. W. (1966) *Aspects of Political Development* (Boston: Little Brown).

Qureshi, E. & Sells, M. A., Eds (2003) *The New Crusades: Constructing the Muslim Enemy* (New York: Columbia University Press).

Roy, A. (2003) Confronting empire, in *War Talk* (Cambridge, MA: South End Press), pp. 103–112. The talk was first presented at the closing rally of the World Social Forum in Porto Alegre, Brazil, 27 January 2003.

Said, E. W. (1993) *Culture and Imperialism* (New York: Alfred A. Knopf).

Sanderlin, G., Ed (1971) *Bartolemé de las Casas: A Selection of His Writings* (New York: Alfred A. Knopf).

Said, E. W. & Hitchens, C., Eds (1988) *Blaming the Victims* (London: Verso).

Sassen, S. (2002) *Global Networks, Linked Cities* (New York: Routledge).

de Sepúlveda, J. G. (1987) *Tratado sobre las justas causas de la guerra contra los Indios* (Mexico City: Fondo de Cultura Economica).

Shavit, A. (2004) White man's burden, *Haaretz*, 12 February.

Sontag, S. (2004) What have we done?, *Guardian*, 24 May.

Strauss, L. (1983) Note on the plan of *Beyond Good and Evil*, in: *Studies in Platonic Political Philosophy*, pp. 174–191 (Chicago: University of Chicago Press).

Sullivan, F. P., Ed and Trans. (1995) *Indian Freedom: The Cause of Bartolemé de las Casas* (Kansas City: Sheed & Ward).

Villa, D. (2001) *Socratic Citizenship* (Princeton, NJ: Princeton University Press).

Wiener, T. (2002) Mexico's influence in security council decision may help its ties with U.S., *New York Times*, 9 November, p. A11.

Zolo, D. (1997) *Cosmopolis: Prospects for World Government*, Trans. David McKie (Cambridge, UK: Polity Press).

Zolo, D. *Invoking Humanity: War, Law and Global Order*, Trans. F. & G. Poole (London & New York: Continuum, 2002).

From Market Globalism to Imperial Globalism: Ideology and American Power after 9/11

MANFRED B. STEGER

Introduction

Soon after the collapse of Soviet-style communism in Eastern Europe, various power elites concentrated in the global North stepped up their efforts to sell their neoliberal version of 'globalization' to the public. While not disavowing some of the coercive measures referred to by Joseph Nye as 'hard power'—particularly the application of economic pressure through international lending institutions like the IMF and World Bank—this phalanx of neoliberal forces preferred enhancing the legitimacy of their worldview by means of 'soft power', that is, the use of cultural and ideological appeals to effect their desired outcomes without commanding allegiance.[1] Seeking to make a persuasive case for a new global order based on their values, these power elites constructed and disseminated narratives and images that extolled the virtues of deregulated and globally integrated markets. Throughout the 1990s, they advanced a globalization discourse sufficiently systematic to add up to a comprehensive political ideology. Elsewhere, I have referred to it as 'globalism'—a market ideology endowing the buzzword 'globalization' with norms, values, and meanings that not only legitimate and advance neoliberal interests, but also seek to cultivate consumerist cultural identities in billions of people around the world (Steger, 2002; 2003; 2004).[2]

For most of the decade, this double-pronged strategy of utilizing the persuasive power of ideas and ideals together with the 'sticky power' of international economic policy seemed to minimize ideological dissent.[3] Many people came to accept globalism's core claims, thus internalizing large parts of an overarching normative framework that advocated the deregulation of markets, the liberalization of trade, and the privatization of state-owned enterprises.[4] Representing what Pierre Bourdieu and Zygmunt Bauman have called a 'strong' discourse, globalism was difficult to resist because it relied on the soft power of 'common sense', that is, the widespread belief that its prescriptive program ultimately derived from an accurate description of 'objective reality' (Bauman, 1999, pp. 28–29, 127–28; Bourdieu, 1998, p. 95). As Judith Butler (1996, p. 112) notes, the constant repetition, public recitation, and 'performance' of an ideology's core claims tend to have the capacity to produce what they name.

By the late 1990s, however, a growing divergence between neoliberal ideological claims and the everyday experience of people in many parts of the world undermined globalism's legitimacy. This, in turn, facilitated the production of counterdiscourses powerful enough to seriously challenge the neoliberal worldview. Disseminated by heterogenous social forces on both the political Left and Right, these competing ideological perspectives found their political manifestation in successive waves of worldwide antiglobalist protests. From the spectacular 1999 anti-WTO demonstrations in Seattle to the street protests at the 2001 G-8 Summit in Genoa, these massive displays of popular dissent elicited two major responses from the hegemonic neoliberal forces.

First, and consistent with their original soft-power strategy, some globalists responded with public admissions that globalization did, indeed, require 'minor reforms', particularly 'better management'. These concessions were often followed by highly publicized assurances to put 'a human face' on globalization. Former wizards of globalism like George Soros, Joseph Stiglitz, Jeffrey Sachs, and Paul Krugman publicly bemoaned the 'excesses of market fundamentalism' that had occurred during the 'Roaring Nineties' (see Stiglitz, 2003; 2002; Soros, 2002). At the same time, however, other globalists recommended hard-power tactics to crack down on dissenters. Yet, in order to justify their strange willingness to activate coercive state powers against protesters, these globalists sought to mobilize the corporate-media in fueling the stereotype of the chaotic, cobblestone-throwing antiglobalizer.[5]

As a result, mainstream television images broadcast from Genoa glossed over the fact that the vast majority of demonstrators were committed to nonviolent means of social change. These attempts to stabilize the neoliberal model by means of generating fear and demands for greater security were increasingly reflected in globalist discourse. Globalizing markets were now portrayed as requiring protection against the violent hordes of irrationalism. In other words, the allegedly 'inevitable' and 'irreversible' unfolding of self-regulating markets suddenly needed to be helped along by strong law enforcement measures that would 'beat back' the enemies of democracy and the free market.

After al-Qaeda's devastating attacks on the world's most recognized symbols of a US-dominated globalized economy and culture, this neoliberal tendency to tolerate or endorse hard-power tactics grew even stronger. In the volatile post-9/11 environment in the United States, neoconservative players in the Bush adminstration drew on the existing climate of fear to promote their vision of a benign American empire leading a coalition of 'allies' in the open-ended War on Terror. President George W. Bush abandoned the mildly isolationist position he espoused during the 2000 election campaign and instead adopted the bellicose views of inveterate hard-power advocates like Dick Cheney and Donald Rumsfeld.[6]

If the liberalization and global integration of markets was to continue as a viable project, many globalists felt they had little choice but to enter into a shaky ideological compromise with the ascending neoconservative forces. If neoliberals accepted that their core ideological claims had to be 'hard-powered' to fit the neoconservative agenda, then, in turn, neoconservatives would continue to support a 'free-market' discourse that also helped to soften their militarism. Indeed, this uneasy and sometimes stormy marriage between the economic neoliberalism of the 1990s and the neoconservative security agenda of the 2000s marked the birth of an 'imperial globalism' with an American face. While the hard-powering of market globalism led to a modification of some of its original claims, it would be a mistake to assume that the neoliberal project came to an end with 9/11. The Bush adminstration's embrace of hard power has been amply documented and analyzed *on the policy level* in today's raging debates over whether or not the post-9/11 United States actually constitutes an 'empire'—formal or informal.[7] However, little attention has been paid to the corresponding *ideological-discursive shift* from the soft power discourse of persuasion centered on the idea of a 'leaderless market' to the tough imperial language of American dominance. What are the major ideological differences between market globalism and imperial globalism? Seeking to shed light on the precise nature of these morphological changes in the dominant ideology, this essay scrutinizes a number of representative utterances and writings of influential advocates of globalism before and after 9/11. Focusing on what I identify as its six core claims of globalism, I analyze these major ideological changes and raise critical questions of ideological continuity. Ultimately, then, this essay seeks to contribute to the larger project of developing a critical theory of globalization by focusing on the shifting discursive power dynamics (for a more detailed discussion of developing a critical theory of globalization, see Steger, 2004, pp. 10–11; Mittelman, 2004, Chap. 4, pp. 34–44.)

Claim No. 1: Globalization is about the Liberalization and Global Integration of Markets

This foundational claim of market globalism seeks to shape global preferences without resorting to verbal threats—and, therefore, represents the essence of 'soft power' (Nye, 2004, p. 5). It activates the neoliberal ideal of the self-regulating market as the normative basis for a future global order. According to this ideological narrative, the vital functions of the free market—its rationality and efficiency, as well as its alleged ability to bring about greater social integration and material progress—can only be realized in a liberal society that values and protects individual freedom. Let us consider some examples.

A passage in a 1990s *BusinessWeek* article (13 December 1999, p. 212) clearly defines globalization in market terms: 'Globalization is about the triumph of markets over governments. Both proponents and opponents of globalization agree that the driving force today is markets, which are suborning the role of government. The truth is that the size of government has been shrinking relative to the economy almost everywhere.' Joan Spiro, US Undersecretary of State for Economic, Business, and Agricultural Affairs in the Clinton administration, stated that 'One role [of government] is to get out of the way—to remove barriers to the free flow of goods, services, and capital' (Spiro, 1996).

Perhaps the most eloquent exposition of the neoliberal claim that globalization is about the liberalization and global integration of markets can be found in Thomas Friedman's bestseller, *The Lexus and the Olive Tree: Understanding Globalization* and its post-9/11 sequel, *Longitudes and Attitudes: The World in the Age of Terrorism*. Indeed, many commentators have emphasized that Friedman's books provide the 'official narrative of globalization' in the United States today (see, e.g, Bole, 1999, pp. 14–16). The award-winning *New York Times* columnist argues that people ought to accept the following 'truth' about globalization: 'The driving idea behind globalization is free-market capitalism—the more you let market forces rule and the more you open your economy to free trade and competition, the more efficient your economy will be. Globalization means the spread of free-market capitalism to virtually every country in the world' (Friedman, 2000, p. 9).

After 9/11, both neoliberals and their opponents emphasized the continued viability of this foundational globalist claim while acknowledging a hardening of the narrative. For example, the Indian writer Arundhati Roy, one of the most eloquent critics of corporate globalization, argues that the language of neoliberalism appears to have absorbed the aggressive idiom of 'breaking open markets' (Roy, 2004, p. 11). This discursive shift is clearly visible in President Bush's public utterances before and after 9/11. During his 2000 presidential campaign, candidate Bush consistently promised to 'work tirelessly to open up markets all over the world' and 'end tariffs and break down barriers everywhere, entirely, so the whole world trades in freedom' (Bush, 2000). After 9/11, Bush still hoped to 'ignite a new area of global economic growth through free markets and free trade', but his 2002 *National Security Strategy of the United States* (NSSUS) explictly merges market language with security slogans, culminating in the credo of imperial globalism: 'Free markets and free trade are key priorities of our national security strategy' (Bush, 2002a).

Bush's post-9/11 understanding of the neoliberal project as part of an overarching security agenda has been dutifully echoed in similar remarks by world leaders as different as Paul Martin, Canada's Minister of Finance, and Goh Chok Tong, Prime Minister of Singapore (see Lien, 2003). Moreover, most importantly, a good number of neoliberal globalists went along with the hard-powerization of their market ideology. For example, Thomas Friedman—initially a strong proponent of the Bush administration's global war on terror in Afghanistan and Iraq— admonished his readers to go along with the neoconservative posture of 'aggressive engagement' in the Middle East. In his view, this was the best strategy for 'leading the Arab world into globalization' (Friedman, 2003, pp. 314–315).

Claim No. 2: Globalization is Inevitable and Irreversible

A study of the utterances of influential globalists in the 1990s reveals their reliance on an economistic narrative of historical inevitability. While disagreeing with Marxists on the final goal of historical development, globalists nonetheless share with their ideological opponents a fondness for such terms as 'irresistable', 'inevitable', and 'irreversible' to describe the projected path of globalization. Let us consider some examples.

In a speech on US foreign policy, President Clinton told his audience: 'Today we must embrace the inexorable logic of globalization ... Globalization is irreversible. Protectionism will only make things worse' (Clinton, 1999; and Clinton cited in Ross, 1997). Frederick W. Smith, chairman and CEO of FedEx Corporation, suggests that 'globalization is inevitable and inexorable and it is accelerating ... Globalization is happening, it's going to happen. It does not matter whether you like it or not, it's happening, it's going to happen' (Smith, 1999). Neoliberal elites in the global South faithfully echoed the globalist language of inevitability. For example, Manuel Villar, the Philippines Speaker of the House of Representatives, insisted that 'We cannot simply wish away the process of globalization. It is a reality of a modern world. The process is irreversible' (Villar, 1998).

Throughout the 1990s, the neoliberal portrayal of globalization as some sort of natural force, like the weather or gravity, made it easier for globalists to convince people that they would have to adapt to the discipline of the market if they were to survive and prosper. Hence, the globalist claim of inevitability neutralized the challenges of antiglobalist opponents by depoliticizing the public discourse about globalization: neoliberal policies were above politics, because they simply carried out what was ordained by nature. This view implied that, instead of acting according to a set of choices, people merely fulfill world-market laws that demanded the elimination of government controls. Since the emergence of a world based on the primacy of market values reflected the dictates of history, resistance would be unnatural, irrational, and dangerous.

In the immediate aftermath of 9/11, this claim came under sustained criticism by commentators who emphasized the 'dark side of globalization'. Some even proclaimed the imminent 'collapse of globalism', worrying that the terrorist attacks would usher in a new age of nationalism (Saul, 2004; see also Roach, 2002, p. 65). Noted neoliberal economists like Robert J. Samuelson argued in his widely read *Newsweek* column that globalization might not be inevitable since previous globalization processes had been stopped by similar cataclysmic events such as the 1914 assassination of the Austrian Archduke Franz Ferdinand in Sarajevo (Samuelson, 2003, p. 41).

On the other hand, the unfolding War on Terror allowed the Bush administration to weave the determinist language of globalism into imperial pronouncements of the inexorable triumph of the forces of 'Good' over the 'Axis of Evil'. The old soft-power discourse of *economic* inevitability reemerged confidently in the new hard power narrative of *military* inevitability. Constant assurances that the United States and its allies would prevail in the War on Terror reverberated through the media landscape. For example, Christopher Shays, neoliberal Republican Congressman from Connecticut and Chair of the House Subcommittee on National Security, publicly expressed his belief that the 'fight against global terrorism' was bound to end in a 'safer world' characterized by 'broad-based free expression and free markets'. After all, Shays added, the 'toxic zeal' of the terrorists 'can only be defeated by market forces, the relentless inevitability of free peoples pursuing their own enlightenend self-interest in common cause' (Shays, 2003).

Claim No. 3: Nobody is in Charge of Globalization

Market globalism's deterministic language offered its proponents in the 1990s yet another rhetorical advantage. If the natural laws of the market have indeed preordained a neoliberal course of history, then globalization does not reflect the arbitrary agenda of a particular social class or group. In other words, globalists merely carry out the unalterable imperatives of a transcendental force much larger than narrow partisan interests. People are not in charge of globalization; markets and technology are. Here are two examples.

Robert Hormats, vice chairman of Goldman Sachs International, emphasized that 'The great beauty of globalization is that no one is in control. The great beauty of globalization is that it is not controlled by any individual, any government, any institution' (Hormats, 1998). In his usual confident tone, Thomas Friedman, too, alleged that 'the most basic truth about globalization is this: *No one is in charge* ... We all want to believe that someone is in charge and responsible. But the global marketplace today is an Electronic Herd of often anonymous stock, bond and currency traders and multinational investors, connected by screens and networks' (Friedman, 2000, pp. 112–113).

After 9/11, it became increasingly difficult for market globalists to maintain the position that 'nobody is in charge of globalization'. While a number of corporate leaders still reflexively referred to the 'leaderless market', neoconservatives close to the Bush adminstration lectured market globalists that global security and a global liberal order 'depend on the United States—that "indispensable nation"—wielding its power' (Kagan, 2002). After all, if America indeed spearheaded the cause of universal principles, then it had a responsibility to make sure that the spread of these values was not hampered by ideological dissenters. The resulting hardening of discourse is obvious in the 2002 NSSUS. For example, Bush ends the preface of this document by glorifying tough US global leadership: 'Today, humanity holds in its hands the opportunity to further freedom's triumph over all these [terrorist] foes. The United States welcomes our [*sic*] responsibility to lead in this great mission' (Bush, 2002a).

If the United States indeed sought to conceal its imperial ambitions in the 1990s behind the soft language of market globalism, then the gloves definitely came off after 9/11, exposing the iron fist of an irate giant. The attacks changed the terms of the globalist discourse in that they enabled neoconservatives to put their global ambitions *explicitly* before a public alarmed by an amorphous terrorist threat and thus vulnerable to what Claes Ryn, Chairman of the National Humanities Institute, calls the 'neo-Jacobin spirit' of the Bush administration (Ryn, 2003, pp. 384–385). The resulting move toward imperial globalism meant that the claim 'nobody is in charge of globalization' had to be abandoned and replaced by Bush's aggressive pronouncement of global leadership.

However, the replacement of claim three with a more aggressive pronouncement of global Anglo-American leadership should not be read as a sign of globalism's ideological weakness. Rather, it reflects its ideational flexibility and growing ability to respond to a new set of political issues. Indeed, like all full-fledged political belief systems, globalism is increasingly bearing the marks of an 'ideational family' broad enough to contain the more economistic variant of the 1990s as well as its more militaristic post-9/11 manifestation.

Claim No. 4: Globalization Benefits Everyone (... in the Long Run)

This claim lies at the very core of market globalism because it provides an affirmative answer to the crucial normative question of whether globalization represents a 'good' or a 'bad' phenomenon. Market globalists in the 1990s frequently connected their arguments in favor of the integration of global markets to the alleged benefits resulting from the liberalization and expansion of world trade. At the 1996 G-7 Summit in Lyon, France, for example, the heads of states of the seven major industrialized democracies issued a joint communiqué that contains the following passage:

> Economic growth and progress in today's interdependent world is bound up with the process of globalization. Globalization provides great opportunities for the future, not only for our countries, but for all others too. Its many positive aspects include an unprecedented expansion of investment and trade; the opening up to international trade of the world's most populous regions and opportunities for more developing countries to improve their standards of living; the increasingly rapid dissemination of information, technological innovation, and the proliferation of skilled jobs. These characteristics of globalization have led to a considerable expansion of wealth and prosperity in the world. Hence we are convinced that the process of globalization is a source of hope for the future. (Economic Communiqué, 1996)

The public discourse on globalization in the 1990s was rife with such generalizations. Even cautious Alan Greenspan, chairman of the US Federal Reserve Board, insisted that 'there can be little doubt that the extraordinary changes in global finance on balance have been beneficial in facilitating significant improvements in economic structures and living standards throughout the world' (Greenspan, 1997).

In addition, globalists often seek to cement their decontestation of globalization as 'benefits for everyone' by coopting the powerful language of 'science' which claims to separate 'fact' from 'fiction' in a 'neutral' fashion, that is, solely on the basis of 'hard evidence'. And yet, the two most comprehensive empirical assessments of changes in global income distributions in the last decade have arrived at sharply conflicting results.[8] Even those globalists who consider the possibility of unequal global distribution patterns nonetheless insist that the market itself will eventually correct these 'irregularities'. As John Meehan, chairman of the US Public Securities Association, puts it, 'episodic dislocations' such as mass unemployment and reduced social services might be 'necessary in the short run', but, 'in the long run', they will give way to 'quantum leaps in productivity' (Meehan, 1997).

Remarkably resilient after 9/11, this claim nonetheless received hard-power treatment. Indeed, the terrorist attacks actually added to the fervor with which imperial globalists speak of the supposed benefits accruing from the rapid liberalization and global integration of markets. For example, in the NSSUS, Bush consistently mentions the alleged benefits of securing the benefits of free markets: 'Free trade and free markets have proven their ability to lift whole societies out of poverty—so the United States will work with individual nations, entire regions, and the entire global trading community to build a world that trades in freedom and therefore grows in prosperity' (Bush, 2002a).

Claim No. 5: Globalization Furthers the Spread of Democracy in the World

This claim is anchored in the neoliberal assertion that *freedom*, *free markets*, *free trade* and *democracy* are synonymous terms. Affirmed as common sense throughout the 1990s, the compatibility of these concepts often went unchallenged in the public discourse. Francis Fukuyama, for example, asserted that there existed a clear correlation between a country's level of economic development and successful democracy. While globalization and capital development did not automatically produce democracies, 'the level of economic development resulting from globalization is conducive to the creation of complex civil societies with a powerful middle class. It is this class and societal structure that facilitates democracy' (Fukuyama, n.d.). Praising the economic transitions towards capitalism in Eastern Europe, US Senator Hillary Rodham Clinton told her Polish audience that the emergence of new businesses and shopping centers in former communist countries should be seen as the 'backbone of democracy' (Rodham Clinton, 1999).

After September 11, this claim, too, became firmly linked to the Bush administration's security agenda. The President did not mince words in 'Securing Freedom's Triumph'—his *New York Times* op-ed piece a year after the attacks: 'As we preserve the peace, America also has an opportunity to extend the benefits of freedom and progress to nations that lack them. We seek a peace where repression, resentment and povery are replaced with the hope of democracy, development, free markets and free trade' (Bush, 2002b). Fourteen months later, he reaffirmed this 'forward strategy for freedom' by referring to his country's unwavering 'commitment to the global expansion of democracy' as the 'third pillar' of the United States' 'peace and security vision for the world' (Bush, 2003).

This idea of securing 'freedom' through an American-led drive for political and economic 'democratization' around the globe—thus connecting the military objectives of the War on Terror to the neoliberal agenda of liberalizing markets—has emerged as the centerpiece of imperial globalism. And nowhere did these hard discursive dynamics of imperial globalism become as apparent as in the corporate scramble for Iraq following the official end of 'major combat operations' on 1 May 2003. Already during the first days of the Iraq war in late March 2003, globalists with strong ties to the Republican party had suggested that Iraq be subject to a radical neoliberal treatment.

Exemplifying this ideological marriage of convenience between many neoliberals and neoconservatives, Robert McFarlane, former National Security Advisor to President Reagan and current chairman of the Washington, DC-based corporation Energy & Communication Solutions, LLC, together with Michael Bleyzer, CEO and president of SigmaBleyzer, an international equity fund management company, co-authored a remarkably brazen op-ed piece in *The Wall Street Journal* bearing the suggestive title, 'Taking Iraq Private'. Calling on 'major U.S. corporations, jointly with other multinationals', to 'lead the effort to create capital-friendly environments in developing countries', the globalist duo praised the military operations in Iraq as an indispensible tool in establishing the 'political, economic and social stability' necessary for 'building the basic institutions that make democracy possible'. Alleging that recent analyses of the 'economic policies of 128 countries' identified neoliberal measures as the 'key drivers for development', the two men reminded the government that 'the U.S. must demonstrate that it is not only the most powerful military power on the planet, but also the foremost market economy in the world, capable of leading a greater number of developing nations to a more prosperous and stable future' (Mcfarlane & Bleyzer, 2003).

It did not take a long time for the Bush administration to heed such advice. In what amounted to a concentrated public relations initiative in autumn 2003, Secretary of State Colin Powell conveyed the administration's view of the matter in countless speeches, Internet messages, and television and radio interviews. For example, in his address to an economic conference on the Middle East attended by hundreds of American and Arab-American business executives, Powell emphasized the adminstration's intention to develop the US–Middle East Free Trade Area (MEFTA) within a decade. Linked to the adminstration's 2002 'US–Middle East Partnership Initiative', the new project also included programs to send Arab college students to work as interns in American corporations (Colin Powell cited in Treaster, 2003; Olivastro, 2002).

In the meantime, in Iraq, the US head of the Coalition Provisional Authority, Ambassador Paul Bremer, had pressured the Governing Council to let Order 39 take effect, permitting complete foreign ownership of Iraqi companies and assets (excluding natural resources) that had hitherto been publicly owned, total remittance of profits, and some of the lowest corporate tax rates in the world (Williams, 2003). No doubt, the military-industrial complex and related enterprises have been the biggest beneficiaries of imperial globalism. For example, in the fiscal year 2002, the 'Big Three' US weapons makers—Lockheed Martin, Boeing, and Northrop Grumman—received a total of more than $42 billion in Pentagon contracts. This was an increase of nearly one-third from 2000, President Clinton's final year in office (Hartung, 2004, pp. 19–21). The Bush adminstration awarded largely without competition or detailed explanations of total costs multi-billion dollar reconstruction contracts to such companies as Bechtel Group Inc., Halliburton Co., and Stevedoring Services of America—all generous contributors to the Republican party with strong personal connections to high-level officials in the two Bush administrations, including Vice President Cheney, former Secretary of State George Shultz, Under Secretary of Defense Douglas Feith, and Defense Policy Board member Richard Perle. Companies headquartered in countries that opposed the Iraq war, like France, Germany, and Russia, were not invited to submit any bids (Mittal, 2003).

Thus, imperial globalism amounts to a neoliberal structural adjustment program by military means. With their economy in complete shambles and burdened with a national debt of nearly $400 billion, the Iraqi people have to come to grips with the emerging reality that debtor countries might be unwilling to write off their loans in their entirety, thus making the privatization of the country's oil industry—either partially or fully—a distinct possibility for fiscal reasons. Moreover, UN Security Council Resolution 1483, adopted on 23 May 2003, incorporated Iraq into the global market, but granted broad power to the United States and United Kingdom to manage Iraq's economic fate for at least a year. It should come as no surprise that Secretary of Defense Donald Rumsfeld has announced that since the American people have already made significant investments in 'liberating and rebuilding Iraq', the administration would turn to the Iraqi regime for funds before further burdening the US taxpayer (Looney, 2003).

In short, the globalist claim of spreading freedom and democracy has become a convenient narrative for the Bush administration and its supporters in Congress to secure and expand its influence and power globally by combining arguments in favor of military interventions with the familiar slogans of market liberalization.

Claim No. 6: Globalization Requires a War on Terror

At this point, it should be obvious why, in the post-9/11 context, it has become necessary for neoliberal globalist forces to make their peace with a hardened narrative. If globalization, understood as the liberalization and global integration of markets, is to remain a viable project then the coercive powers of the state have to be employed against those who threaten it—both internal antiglobalist dissenters and external terrorist foes. Hence the addition of a new globalist claim: globalization requires a war on terror.

Two representative samples of how this new claim has been circulating in the public discourse are Thomas Barnett's 'The Pentagon's New Map', published in the March 2003 issue of *Esquire* magazine, and Robert Kaplan's 'Supremacy by Stealth' featured in the July 2003 issue of *The Atlantic Monthly*. Both publications reach a mass readership and its authors are respected professionals in their fields. Thomas Barnett, a Harvard-educated professor of military strategy at the US Naval War College, has been advising the Office of the Secretary of Defense for some time. Within weeks of September 11, he was called to the Pentagon and installed as the assistant for strategic futures in the Office of Force Transformations. Since then, he has been giving his briefings regularly at the Pentagon, in the intelligence community, and to high-ranking officers from branches of the military.

In his much-debated *Esquire* article, which he later expanded into a best-selling book, Barnett argues that the Iraq War marks 'the moment when Washington takes real ownership of strategic security in the age of globalization'. He breaks the globe down into three distinct regions. The first is characterized by 'globalization thick with network connectivity, financial transactions, liberal media flows, and collective security', yielding nations featuring stable democratic governments, transparency, rising standards of living, and more deaths by suicide than by murder (North America, most of Europe, Australia, New Zealand, and a small part of Latin America). He calls these regions of the world the 'Functioning Core', or 'Core'. Conversely, areas where 'globalization is thinning or just plain absent' constitute a region plagued by repressive political regimes, regulated markets, mass murder, and widespread poverty and disease (the Caribbean Rim, virtually all of Africa, the Balkans, the Caucasus, Central Asia, the Middle East and Southwest Asia, and much of Southeast Asia). The breeding ground of 'global terrorists', Barnett refers to this region as the 'Non-Integrating Gap', or 'Gap'. Between these two regions, one finds 'seam states' that 'lie along the Gap's bloody boundaries' (Mexico, Brazil, South Africa, Morocco, Algeria, Greece, Turkey, Pakistan, Thailand, Malaysia, the Philippines, and Indonesia).

For Barnett, the importance of September 11 is that the attacks forced the United States and its allies to make a long-term military commitment to 'deal with the entire Gap as a strategic threat environment'. In other words, the desired spread of globalization requires a War on Terror. Its three main objectives are: '1) Increase the Core's immune system capabilities for responding to September 11-like system perturbations; 2) Work on the seam states to firewall the Core from the Gap's worst exports, such as terror, drugs, and pandemics; and, most important, 3) *Shrink the Gap* . . . The Middle East is the perfect place to start'. The third point is particularly important, because 'the real battlegrounds in the global war on terrorism are still *over there*'. As Barnett emphasizes, 'We ignore the Gap's existence at our own peril, because it will not go away until we as a nation respond to the challenge of making globalization truly global'.

At the end of his article, Barnett offers a nod to neoliberals by conceding 'it will take a whole lot more than the U.S. exporting security to shrink the Gap', because 'the integration of the Gap will ultimately depend more on private investment that anything the Core's public sector can offer. But it all has to begin with security, because free markets and democracy cannot flourish amid chronic conflict' (Barnett, 2003; 2004).

This celebration of hard-power US hegemony is precisely the starting point of Robert D. Kaplan's recent essay. Simply taking for granted that 'the United States now possesses a global empire', the award-winning journalist and best-selling author urges his readership to 'move beyond a statement of the obvious' and instead join him in pondering how America should 'manage an unruly world' after 9/11:

> The purpose of [US] power is not power itself; it is the fundamentally liberal purpose of sustaining the key characteristics of an orderly world. Those characteristics include basic political stability; the idea of liberty, pragmatically conceived; respect for property; economic freedom; and representative government, culturally understood. At this moment in time it is American power, and American power only, that can serve as an organizing principle for the worldwide expansion of a liberal civil society. (Kaplan, 2003a)

What does Kaplan mean by 'the idea of liberty, pragmatically conceived'? It turns out that Kaplan's pragmatics of liberty refer chiefly to hard-power military tactics designed to maintain American pre-eminence: fast-track naturalization for foreign-born soldiers fighting for the empire; training special forces to be lethal killers one moment and humanitarians the next; using the military to promote democracy; not to let military missions be compromised by diplomacy; the resolve to 'fight on every front', including the willingness to strike potential enemies pre-emptively on limited evidence, deal with the media 'more strictly', and crack down on internal dissent, especially anti-war demonstrators. Kaplan suggests 'Ten Rules' for running the world, which culminate in the idea that the best way for the United States to maintain and expand its empire is to adopt the 'pagan warrior ethos of second-century Rome'. What Kaplan seems to forget in the heat of his argument, however, is that neither Emperors Trajan nor Hadrian were renowned for their liberal inclinations. This, of course, is the central problem of the uneasy compromise between neoliberalism and neoconservatism: once empire gets hold of market globalism, it may turn it into a very different ideological creature. No wonder, then, that Kaplan closes his article with a panegyric to Winston Churchill and his assessment of the United States as 'a worthy successor to the British Empire, one that would carry on Britain's liberalizing mission' (Kaplan, 2003a).

From Market Globalism to Imperial Globalism: Ideological Continuity or Rift?

As capitalist liberalism reinvented itself in the last two decades, it drew largely on the basic ideas of nineteenth-century British free-market philosophers. Still, it represented a remarkable ideological achievement of neoliberal globalists in the 1990s to re-energize these quaint arguments with the buzzword 'globalization', thereby bestowing new currency upon their antiquated vision. The Anglo-American framers of market globalism spoke softly and persuasively as they sought to attract people worldwide to their vision of globalization as a leaderless, inevitable juggernaut that would ultimately engulf the entire world and produce liberal democracy and material benefits for everyone.

In the harsh political climate following the attacks of September 11, however, many market globalists struggled to maintain the viability of their project. One obvious solution was to toughen up their ideological claims to fit the neoconservative vision of a benign US empire relying on overwhelming military power. As a result, market globalism morphed into imperial globalism. Claims one (globalization is about the liberalization and global integration of markets) and four (globalization benefits everyone)—the backbone of market globalism—are still largely intact but had to undergo hard-power facelifts. The determinist language of claim two found its new expression in the proclaimed 'inevitability' of America's military triumph over its terrorist nemesis. Claim three (nobody is in charge of globalization), however, was dropped in favor of Bush's ostentatious pronouncement of US global leadership. Claim five (globalization furthers the spread of democracy in the world) ascended to new heights with the hard power mission of 'building democracy' in the Gap regions. The neoconservative commitment to 'American values' of freedom, security, and free markets made it necessary to add claim six (globalization requires a War on Terror) to globalism's discursive arsenal. Robert Kaplan best captures the new logic of imperial globalism: 'You have to have military and economic power behind it, or else your ideas cannot spread' (Kaplan, 2003b).

But this changing morphology of globalism raises the legitimate question of ideological continuity: how much of 'neoliberalism' remains in imperial globalism? After all, in recent years, leading neoliberal voices like George Soros and Paul Krugman fiercely denounced the hard-power approach of neoconservatives. At first glance, then, it appears that there has been more of a split than a convergence between market globalism and imperial globalism, with some neoliberal globalist elites openly expressing both their dislike for and mistrust of the unilaterist imperialist drive of the Bush government. After all, they argued, their 1990s brand of globalism had been very different from its imperial version: fundamentally multilateral, it was strongly committed to the mutual effort of creating military stability, a transnational trade regime, and comprehensive international treaties (see Soros, 2003; Krugman, 2003).

There is no question that a number of prominent neoliberals have refused to make ideological compromises with neoconservatives, especially on the subject of unilateralism. Combining their hands-off attitude toward Big Business with intrusive government action for the regulation of the ordinary citizenry in the name of public security and traditional values, neoconservatives have advocated a more assertive and expansive use of both economic and military power than neo-liberals—ostensibly for the purpose of promoting freedom and democracy around the world. These sentiments seem to imply a strong commitment to universalistic principles, but, as one commentator puts it,

> Unlike liberal Wilsonians, their [neoconservatives'] promotion of democracy is not for the sake of democracy and human rights in and of themselves. Rather, democracy-promotion is meant to bolster America's security and to further its world preeminence; it is thought to be pragmatically related to the U.S. national interest. The principles of these neocons[ervatives] are universalistic, but not so their policy, which steers clear of international organizations and is nationalist and unilateralist. (Wolfson, 2004; see also Lind, 2004)

On the other hand, it is crucial to bear in mind that neoliberalism and neoconservativism in the United States are not ideological opposites. In fact, they represent variations on the same liberal theme, and their similarities often outweigh their differences. Contemporary American neocon-servatives are far removed from classical British traditionalists who expressed a fondness for aristocratic virtues and bemoaned radical social change, disliked egalitarian principles, and dis-trusted progress and reason. Rather, American neoconservatives subscribe to a variant of liberal-ism they relate to the world views espoused by Ronald Reagan, Theodore Roosevelt, Abraham Lincoln, and James Madison.

In fact, the militaristic display put on at the 2004 Democratic Convention in Boston showed that despite persisting differences with the Bush administration's crude unilateralism, prominent neoliberals like John Kerry and Hilary Rodham Clinton have embraced large portions of the Republican hard-power security agenda, including the neoconservative dogma that the United States does not 'ask anybody's permission' in pursuit of its national interests. Finally, on major issues of economic globalization such as trade liberalization, deregulation, and privatiza-tion, the ideological differences between neoliberals and neoconservatives have been negligble for years. Like the late nineteenth-century context that gave rise to American imperialism, the post-9/11 landscape seems to call for a hard-power globalism that unites the twin goals of global economic and political hegemony in the name of high-sounding ideals like strength, security, just peace, democracy, development, free markets, and free trade.

Overall, then, my argument in favor of considerable ideological continuity between 1990s market globalism and 2000s imperial globalism leaves room for the dangerous possibility of an ideological turn toward US nationalism and right-wing militarism. In my view, claim six best captures this ominous potential. On one hand, the claim that globalization requires a global war on terror attests to globalism's political responsiveness and conceptual flexi-bility—qualities that characterize mature political belief systems (for possible criteria of 'mature' ideologies, see Freeden, 2003). On the other hand, however, claim six possesses a paradoxical character. If global terror were no longer a major issue, it would disappear without doing damage to the overall conceptual coherence of globalism. Hence, it appears that claim six is a contingent one and thus *less important* than the previous five. If, however, the global War on Terror turns out to be a lengthy and intense engagement—as suggested by the Bush administration—then it would become actually *more important* over time. No wonder, then, that some commentators who seize upon the second option have claimed to detect a dangerous turn of globalism toward fascism (Falk, 2003).

To be sure, throughout the 1990s there had been sinister warnings on the part of some cultural theorists that globalization was actually 'Americanization' or 'McDonaldization' in universalist and rationalist disguise (see, e.g., Latouche, 1996; Ritzer, 1993). But US unilaterism and belligerence in the wake of 9/11 constitutes a much more serious manifestation of the same phenomenon. Indeed, the problem with globalism's turn toward nationalism has been as much conceptual as political. After all, bestowing meaning on 'globalization' by connecting it to the idea of a necessary global War on Terror has created serious logical contradictions. First, the globalists' reliance on the coercive powers of the state to secure their project undermines both the idea of the 'self-regulating market' and the claim of historical 'inevitability'. Second, the belligerent vision of enforcing 'democracy' and 'freedom' at gunpoint conflicts with the common understanding of liberty as absence of coercion. Third, as noted above, the Anglo-American unilateralism contradicts the cosmopolitan, universal spirit associated with the concept 'globalization'—hence the criticism of 'reformed' neoliberals like George Soros.

In short, introducing claim six as an ideological pillar of globalism runs a considerable risk of causing irreparable damage to the political belief system. After all, the celebration of globalization in American imperialist terminology invites a conceptual contradiction that may eventually prove to be fatal to globalism. And yet, if the political issues of our time indeed favor an ideology that boldly arranges seemingly conflicting pieces of three major political belief systems—liberalism, conservatism, and nationalism—around the idea of 'globalization', then imperial globalism might actually achieve a level of ideological dominance unprecedented in modern history.

Notes

1   The terms 'hard power' and 'soft power' have been coined by Joseph S. Nye. However, the power dynamics in question have been described and analyzed in different terms by generations of political thinkers influenced by the writings of Antonio Gramsci. For the latest elaboration of his perspective on power, see Nye (2004).

2   As I point out in these studies, these power elites consist chiefly of corporate managers, executives of large transnational corporations (TNCs), corporate lobbyists, high-level military officers, prominent journalists and public-relations specialists, intellectuals writing to a large public audience, state bureaucrats and influential politicians. It is questionable whether these social elites constitute a coherent 'transnational capitalist class' (in an orthodox Marxist sense), as Leslie Sklair suggests. In my view, Mark Rupert's neo-Gramscian concept of a 'transnational historic bloc of internationally-oriented capitalists, liberal statesman, and their allies' seems to come closer to an accurate description of the loose, heterogeneous, and often disagreeing global alliance of neoliberal forces that I have in mind (see Sklair, 2001; Rupert, 2000, pp. 16–17, 154).

3   A *BusinessWeek*–Harris poll on globalization conducted by Harris Interactive between 7 and 10 April 2000 found that 65% of 1,024 American respondents thought that globalization was a 'good thing' for consumers and businesses in both the United States and the rest of the world. More recent polls are still showing a slim majority holding these views. For example, a 2004 University of Maryland Center on Policy Attitudes poll shows that slightly more than 50% of respondents saw globalization as 'positive' or 'somewhat positive'. At the same time, however, this number confirms a significant decline in positive attitudes since the late 1990s. See http://americans-world.org/digest/global_issues/globalization?gz_summary.cfm.

4   Walter Russell Mead argues rather convincingly that the military and economic dimensions of Nye's 'hard power' concept are sufficiently different to warrant separate terms. Thus he refers to military power as 'sharp power', and to economic power as 'sticky power', which he defines as a more coercive 'sort of soft power' comprised 'by a set of economic institutions and policies that attracts others toward U.S. influence and then traps them in it' (see Mead, 2004, pp. 46–53).

5   For example, at the G-8 Summit in Genoa, the Italian government employed a contingent of over 16,000 police and military troops to 'guarantee the safety' of delegates who pondered new neoliberal measures.

6   Joseph Nye (2004, p. ix) reports that Secretary Rumsfeld responded to a question about the relevance of 'soft power' in the US foreign policy by claiming that he did not know what the term meant.

7   The post-9/11 literature on the power dynamics of 'American Empire' is vast and rapidly growing (see, e.g., Johnson, 2004; Boggs, 2004; Todd, 2003; Soros, 2003; Schmemann, 2003; Mann, 2003; Harvey, 2003). Michael Walzer, for example, suggests that the post-9/11 American empire constitutes a 'new beast' characterized by 'a looser form of rule, less authoritarian than empire is or was, more dependent on the agreement of others'. At the same time, Walzer acknowldges the administration's shift to hard power by conceding that 'George W. Bush's unilateralism is a bid for hegemony without compromise; perhaps he sees America playing an imperial—perhaps also messianic—role in the world' (see Walzer, 2003, pp. 27–30).

8   Columbia University economist Xavier Sala i-Martin argues that his evidence shows that inequality of individuals across the world is declining; but according to World Bank economist Branko Milanovic, global inequality has risen (see Secor, 2003).

References

Barnett, T. P. M. (2003) The Pentagon's new map, *Esquire* (March). Available at http://www.nwc.navy.mil/newrulessets/ThePentagonsNewMap.htm.

Barnett, T. P. M. *The Pentagon's New Map: War and Peace in the 21st Century* (New York: Putnam, 2004).

Bauman, Z. (1999) *In Search of Politics* (Stanford, CA: Stanford University Press).

Boggs, C. (2004) *The New Militarism: U.S. Empire and Endless War* (Lanham, MD: Rowman & Littlefield Publishers).

Bole, W. (1999) Tales of globalization, *America*, 181(18), 4 December, pp. 14–16.

Bourdieu, P. (1998) *Acts of Resistance* (New York: The New Press).

Bush, G. W. (2000) speech at the Republican Primary debate in West Columbia, SC, 7 January. Available at http://www.issues2002.org/Background_Free_Trade.htm.

Bush, G. W. (2002a) *National Security Strategy of the United States* (NSSUS). Available at http://www.whitehouse.gov/nsc/print/nssall.html.

Bush, G. W. (2002b) Securing freedom's triumph, *New York Times*, 11 September.

Bush, G. W. (2003) Speech in London on Iraq and the Mideast, printed in *New York Times*, 19 November.

Butler, J. (1996) Gender as performance, in P. Osborne (Ed) *A Critical Sense: Interviews with Intellectuals* (London: Routledge).

Clinton, W. (1999) Remarks by the President on Foreign Policy, San Francisco, 26 February. Available at http://www.pub.whitehouse.gov/urires/12R?urn:pdi://oma.eop.gove.us/1999/3/1/3.text.1.html.

Economic Communiqué (1996) G-7 Summit, Lyon, June 28. Available at http://library.utoronto.ca/www/g7/96ecopre.html.

Falk, R. (2003) Will the empire be fascist?, *The Transnational Foundation for Peace and Future Research Forum*, 24 March. Available at http://www.transnational.org/forum/meet/2003/Falk_FascistEmpire.html.

Freeden, M. (2003) Editorial: ideological boundaries and ideological systems, *Journal of Political Ideologies*, 8(1), pp. 1–8.

Friedman, T. (2000) *The Lexus and the Olive Tree: Understanding Globalization* (New York: Anchor Books).

Friedman, T. (2003) *Longitudes and Attitudes: The World in the Age of Terrorism* (New York: Anchor Books).

Fukuyama, F. (n.d.) Economic globalization and culture: a discussion with Dr. Francis Fukuyama. Available at http://www.ml.com/woml/forum/global2.html.

Greenspan, A. (1997) The globalization of finance, 14 October. Available at http://cato.org/pubs/journal/cj17n3-1.html.

Hartung, W. H. (2004) Making money on terrorism, *The Nation*, 23 February, pp. 19–21.

Harvey, D. (2003) *The New Imperialism* (Oxford, UK: Oxford University Press).

Hormats, R. (1998) PBS interview with Danny Schechter, February. Available at http://pbs.org/globalization/hormats1.html.

Johnson, C. (2004) *The Sorrows of Empire: Militarism, Secrecy, and the End of the Republic* (New York: Metropolitan Books).

Kagan, R. (2002) The U.S.–Europe divide, *Washington Post*, 26 May.

Kaplan, R. D. (2003a) Supremacy by stealth, *The Atlantic Monthly* (July/August). Available at http://www.theatlantic.com/issues/2003/07/kaplan.htm.

Kaplan, R. D. (2003b) The hard edge of American values, *The Atlantic Monthly Online*, 18 June. Available at http://www.theatlantic.com/fc...com/unbound/interviews/int2003-06-18.htm.

Krugman, P. (2003) *The Great Unraveling: Losing Our Way in the New Century* (New York: Norton).

Latouche, S. (1996) *The Westernization of the World* (Cambridge: Polity Press).

Lien, J. (2003) Open trade doors in East Asia, *Business Times Singapore*, 9 May.

Lind, M. (2004) A tragedy of errors, *The Nation*, 23 February, pp. 23–32.

Looney, R. (2003) Bean counting in Baghdad: debt, reparations, reconstruction, and resources, *Middle East Review of International Affairs Journal*, 7(3). Available at http://meria.idc.ac.il/journal/2003/issue3/jv7n3a4.html.

Mann, M. (2003) *Incoherent Empire* (London: Verso).

Mcfarlane, R. & Bleyzer, M. (2003) Taking Iraq private, *The Wall Street Journal*, 27 March.

Mead, W. R. (2004) *Foreign Policy* (March/April), pp. 46–53.

Meehan, J. J. (1997) Globalization and technology at work in the bond markets, Speech given in Phoenix, AZ, 1 March. Available at http://www/bondmarkets.com/news/Meehanspeechfinal.html.

Mittal, A. (2003) Open fire and open markets: strategy of an empire, *Common Dreams*, 6 September. Available at http://www.ccmep.org/2003_articles/090603_open_fire_and_open_markets.htm.

Mittelman, J. H. (2004) *Wither Globalization? The Vortex of Knowledge and Ideology* (New York: Routledge).

Nye, J. S. (2004) *Soft Power: The Means to Success in World Politics* (New York: PublicAffairs).

Olivastro, A. (2002) Powell announces U.S.–Middle East partnership initiative, *The Heritage Foundation*, 12 December. Available at http://www.heritage.org/research/middleeast/wm179.cfm.

Ritzer, G. (1993) *The McDonaldization of Society: An Investigation into the Changing Character of Contemporary Social Life* (Thousand Oaks, CA: Pine Forge Press).

Roach, S. (2002) Is it at risk?—globalisation, *The Economist*, 2 February, p. 65.

Rodham Clinton, H. (1999) Growth of democracy in Eastern Europe, Warsaw, 5 October. Available at http://www.whitehouse.gov/WH/EOP/FirstLady/html/generalspeeches/1999/19991005.html.

Ross, S. (1997) Clinton talk of better living, *Associated Press*, 15 October. Available at http://more.abcnews.go.com/sections/world/brazil1014/index.html.

Roy, A. (2004) The new American century, *The Nation*, 9 February, p. 11.

Rupert, M. (2000) *Ideologies of Globalization: Contending Visions of a New World Order* (London: Routledge).

Ryn, C. (2003) The ideology of American empire, *Orbis* (Summer), pp. 384–385.

Samuelson, R. J. (2003) Globalization goes to war, *Newsweek*, 24 February, p. 41.

Saul, J. R. (2004) The collapse of globalism and the rebirth of nationalism, *Harper's Magazine* (March), pp. 33–43.

Schmemann, S. (2003) *America Unbound: The Bush Revolution in Foreign Policy* (Washington: Brookings Institution Press).

Secor, L. (2003) Mind the gap, *The Boston Globe*, 5 January.

Shays, C. (2003) Free markets and fighting terrorism, *The Washington Times*, 10 June.

Sklair, L. (2001) *The Transnational Capitalist Class* (Oxford, UK: Blackwell).

Smith F. W. (1999) cited in International Finance Experts Preview Upcoming Global Economic Forum, 1 April. Available at http://www.econstrat.org/pctranscript.html.

Soros, G. (2002) *George Soros on Globalization* (New York: PublicAffairs).

Soros, G. (2003) *The Bubble of American Supremacy: Correcting the Misuse of American Power* (New York: PublicAffairs).

Spiro, J. E. (1996) The challenges of globalization, speech at the World Economic Development Congress in Washington, DC, 26 September. Available at http://www.state.gov/www/issues/economic/960926.html.

Steger, M. B. (2002) *Globalism: The New Market Ideology* (Lanham, MD: Rowman & Littlefield Publishers).

Steger, M. B. (2003) *Globalization: A Very Short Introduction* (Oxford, UK: Oxford University Press).

Steger, M. B., Ed (2004) *Rethinking Globalism* (Lanham, MD: Rowman & Littlefield Publishers).

Stiglitz, J. (2002) *Globalization and Its Discontents* (New York: Norton).

Stiglitz, J. (2003) *The Roaring Nineties* (New York: Norton).

Todd, E. (2003) *After Empire: The Breakdown of the American Order* (New York: Columbia University Press).

Treaster, J. (2003) Powell tells Arab-Americans of hopes to develop Mideast, *New York Times*, 30 September.

Villar, M., Jr. (1998) High-level dialogue on the theme of the social and economic impact of globalization and interdependence and their policy implications, New York, 17 September. Available at http://www.un.int/philippines/villar.html.

Walzer, M. (2003) Is there an American empire?, *Dissent* (Fall), pp. 27–31.

Williams, S. (2003) The seeds of Iraq's future terror, *The Guardian*, 28 October.

Wolfson, A. (2004) Conservatives and neoconservatives, *The Public Interest* (Winter). Available at http://www.thepublicinterest.com/current/article2.html.

Dr. Manfred B. Steger is Professor of Global Studies and Head of School of International and Community Studies at the Royal Melbourne Institute of Technology, Australia. He is also a Research Fellow at the Globalization Research Center at the University of Hawai'i-Manoa. His academic fields of expertise include global studies, political and social theory, and theories of nonviolence. His most recent publications include *Globalism: Market Ideology Meets Terrorism*, 2nd ed. (Rowman & Littlefield, 2005: 1st ed. 2002); *Judging Nonviolence: The Dispute Between Realists and Idealists* (Routledge, 2003); *Globalization* (Oxford University Press, 2003); *Gandhi's Dilemma: Nonviolent Principles and Nationalist Power* (St. Martin's Press, 2000); and *The Quest For Evolutionary Socialism: Eduard Bernstein and Social Democracy* (Cambridge University Press, 1996). He is currently working on a book manuscript titled, *Ideology in the Global Age: The Transformation of the Modern Imaginary* (under contract with Oxford University Press).

Capital, Class and the State in the Global Political Economy

WILLIAM K. TABB

It is as true for Marxists as it is for everyone else that making sense of globalization is the great Rhorshak test of our time. Matters of the relation of state theory and capital logic need to be interpreted in terms of the governance of the contemporary imperialist system, its contradictions and oppositional potentialities. Issues of accumulation and class must be retheorized in the historical conjuncture in which we live. While mainstream discourse stresses the inevitability and desirability of globalization variously defined, Marxism invites us to see such phenomena in historical perspective, to examine institutions and social relations—whether changing legal definitions of property or financial contracts and more broadly rights claims of capital and labor. This hardly means that Marxists are in agreement on the meaning for our time of such basic constructs as class, the theory of the state, imperialism or tendencies and contradictions of accumulation on a world scale. I think however that this is a particularly fertile time for such theorizing and a great deal of fruitful work is being produced by Marxists and others. In this paper I discuss the relation of state logic and capital logic in the contemporary global political economy, a period in which the use of the term imperialism has come back into fashion along with discussion of the merits of a presumed benign American Empire.

I use the term imperialism in its broadest sense to describe the process whereby leading fractions of the ruling class or, in a more sanitized framing, policy makers of more powerful countries use economic and military capacities to appropriate the land, labor, natural resources and markets of other countries to foster capital accumulation under the control of wealthy interests at home and abroad. I am surely not alone in seeing imperialism as always about the process of expropriation/appropriation by metropolitan capital of the resources, assets, and wealth of other countries, nationality groupings, and indigenous peoples all over the planet. The different phases of imperialism are to be distinguished by the precise manner in which this process takes place, the degree of success it has, the resistance it encounters, and the alternative visions of transnational social relations which are generated (Parenti, 2002; Patnaik, 2004). It is this need for historical specificity in the context of broader theory which drives my research.

This paper is organized into four sections. The first lays out the theoretical priors , the starting point of what is to follow. A second section examines the agenda of core capital as embodied in the unannounced goals of what I have termed the global state economic governance institutions (Tabb, 2004) as they apply to the less developed and newly industrializing economies. Part three addresses the interests and actions of the US more directly in state power terms suggesting how financialization has preferentially benefited American capital and financial over-extension threatens the United States and the world financial regime. A fourth part of the paper discusses regional tensions and the emergence and trajectory of bloc competition prompted by desire to contest US ambition to govern a unipolar global political economy. The paper ends with some concluding thoughts on these developments.

Conceptual Framings

Concretely theorizing imperialism involves choosing both an approach to the theory of the state and the logic of the accumulation process specific to the conjuncture under study. In looking at American imperialism today I find it useful to think in terms of two wings of the imperial eagle, two logics in capitalist exploitation not totally separate of course, for they together impel the bird of prey, but in the emphases on one or the other logics as part of a larger division of labor between, as Ellen Wood (2002, p. 30) has put the matter, 'the economic moment of appropriation and the extra-economic or political moment of coercion', qualifying her formulation to underline that the political moment of coercion is never absent from the economic moment of appropriation. I would stress that the moments analytically separable are always connected. The economic moment of appropriation requires coercion to impose not simply something called 'the rule of the free market' but the specific ways in which particular exchange norms and regulations are established and enforced. None the less, the dynamic of the market and the political use of threat and of military coercion certainly represent a range of policy alternatives for the more powerful capitalist state of our day.

Global state economic governance institutions represent one wing of the imperial eagle, that of the liberal internationalists who favor multilateral negotiation as a method of regulation and expansion of the territorial basis and the spheres of exchange in which norms and rules favoring the interests of transnational capital are applied and enforced. They are globalist in their outlook, seeing the world political economy as the unit of analysis framing the jockeying to gain relative advantage. They tend to be instrumentally multilateralist and liberal institutionalists. The other wing, to mix metaphors a bit, is the iron fist ready to crush resistance and harshly bring back the disobedient into the fold. That the propaganda machine defining rogue states as enemies posing threats to the legal order and to the global hegemon's own security may seem laughable, but invasion of tiny Grenada or the overthrow of Sandinista Nicaragua proceed on such a basis no less than regime change in Iraq. George W. Bush White House's muscular assertiveness of the right to preemptively attack any it chooses is an extreme version. This wing sees an inter/ national political economy in which power is more of a zero sum game. They are nationalist and realist in focus. The previous administration of Bill Clinton, in which the key cabinet player was Robert Rubin as Secretary of the Treasury rather than as under Bush Donald Rumsfeld the Secretary of Defense, signaled its preference for exercise of power through mediating multilateral institutions. All presidencies reflect some balance of these two strategic orientations produced by the unique interest coalition in power, in the case of Bush above all the oil and military contractor sectors and driven as well by the ideological leanings of its key operatives which influence ways of seeing conjunctural risks and opportunities a particular administration faces.

The set of relationships which frame policy-making involve class and the way state power and accumulation strategies interact. These are conjunctural. Military intervention and regime change are much more likely when more is at stake: recalcitrant leaders in oil-producing states who cannot be effectively controlled through economic coercion and states where rent seeking is the road to quick wealth and so local elites are uncongenial to the priorities of foreign investors, so-called rogue states and failed states which harbor terrorists or drug dealers are more likely to face military invasions. The likelihood of such regime change initiative and the type and extent of guided state building will depend on the character of the administration in power in Washington. Further, the success or failure in recent outings will influence willingness to engage in what may turn out to be ill-conceived adventurist undertaking. There is inevitable tension between the innate tendencies to seek out foreign investment by corporate interests, by states in imperialism, and hegemons in empire and the chances of success at acceptable cost which are always contingent.

Capitalists always and everywhere are involved in an intricate dance of competition *and* cooperation, competition for a greater share of profit, wealth and power appropriated through market interactions and statist favoritism, and cooperation as a class against labor's demands and citizen efforts to limit their class prerogatives over a wide range of existing and potential social regulation of their freedoms naturalized within a hegemonic understanding of capitalism in a conjunctural social formation. This dialectic tension has long existed at the level of the world system (and was certainly central to Marx's understanding of capitalism). It has been further internationalized or globalized in our own time, raising the issue of whether there is an emergent transnational capitalist class. I certainly see evidence of increased cross-border cooperation among leading elements of the capitalist class but would insist on the continued centrality of the tension among the interests of capitalists based in different states as we trace out the manner in which global state governance institutions are in fact emerging and gaining purchase over nation state level decision making. I also see a continued tension between reorganization of the world system political economy in the current stage of globalization and the importance of individual states and their capacity to assist and constrain 'their' capitalists in the present context of greater openness enforced by global state economic governance regimes (Tabb, 2004).

I do not see a cohesive transnational capitalist class eclipsing nation state based interests. The centrality of the state for organizing politics and containing class contradictions remains the dominant reality. States, because of the pressures of local elite governing coalition members and also because they must meet revenue needs essential to their legitimation, are inclined to favor national economic interests to the maximal extent they safely can, given the pressures of global market forces and the demands of governments more powerful than their own, remain essential players. When we look at local coalitions which influence state policies in both the core and in non-core social formations we see the way corporate interests influence the kind of liberalization which occurs. There are very few if any truly transnational corporations in the sense of firms which are not primarily associated with particular nation state locations and politics. They use both their own state's resources and, where they can, the abilities 'their' state has to apply pressure elsewhere.

Class Goals of the Global State Economic Governance Institutions

Such considerations bring us back to the relation of state logic, capital logic and the larger moment of imperialism in the global political economy because, for all the talk of an interstate system, the heritage of Westphalia and all that, few of the 200 or so governments which exist today now, or in their previous incarnations as colonies and vassals, were ever sovereign in the idealist international relations model sense. Territorially based states are always part of a system which rests on economic exploitation. It is this structured inequality which should frame contemporary discussion of global neoliberalism. 'Policy failure' needs to be theorized in the context of the goals of policy makers, what class interests they represent, and so how 'bad' policies may be the best possible policies available given the contradictions of capitalism. It is an economic and political system structured not only by class domestically but by North–South relations put in place by colonial and neocolonial power asymmetries. In the present epoch the interrelation between debt and the single-minded export orientation pushed by the global state economic governance institutions combine to effect the stranglehold debt repayment has over economic policy making which forces and enforces the need to increase exports to earn foreign exchange to meet debt obligations. What was achieved directly by colonial administrators and direct appropriation of land and labor is now achieved indirectly by constraining development possibilities. Financialization generalizes this form of extraction and appropriation.

Contrary to official assertions and much mainstream social science based on the premise of efficient markets and public choice theory, the policy initiatives of the global state economic governance institutions—collectively labeled neoliberalism—have been failures in terms of their announced goals. The IMF accepts, as in the findings of a technical report co-authored by its US-appointed chief economist Kenneth Rogoff, that 'The empirical evidence has not established a definitive proof that financial integration has enhanced growth for developing countries. Furthermore, it may be associated with higher consumption volatility' (Prasad et al., 2003: 58). That is to say, collapsing financial bubbles leaving economies in depression with rising unemployment, falling incomes, and extensive social suffering, are the logical outcome or at least their impacts correlate closely with financial liberalization. It is now widely recognized that overall economic performance and social development in the world economy has been substantially inferior in the last two decades of what we might call 'High Globalization' compared to the two decades before that, in which the dominant social structure of accumulation under national Keynesianism in the core and state-led development regimes in the periphery exhibited far stronger growth in economic and social indicators (Weisbrot et al., 2001). Political economists have detailed the harm done by neoliberal policies to the point where the Washington 'Consensus' has lost credibility. Work now focuses on why since the medicine has had iatronic results the debt doctors continue to force it down the throats of unwilling patients. Seen as a tool bag of imperialism, the assurance that more pain is good for these devastated economies victimized by the normal working of the world capitalist system and the insistence that these countries stay the unsound course is more understandable.

Attention has specifically focused on the rise of financialization as a dominant force in transnational capitalism. It offers an explanation of why, despite poor performance, state intervention in demand management has been forbidden and addressing demand constraints to global growth and issues of redistribution has been out of bounds. This remains the case despite the incredible costs of such policies. They have however brought forth substantial popular resistance. There is now much talk in official circles about the need for safety nets (even as the policies imposed do not allow for other than rhetorical endorsement of such a necessity). The competitiveness discourse and accompanying framings of New Classical Economics, supply-side economics, monetarism, real business cycle theory and the more overtly right wing political theorization of the state in public choice, rent seeking, crony capitalism, and so on, support deflationary tendencies as well. All of these approaches by conservative economists and political scientists favor overt class-based redistributive growth as scientifically self-evident despite evidence to their extreme social cost. Nor have such policies been at all successful compared to the earlier demand side regimes and state-led industrial policy approaches of the National Keynesian social structure of accumulation that produced far more rapid as well as equitable growth. Without alleging planned conspiracies it remains the case that each financial crisis is an opportunity for the more powerful market participants with deeper pockets to appropriate the resources of debtors. Debt is the modern day cannon breaking down the walls put up by the developing countries during the period of nationalist development strategies. Debt peonage allows imposition of conditionalities and structural adjustment programs transferring ownership and often dramatically redefining property rights. The fables of neoclassical economics, perfect competition, and the rest obscure the transference of wealth accomplished by financial crises and the manner in which they are resolved.

There is a complex relation between development strategies in the sense of building production capacity controlled locally and the way developmentalist states deal with the relation between national production and international trade, on the one hand, and financialization on the other. There are tensions and contradictions within each of these processes as well as between them that involve conflict between class fractions both within peripheral formations and between states of the periphery and the core, and among core formations as well. What free trade, specialization, and the division of labor promise is increased global efficiency and mutual gain based on comparative advantage. In the real world, in which adjustment costs are sizable and path dependent choices make some decisions to structure an economy around such specialization irreversible within a practical political time frame and at realistically manageable costs, the neoliberal model produces dependency and an inability to reverse overspecialization, even as the terms of trade over long periods go against primary producers and exporters of commodity manufactures. It has not been given comparative advantage that has been key to the development of the now successful economies, but rather success was based on subsidies and the borrowing of technology from industrial leaders while closing off domestic markets until local producers' capacity to compete matured. The literature on late industrializers (Gershenkron, 1962) and the late-late industrializers (Wade, 1990; Amsden, 1989) make this evident. Such successes can be counterposed to other efforts at state-led development (India's for example) which were far less successful and to many experiences which resulted in costly failure to become competitive behind protectionist barriers, but it can be questioned whether the eagerness to close off, indeed outlaw, such an approach is not in fact a form of protectionism on the part of the already advanced economies working through the global state governance institutions. The ever expanding agenda being pushed by the US and the EU at the World Trade Organization ministerial meetings bear witness to an ambition to prevent use of the very tools which were responsible for successful development in the past. The extension of trade issues to so-called trade related investment measures (TRIMs), trade related intellectual property rights (TRIPs) and now the Singapore issues (which demand still further reduction in the scope of state tools to promote domestic development) are being resisted as the impact of such development unfriendly rules become clear to the countries which naively signed on to the Uruguay Round agreements and many extensions of rules designed to favor the rich economies of the global trading system. The World Trade Organization has expanded its remit to cover just about every aspect of state–market relations that the IMF and the World Bank do not govern. And of course the conditionalities imposed by the IMF on particular dependent countries now run to well over a hundred very specific items in the micro management demands made on debtor economies. That the Brazil-led G-20 (called the G-22, G-23, and other designations as its membership grew and later contracted under pressure on some smaller states from the United States is a confusing designation given a second G-20 created by an expanding of the G-7 for some purposes—see Tabb, 2004, p. 390) was able to unite and proclaim a collective 'Enough!' to further one-sided concessions is encouraging, and I shall discuss such opportunities a bit later, but we should not be overly optimistic. Class relations and class recomposition in much of what was once thought of as the Third World must be considered with a skeptical intelligence.

Many on the left have noted the continued importance of the nation state to disciplining labor and the control of opponents of neoliberalism. The reassertion of state power in the presence of privatization and economic liberalization in the service of imperialism, however, also involves a fundamental restructuring of the political economy in ways which serve the interests of local elites, and not simply as junior partners of foreign capital. The empowerment of new domestically hegemonic coalitions is about a respecification of property rights, appropriation of resources, and a reordering of government spending processes and revenue collection. These should be seen as state building. They involve self-interested activity by class fractions which benefit from a seeming sweeping aside of protectionism, subsidies, and regulation. Specifically, a second generation governance discourse is revisiting the historical experience of the now developed nations and comparing the quality of their markets and institutions during the decades and over the centuries in which they achieved impressive economic growth. The introduction of key features of democracy and good governance came very late in the process of economic development. Crony capitalism, widespread nepotism, the spoils system, open sale of public office, and disenfranchisement of women, racial minorities and working men without sufficient property characterized political systems for most of the period of advancing per capita income in today's richer nations. Violation of property rights, irresponsible financial institution behavior and far from adequate corporate governance, and the absence of human rights including labor rights characterized the early to fairly late stages of economic development of the West (Chang, 2003).

To expect today's less economically developed countries to immediately overcome such problems as a condition for aid therefore seems farfetched. But there is another more central consideration. It has been only when a maturing capitalist economy creates a working class capable of self-organization and mature political unification that broad system reforms are won through struggle that such a political thrust invites a response on the part of the more farsighted sections of the ruling class who offer reform from above to contain self-organization and political mobilization from below. In the vast literature demanding reforms, little is said about the need to support broad-based popular movements which challenge class domination. Working class self-organization is discouraged by elites of the core as much as the periphery's ruling classes. The form of democracy being encouraged and suggestions for institutional reform and good governance rather can be understood as reflecting a strategy to remake these states in ways conducive to more effective foreign penetration and to distract attention from the structural inequalities of unequal exchange between and within core and periphery of the world system.

While the economies of Northeast Asia and some other of the larger states of the semi-periphery have developed a significant class of domestic industrial entrepreneurs, most of the poorer states have elites concentrated in non-tradable activities and, importantly, in finance. After the crises in East Asia it became clear that financial interests had been influencing government policies in ways detrimental to development. The policy most followed of continuing to peg the value of local currencies to the US dollar, a peg which could not be maintained and when finally abandoned in economic collapse had painful consequences. The financial interests which dominate public policy in many developing countries did not need the global state economic governance institutions to impose financial liberalization upon them from the outside, they embraced such policies out of self-interest harmful to the public good. These elites, as K. S. Jomo (2002, p. 6) writes of the case of the nations of Southeast Asia,

> insisted on retaining the pegs, even though it was adversely affecting competitiveness in the real economy, because they were heavily leveraged in dollars (often without hedging their debt), and did not want the pegs to change. Because of their growing influence public policy generally, and financial policies in particular, have been increasingly influenced by such financial interests, who sought to protect the value of their financial assets … As a consequence, they tended to propose, favour and insist upon policies with deflationary macroeconomic consequences. Elite influence on public policymaking also favoured partial financial liberalisation, which eventually led to conditions culminating in the region's debacle in 1997–98.

Such policies were and continue to be profitable for local financiers who speculate with borrowed funds helping to produce the asset bubbles which then so painfully collapse in the context of socialized losses. It is not only the foreign hedge funds which are responsible for these repeating cycles but an engorged local financier class.

The deflation which follows the collapse of the currency and of government finances is solved through IMF austerity even where, as in the case of East Asia in the late 1990s, Japan was ready to fund a reflation so that these local economic depressions could be avoided and output levels resumed with far less disruption to the productionist base of the economies involved. The US blatantly told Japan this alternative to forced austerity would not be allowed. Instead these assets were to be sold at bargain basement prices and states wrenchingly forced to abandon the model heavily reliant on state-led development and local autonomy. Under such 'solutions' to crisis, the extent to which state apparatuses are systematically being reorganized around a strategy of competitive austerity in anti-working class ways enforcing wage compression and tax cutting for the wealthy has spelled declining public services and living standards.

In such a context privatization of state assets whether in Russia, Chile, or elsewhere can be understood not simply as a movement from public to private, but in important ways from non-state to state. The latter is crucial. Such institutional change can increase state capacity for defining and enforcing property rights, extracting revenue for privileged capitalists, and fostering the centralization of administrative and political resources. Case studies of the experience of privatization show public and private are neither contradictory nor mutually exclusive terms and that power relations are not at all negative sum games in which state capacity is lost to private capitalists. Efforts to impose neoliberalism have been met by local elites showing strong capacities to carry out privatization and deregulation in ways which increase their own wealth and power at the expense of foreign capital (Schamis, 2002). In terms of the allegation of an emergent transnational class, the assertion of nationalist capitals' prerogatives can *either* be read as a sign of continued division within a single transnational capitalist class or, on the contrary, as evidence of continued separation between these national capitalists in local state formations and the capitalist interests of the core. The possibility of 'spinning' the story either way underlines the difficulties inherent in unproblematically endorsing either side in this intra-Marxist debate. I think it is in reality a matter of different levels of analysis of capitalism. At the level of mode of production it would seem legitimate to say there is a transnational capitalist class. The advocates of the position claim more than this however. They assert that globalization has qualitatively changed the nature of class relations so that this mode of production level corresponds to the conjunctural state of the present world system. It is here that I see an overreaching and would assert continuing centrality of class as rooted in nation state formations for study of the concrete world political economy of our time.

The US State and Financialization

The creation of fiscal crisis as a way to force privatization and further liberalization is the result not merely of imposition by the IMF and World Bank but of financialization strategies by local elites consistent with class warfare tactics of public finance. In the United States, Ronald Reagan and George W. Bush also created huge government deficits and unsustainable public debt to produce conditions for the emasculation of the public sector's capacity to provide goods and services to the working class. By starving the state sector, punishing the progressive redistributional coalition including teachers and other public sector workers, selling off public assets or giving generous contracts to favored supporters, the progressive base is weakened and the coalition which has been empowered by state policies of privatization and liberalization are rewarded. Global neoliberalism acts to produce recessionary trends as a result of its class war policies, in the austerity it forces on those whose economies are effectively constrained by the IMF and World Bank, and also in the fiscal constraints in Europe under Maastricht, and the punishing inequalities of Bush tax cuts and spending austerities in the United States. It is possible the foundations are being laid for a wider crisis of the political economy. The United States built up an unsustainable debt to the rest of the world by running annual balance of payments deficits of 5% and more of gross domestic product, sinking the country deeper into debtor status. The US state and transnational capital benefited from financial breakdown in Latin America, Russia, Eastern Europe, East Asia, and elsewhere where financial crisis was resolved so as to increase foreign control and to undermine nationalist development. The United States through its deficits sucked in capital to an extent which poses potential dangers to the global financial order. Did this signal weakness of the US economy or rather strength? Dependence and so weakness? Or the power to attract and command resources and wealth from the rest of the world?

The United States plays a central role supported by the British: militarily as in Iraq, in the larger Bush regime-change agenda, and in pushing financial liberalization. Both the British and US economies depend on finance and oil as key sectors of accumulation and appropriation. The United States can print dollars and, given its hegemonic status, can pressure other states to continue to finance its penchant for living well beyond its means. The United States gains relative strength as actions and institutional policies it initiates undermine social stability and development prospects elsewhere. It may continue to be the safe haven for capital flight and the financial market offering high and more secure returns and so run balance of payment deficits inconceivable for any other nation. At the same time, there are grounds to be seriously worried. US power means that the imbalance will hardly be addressed solely as the financial equations of traditional modeling would predict.

Important voices on the left including Immanuel Wallerstein and Samir Amin argue the structural weakness of the US economy on the grounds that its productive system is far from the most efficient in the world. On the contrary, it enjoys comparative advantage only in the arms sector. It is certainly true that its trade deficit cuts across virtually all segments of the production system. The national savings rate in the United States is virtually zero. Its advantage is its ability to bully, specifically to maintain its ascendancy over oil producers, and mandate that oil payment be made in dollars. Its role of consumer of last resort through debt fuels effective demand in a world forced by financialization into stagnationist pressures. World economic growth, which averaged almost 5% in the golden age, 1950–1973, fell to 3% between 1973 and 1992 and fell still further in the years since. The relatively better performance of US investments must be seen in the context of global lack of real growth, the vast build-up in US debt, and the competitive weakness of real production in the United States. All of this points to the centrality of the US state in the global political economy and suggests again that methodological assumption of a unified transnational capital class is lacking in analytical purchase.

Perhaps more importantly, it should enlarge debate on two aspects of the contemporary world capitalist system. The first is with respect to the impacts of aging populations on fiscal capacities and priorities. In the United States there is the attempt to create 'the ownership society' (as in 'A paternalistic state will not control your retirement, you will'). The retreat of the state takes different forms in other societies, but the direction is widely evident. Secondly, the particulars through which the welfare state is being challenged are a rebalancing of the larger process of redistributive growth which always accompanies changes at the level of the forces of production as they re-form classes and impact on the bargaining power and consciousness of class fractions within state formations. Central to such a restructuring of global capitalism in our time is the centrality of finance. As was the case at the last turn of the century, the relation of finance capital to productive capital is central.

The questions of the weakness of the traditional domestic sectors of the US economy (aside from finance, real estate, and of course military contracting) combined with the power of finance transnationally and of the US state raise complex analytic issues which have only begun to be addressed. Scholars might do well to examine current financialization in a longer perspective of US power and financialization strategies which extend over many decades. In the 1960s and 1970s US presidents could invite German chancellors down to the LBJ ranch and over a barbeque tell them what the dollar required. It unilaterally put an end to the Bretton Woods system with what the Japanese refer to as the Nixon *shocku*. The imposition of America's solution to the Latin American debt crisis in the early 1980s and the Asian financial crisis in the late 1990s further suggests the need for a revisionist international political economy which puts financialization at its center. The parallel to a century ago in both the domestic consolidations of national industrial economies and to debates over finance capital which were a central topic of Marxist and liberal theorists. These debates reflected the jockeying for position internationally among competing fractions of capital. In a very different context, the nature of financialization in our time and the way governments as containers of populations, unique institutions, and of electoral decision making come under pressure from markets and global state economic governance institutions are the larger frame for contemporary debate. The power of the United States inextricably linked to the position of the dollar as the international medium of exchange and the dominance the right of seigniorage conveys. The discussion should be about not just the debtor position of the non-core nations and their need to hold dollar reserves in the presence of a destabilizing and disorderly financial regime but the ability of the United States to force liquidity on the rest of the world while running outsized balance of payments deficits of is own.

While we have come to think of the International Monetary Fund and other global state economic governance institutions as creatures of American policy, the IMF often acts in a capacity beyond fealty to the occupant of the White House as a global state economic governance institution with a wider steering perspective for transnational capital. Its grim warnings of long-term fiscal disaster show a perspective hardly consistent with a slavish political loyalty to Washington's currently dominant politics. Such actions signal a degree of transnational state construction. The International Monetary Fund and the OCED have quite publicly criticized the Bush tax cuts for example. Their economists anticipate the impact will be to lower US productivity in the long run by increasing deficits and by pushing up interest rates. In March 2003 the IMF, joined by the OECD, issued such a warning which pointed out that the 7% deterioration in the ratio of the US fiscal deficit to GDP since 2000 is the largest deterioration since World War II and is currently equal to about 6% of world gross savings. In evaluating the strength of the US economy, financial and other asset markets from equities to housing have fueled dramatic wealth creation and the strongest economic growth among the advanced nations. This in turn has been based on debt creation. Their warnings have grown increasingly shrill. In January 2004 the IMF warned that the US record-breaking level of debt was threatening global stability and could soon play havoc with international exchange rates, and that higher borrowing costs abroad would spill over into global investment and output.

Regional Bloc Competition and Negotiating the Global Political Economy

The United States remains hegemonic and, in this post-9/11 era, foregrounded its war on terrorism which it is busy expanding as a mechanism of increasing its control. This impacts on those declared its enemies and those it would intimidate with a 'you are either with us or with the terrorists' rhetoric. It redirects the debate over globalization at a time when the failure of the neoliberal agenda to help the poor had been gaining increased purchase. Global growth has been very uneven, with over fifty countries suffering falling real per capita GDPs during the 1990s. It has become obvious that the distribution of the benefits of growth and costs of stagnation are less and less within the power of individual states to control. It is widely recognized that a process of combined and uneven development is in significant measure a matter of the way power is exercised in a markedly unilateralist manner so that a war on terror which distracted from a focus on global justice concerns is itself meeting strong resistance. The United States, as a result of what looks more and more like overreaching, has found itself meeting more effective resistance not simply in Iraq but in terms of economic diplomacy across a wide set of issues and negotiating fora as it attempts to impose its restructuring visions on the world.

While it remains true that when the United States sits down to international negotiations it is the most powerful actor in the process, this does not mean it always gets what it wants or even gets what it wants as often as it has in the past. As it has been rebuffed in the economic realm, most pointedly at the WTO ministerials, the Bush II White House has adopted a strategy of negotiating bilateral investment treaties with small, weaker countries which US Trade Representative Robert Zoellick calls the 'can do' countries. This process is seen by Zoellick as 'competition in liberalization'. The United States planned bilateral negotiations with eleven countries which are prospective FTAA members (it already has agreements with Mexico and Chile). The US still seeks to put itself at the center of a trade bloc, the Free Trade Area of the Americas, by isolating Brazil by lining up Central American states, once referred to by our government officials as banana republics. Yet it finds it cannot even get all of these states on board. When time came for the Miami meeting in late 2003, a breakdown of negotiations would have been particularly bad for the brothers Bush. Miami had been the city chosen for the headquarters of the trade agreement. Florida was a key state in the upcoming presidential election and the one which facilitated his ascendancy to the presidency in 2000 thanks in part to the activities of the president's brother, Jeb Bush, the state's governor. An empty agreement on an 'FTAA-lite' was an effort to save face after the embarrassing breakdown of the WTO talks in Cancun only a short time earlier. The breaking off of negotiations in Miami was also necessary to keep any possibility of lowering barriers to Brazil's low-cost orange juice, a threat to Florida's citrus industry (being protected by a 29 cent tariff on each gallon imported), off the voters' political radar screen. These domestic considerations aside, the setback for US aspirations to the economic integration of the Western Hemisphere was significant.

Perhaps the historically more serious threat comes from the development of the ASEAN plus three (China, South Korea, and Japan) grouping. There is movement toward what Japanese Prime Minister Koizumi calls an 'East Asian Community' which would be still further expanded to include New Zealand and Australia. Japan, which extended 80 billion dollars to its neighbors impacted by the financial crisis of 1997–98, and uses its official development assistance to strengthen its leadership in the region, competes with China which has offered the ASEAN nations trade concessions going well beyond what Japanese constituencies have been willing to allow with regard to agriculture and other sector protectionism. China's 'charm offensive' in the region is paying dividends and, while Japan and China remain rivals (it may prove hard to undo the anti-Japanese feelings among Chinese of all ages as memories of World War II atrocities are very much alive and Japan's fear of a rising region hegemon are strong), the integration of Asia offers a serious challenge to the United States. Japan's imports from China exceeded its imports from the United States for the first time in 2003, and political relations at the governmental level have improved substantially. China has also become South Korea's largest trading partner so that despite rivalries, and in a way spurred by them, there has been a great deal of movement in such areas as energy, security, and technology leading to increased expectations of a Northeast Asian economic community of some potency centered around China, Japan and South Korea and expanding south rivaling in size and influence the EU or NAFTA and the FTAA. The three, along with Hong Kong and Taiwan, account for about 20% of world GDP, compared to 30% for Europe and 34% for North America, and growing much faster than either. With ASEAN countries such a regional grouping would be more powerful still. China's importance to the global political economy cannot be questioned (although its economic and political stability are rightly grounds for some doubt and speculation) and Asia is now an important center of accumulation and, growing political, these tensions may intensify and reorient world attention eastward.

While much discussion of US–Europe relations stresses overwhelming US military and political power, the simmering differences between the United States and the European Union are significant, and have potential to disrupt the global trading system despite efforts on both sides to avoid a breakdown. World Trade Organization arbitration panels have repeatedly ruled that tax breaks to US exporters are illegal under its rules and granted the EU the right to impose sanctions each time the United States has tried to modify its subsidy program and failed to win WTO approval. The punitive import tariffs the EU can impose (approximately $4 billion-worth) have not yet been implemented out of fear that such an action could seriously damage EU–US trade relations and indeed the international trading system which has been built up under US leadership of the GATT and the WTO.

The WTO has also ruled the 1916 US anti-dumping act illegal. But here too the EU has put off retaliatory measures to presumably give the United States more time but actually out of concern that the US would simply leave the WTO and the world would return to the law of the trade jungle. The EU won the right to impose punitive import tariffs worth $2.2 billion in 2003 in the steel case but feared escalation, and the Bush people finally backed down on the issue in significant measure at the behest of domestic users of steel who had become less competitive as a result of Washington's protection of high cost domestic producers in politically sensitive states. Further, despite all the talk of 'Old Europe' being non-competitive, Germany is the world's biggest exporter currently, ahead of the United States in dollar terms. France also exports much more than it imports, unlike the United States. By conventional measures Europe is as productive as the United States. Europe's growth rate is being held back not so much by social spending and labor protections—indeed it has restructured quite a lot—as by EU rules which make fighting inflation the only economic target and by not promoting growth and stimulating employment as it copies Anglo-American policy priorities. Much of the politics of the rightward drift in Europe is related to continued acceptance of Maastricht handcuffs, immigration, globalization more broadly, and the inability or unwillingness of Third Way and other social democratic parties to offer real alternatives to neoliberalism.

It is this lack of a serious alternative to continued necessity to compete within the neoliberal framework which is the problem for those who worry about the social costs and environmental collapse as well of the present pattern of accumulation in the world system. Within Europe and elsewhere the continued growth of what is called the anti-globalization movement, but which is better described as a global justice movement, is questioning the core rules of corporate capitalism's version of globalization, a set of rules and regimes which are hostile to widely shared concerns and which favor a globalization from below based on solidarity and not competition.

I would conclude this roundup of regional developments by commenting on state failure in the Middle East, Africa, and Central Asia, where economic growth has been slow, unemployment high, and both a sense of government incapacity and corruption and of being victimized by globalism prevail. Over an extended part of the globe, poverty and state fracturing and failure to do much to address pressing human need has created political conflict and social breakdown. As Aijaz Ahmad (2003, p. 57) reminds us, 'The defeat and/or decline of the democratic, secular, anti-colonial nationalism has given rise, in a host of countries, from India to Egypt to Algeria, to hysterical, irrationalist forms of cultural nationalism and atavistic hysteria'. The United States has played no small part in conjuring these forces to prominence by funding, training, and broadly encouraging religious fundamentalists to defeat communists and left-wing forces in the Middle East. From CIA sponsorship of Saddam Hussein, Osama bin Laden, and the Taliban the United States created the threats it now faces.

At another level, the connection between globalization and support of terrorism as well as the spawning of savage civil wars can be found in responses to downward mobility and a sense of humiliation. Being held in contempt in some cases is turned inward so that drugs, crime, and the violence of self destruction dominate. In others the response is a heightening of ethic chauvinism and religious fundamentalisms where such identity politics gives meaning to lives. Capitalism in general, and globalization in particular, erodes societal stability. When progressive movements of global civil society counterpose social justice and human dignity to the false measures of private benefits and the efficiency criteria the global state economic governance institutions impose, they challenge the instrumental rationality of capitalism with its inevitable pressure on community and democratic practice.

The reaction to unmediated economic rationality as it affects the place of particular economic formations within a changed world system alters the nature of war so that more and more conflicts do not primarily involve national armies but more often terrorists, militias, mercenaries, and criminal gangs. They are more often now about ethnic exclusion and identity politics constituted as squabbles over limited resources in which violence is directed against civilians using atrocities—torture, rape, mutilation, and famine—as tools of war. The Bush Administration's claim that societies can somehow be rebuilt from 30,000 feet in 'shock and awe'-induced regime change is widely met with skepticism. Despite what might be called 'the Great Celebration' of globalization as an unambiguous good, protests of wars of empire and of neoliberalism gain strength.

Conclusion

The erosion of state capacities, loss of legitimacy as governments have been less able to deliver basic security, economic and even physical security, or even hope, reflects the workings of the global regimes of our time. To summarize our perhaps overly ambitious framing, the growing power of global state economic governance institutions, which have been so centrally the target of civil society social justice movements, are indeed enforcing a global neoliberalism and globalized state control institutions on the world's peoples. Behind these organizations are class relations and agendas which are not free of competitive negotiation among nationally based capitals. The role of the United States has been central to their formation and evolution. The hegemon's imperial power needs to be further theorized in terms of competing class fractions and continuing struggles with both other nationally based capitals and popular movements. The extent of popular disillusion varies, but disappointment with most post-colonial nationalist governments, whether corrupt and/or ineffective, despotic or presumably democratic, fuel disintegrative trends. Their impacts are felt in extremist politics and popular despair in some parts of the world. US hyperpower practices also encourage regional bloc formation in other centers of potential market integration, producing new patterns of rivalries and redefining the dialectic between class struggle and nationalism (and market-driven regionalism). Such developments in turn call for alternative explanations of the way things can be and what needs to be done. The logic of capitalist development suggests that economies have outgrown the container of existing states and that reorganization of the global political economy is propelling the growth of regional blocs to 'bulk up' to better take on the one remaining superpower. The United States—which had favored the creation of a unified European market which would favor the penetration of its multinational corporations, an Asia-Pacific Economic Cooperation of which it would be a key player, and a Free Trade Area of the Americas which it could lead and control—finds itself faced with resistance from the central players of 'Old Europe', an ASEAN plus three formation from which it is excluded, and in its own backyard a Brazilian-led Mercosur which is looking for alliances with other Latin American nations to increase bargaining power in negotiations with the Colossus of the North. Further, while the traditional working class trade union formations have been weakened, the growth of international civil society and the interventions of the global justice movement and the more central role of global state governance institutions are redefining state power and re-forming class consciousness in a global framework.

Acknowledgements

This paper is a revised version of a presentation at the plenary session of the Global Studies Association, Brandeis University, 24 April 2004. Some clarifications have been added prompted by the comments of Stephen Mikesell, Jerry Harris, and Sam Gindin. I thank them for their perceptive readings of the paper.

References

Ahmad, A. (2003) Imperialism in our time, pp. 43–62 in L. Panitch & C. Leys (Eds) *The New Imperial Challenge—Socialist Registrar 2004* (New York: Monthly Review Press).

Amin, S. (2004) International Development Associates Conference on the Economics of the New Imperialism, 22–24 January, Jawaharlal Nehru University, New Delhi.

Amsden, A.H. (1989) *Asia's Next Giant: South Korea and late Industrialization* (New York: Oxford University Press).

Chang, H.-J. (2002) *Kicking away the ladder: Development Strategies in Historical Perspective* (London: Anthem Press)

Gershenkron, A. (1962) *Economic Backwardness in Historical Perspective* (Cambridge: Harvard University Press).

Jomo, K. S. (2002) Globalization for whom? A world for all, Ishak Shari Memorial Lecture, 11 June. Available at http://www.networkideas.org.

Parenti, M. (1995) *Imperialism, Against Empire* (San Francisco: City Lights books), Chapter 1.

Patnaik, P. (2004) The New Imperialism, International Development Associates Conference on the Economics of the New Imperialism, 22–24 January, Jawaharlal Nehru University, New Delhi.

Prasad, E., Rogoff, K., Wei S.-J. & Ayhan Kose, M. (2003) Effects of financial globalization on developing countries: some empirical evidence, International Monetary Fund, 17 March.

Schamis, H. E. (2002) *Re-forming the State: The Politics of Privatization in Latin America and Europe* (Ann Arbor: University of Michigan Press).

Tabb, W. K. (2004) *Economic Governance in the Age of Globalization* (New York: Columbia University Press).

Wade, R. E. (1990) *Governing the Market Economic Theory and the Role of Government in East Asian Economic Industrialization* (Princeton: Princeton University Press).

Wallerstein, I. (2002) The Eagle has Crash Landed, *Foreign Policy*, July/August.

Weisbrot, M., Naiman, R. & Kim, J. (2001) The emperor has no growth: declining economic growth rates in the era of globalization (Washington: Center for Economic Research and Policy), May.

Wood, E. M. (2002) Global capital, national states, pp. 17–39 in M. Rupert & H. Smith (Eds) *Historical Materialism and Globalization* (London: Routledge).

William K. Tabb teaches at Queens College of the City University of New York. Tabb's writing on globalization includes: *The Amoral Elephant: Globalization and the Struggle for Social Justice in the Twenty-First Century* (Monthly Review Press, 2001); *Unequal Partners: A Primer on Globalization* (New Press, 2002); and *Economic Governance in the Age of Globalization* (Columbia University Press, 2004).

The Long Downward Wave of the World Economy and the Future of Global Conflict

HEIKKI PATOMÄKI

Introduction

Globalization as a political project rests on claims about peace and prosperity. The economic claim is that orthodox economic policies—particularly those associated with 'the Washington consensus'—generate economic growth and thereby benefit also the poor of our planet. The political claim is basically two-fold. Firstly, the world is united in its interest to promote economic liberalism (the harmony of interests thesis). Secondly, globalization of liberal democratic rule implies that there will be no more wars between states (the democratic peace theory).

Simple economic evidence seems to question the first two claims. Average per capita economic growth has actually slowed down if not come to a halt. In retrospect, the oil crisis of 1973–74 appears as the starting point of a long and gradually deepening recession. There are many indications that decade after decade there has been, globally, less growth and more un- and under-employment of industrial and human capacities. To put it provocatively, more 'globalization' seems to mean less economic growth. Also the harmony of interests thesis looks rather weak. Following the second oil crisis in the early 1980s, an increasing number of countries and people have been impoverished also in absolute terms. Many parts of the world have experienced long-term economic decline. Moreover, inequalities have been on the rise also within most countries. Although the OECD world remains mostly affluent in world historical standards,[1] and although some Asian countries have grown and developed (as long as their 'globalization' remained or remains selective), the harmony of interests thesis seems to rest on a fairly weak ground.

In the following, I will explore two sets of issues (tentatively, to be discussed further and in more detail in a book in progress: see Patomäki, forthcoming). Firstly, what are the causes of the on-going downward phase of the world economy? Have orthodox economic policies played a role in these developments? What kind of a role? How should we then explain the adoption of these policies? Secondly, what does all this mean politically? What are the implications of sluggish, ambivalent and unequal growth to democratic peace? Apart from violent conflicts in the global South, is it possible that the logic of violence and war returns also to the core areas of the world economy? Will the liberal dream of eternal peace collapse once again?

By taking some steps towards explaining the past and present trends, I hope also to be able to shed some light on possible futures. Anticipation of the future is a necessary part of social action, and particularly so in the world of modern organizations. Therefore, I indicate also some possible and likely consequences of the world economic (mal)developments.

Economic Developments since the 1960s

In retrospect, the oil crisis of 1973–74 appears as the beginning of a long and gradually deepening recession. Although relatively few economists have actually studied long-term global trends in any systematic fashion, there have been some exceptions. For instance, David Felix (1995, pp. 5–9) has compared relevant figures for the G7 countries in the periods 1946–58, 1959–70 and 1974–89. In the Bretton Woods era the real per capita growth rate was about 4.5%, whereas for 1974–89 it declined to 2.2%. A much bigger sample of 57 countries points to the conclusion that this has been a general world-wide trend. Moreover, the remaining growth has also become more volatile and sensitive to disturbances (ibid., p. 8).

In particular in the OECD countries and Latin America also the ratio of investments to GDP has declined rapidly. Oil-exporting countries and sub-Saharan Africa were only very partial exceptions, largely following the trend. Only a number of Asian countries provided a true exception in this period, sustaining a high and relatively stable growth with a rising ratio of investments to GDP (ibid., pp. 8–9). Also in Japan, profit rates were halved as compared to the period before 1970 and at the same time the growth of net capital stock, productivity and wages declined steeply (see Brenner, 2002, pp. 7–9). This may, of course, have been in part due to the fact that Japan was undergoing a technological transformation and massive reinvestment and early outward investment which stimulated growth elsewhere in the region in this period.

It seems that at the turn of the 1990s per capita growth came to a halt (or at least dropped to something like 1% or less). There are of course different ways of calculating average per capita growth, yielding different results. For instance, Alan Freeman (2003) uses constant per dollar values and IMF data. According to his calculations, whereas in the 1970s the per capita growth was, on average, more than 3.7%, it was slightly negative in the 1990s and early twenty-first century (in constant 1995 US dollars, converted from national currencies at current exchange rates). In 1988 global GDP/capita was US$4,839; in 2002 it was US$4,748. Obviously, the situation is not similar in every country. In some places—particularly in some OECD countries, China and India—there has been and may continue to be some real economic growth, yet more and more people are living in countries with declining standards of living. Measured in these terms, the absolute world GDP began to decline only in the mid-1990s. The Asian crisis of 1997–98 that spread also to Russia and Brazil pressed a hollow in the graph that otherwise shows steady stagnation. Consequently, per capita world economic output in 2002 was essentially the same as in 1980 and, as indicated, slightly less than in 1988.

What is also important is that the slackening global conditions have been accompanied by growing disparities between countries and regions, and between different social classes. The ratio of the richest fifth of countries to the poorest fifth was 30:1 in 1960, 60:1 in 1990 and almost 90:1 at the end of the 1990s. It seems that the global poor have remained as poor as they were in 1820, and that the fruits of industrialization have been experienced only by some countries and people (UNDP, 1999, pp. 2–3, 38–29). Moreover, in 1980 about 120 million people lived in those nine countries where per capita income declined in the previous decade. In 1998 there were 60 such countries, with a total of 1.3 billion inhabitants. This is also a qualitative change as compared to the Bretton Woods era. For the first time since World War II the world economy seems to have become a constant (or negative) sum game where many are losing also in absolute terms. Although relative inequality has steadily risen since the industrial revolution, the average citizen in the 1950s and 1960s seemed to have bene- fited from economic developments to at least some degree in most countries. Following the second oil crisis in the early 1980s, the situation has become quite different. An increasing number of countries and people have been impoverished also in absolute terms (Freeman, 2002).

Moreover, inequalities have been on the rise also within countries. Research based on the World Income Inequality Database (WIID), co-developed by World Institute for Development Economics Research (WIDER) and United Nations Development Programme (UNDP), includ- ing information of about 73 major countries that represent most of the world's population, show that a general fall in inequality during the Bretton Woods era (except in Latin America and parts of sub-Saharan Africa) has been followed by a clear rise particularly over the last two decades (see Cornia, 2004; Cornia et al., 2004). In the 1980s and 1990s, wage and income differentials grew in most of the OECD countries, particularly in the US and the UK but also in such tradition- ally egalitarian countries as Sweden or Japan. However, the fastest ever recorded changes in income inequality took place in Eastern Europe and the Commonwealth of Independent States (CIS) (including the former Soviet states in Central Asia).

The same trend is evident also in the countries of the global South. All but three Latin Amer- ican countries experienced a rise in the already very high inequality levels. In the Southeast and East Asian economies, the reversal of the stable-declining inequality trends started in the late 1980s and was exacerbated by the 1997 Asian crisis. In sub-Saharan African the picture is more ambiguous and the figures also less reliable. It seems, however, that while in some countries the urban–rural divide has become less severe, inequalities in general between households are rising in others (the overall context in Africa, however, is that of general economic decline).

North Africa and the Middle East are less well documented by WIID, yet also countries of these regions seem to concur with the general trends of economic decline and/or rising inequalities. Of the 73 major countries surveyed by WIID, only 5% of the population were living in countries with declining inequality. The use of purchase power parity (PPP) values does not affect the picture of growing disparities within countries in any way. The number of relatively poor has been rising in many, including the poorest, countries, not to speak of income inequalities per se.

It is possible to use PPP values instead of constant dollars.[2] Consequently, the world economic growth would seem somewhat higher and the differences between countries significantly less dramatic than in Freeman's or UNDP's calculations. This is because the price level in less well-off countries tends to be lower than in better-off countries and thus dollar-converted values make them look poorer than they actually are. The difference is particularly striking in the case of India and China. Nevertheless, the use of PPP values does not really change the general picture. Apart from India and China, there has been a wide-ranging slowdown of per capita economic growth. For instance, the 2004 Report of the World Commission on the Social Dimension of Globalization (World Commission, 2004), which was set up by International Labour Organization (ILO), uses the World Bank figures measured in PPP terms and include China and India. Figure 10 on page 36 shows that the growth of world GDP per capita was 4% in the 1960s, 2% in the 1970s, 1% in the 1980s and 1990s, and declining. Similarly, according to PPP-figures, there has been an increasing inequality at least between the richest 10% and the poorest 10% of countries.

What matters for the purpose of establishing a research problem is whether there has been a general pattern or not, not the exact figures. Global GDP and income inequality data form only two synthetic series in representing the variation of a complex monetized 'quantity' that is in a sense the creation of a statistician (Schumpeter, 1939a, p. 18). At best, a general trend of this kind can only be taken as a possible surface level indicator of some real processes.

GDP and Gini coefficient calculations do not, of course, tell any unambiguous truth about world economic developments. Forming a global picture of the world economic growth and inequalities based on statistics requires a number of methodological and interpretative choices. For instance, what is the base year? How should the currency conversions be done? What weight is thereby (implicitly) given, for instance, to the rather significant economic growth that occurred in India (3–4% per capita per annum) and China (6% per capita per annum) in the 1990s? And how should we interpret developments e.g. in India and China? India and China are among the few countries in the global South that have thus far spared themselves the debt crisis, maintained capital controls, and developed large sectors of heavy industry. Freeman (2002, p. 13; 2003, pp. 158–159) argues that an exception should in fact be made of China, particularly when the focus is on the effects of neoliberal globalization, since 'the Chinese state has dominated over market and global processes'. However, in terms of internal inequality, China and India do not necessarily constitute exceptions to the rule. Although absolute poverty has been declining in China during the era of high growth (World Commission, 2004, p. 45, fig. 19), at least until 2003 when a reversal seems to have taken place despite further growth, it is in addition clear that income inequalities between households and regions grew also in China already in the 1990s.[3] The trends in India are ambiguous and difficult to interpret. However, household surveys in India do not show increased per capita consumption and, at any rate, developments in India have involved a moderate rise in recorded consumption inequality and, possibly, by a larger one in unrecorded inequality (Cornia, 2004, p. 7).

Despite these methodological reservations and interpretative qualifications, we can nonetheless conclude on the basis of various GDP per capita and Gini coefficient statistics that the world economic growth has steadily slowed down, probably drastically, and that inequalities have been on the rise—and in many contexts quite dramatically so—since the 1970s. In the following, I will try to answer two sets of questions. Firstly, what has caused the decline of world economic growth and rise of inequality? Are there reasons to expect a new era of growth or, on the basis of the model, are there reasons to anticipate further crises? Secondly, I shall also indicate tentatively some of the social and political consequences of slackening global economic conditions and growing disparities. What sorts of connections are there between the long-term world recession and related economic crises, on the one hand, and conflicts, foreign policies of states, and even wars, on the other?

The Long Wave Cycles

In the early twentieth century, a number of economists noted that it seems that in the capitalist world economy there are not only various short-term cycles but also longer wave cycles. The longest waves seem to take about half a century. This idea was articulated most clearly by Nikolai Kondratieff (1984/1928). Kondratieff found the long wave cycles by studying time-series of various data. His conclusions also appeared to be in line with the contentions of qualitative historians (ibid., p. 64).

However, in social and economic phenomena neither short nor long cycles are strict in any sense. The long wave cycles seem to last from 48 to 60 years but even this generalization was originally—in the 1920s—based on the observation of a time span including two and a half cycles only. At any rate, during a rising wave booms are more frequent than recessions; during a downward wave recessions and depressions dominate. Kondratieff's (ibid., pp. 32–59) data covered price and value series as well as physical volume series of production and consumption in England, France, Germany and the US from the late eighteenth century until the early 1920s. In order to bring out the long cycles in their pure form, he fitted a theoretical curve to each empirical series of data (by using the least square method) and then processed the data and smoothed the deviations, using the method of moving average. Whenever possible, Kondratieff also used per capita rather than absolute values. The long wave cycles were most clearly visible in prices, interest rates and wages. They could be seen also in international trade. However, in other cases, and particularly in the physical volume series, the data was too incomplete to allow for very far-reaching conclusions. Table 1 summarizes the Kondratieff cycles until the early twenty-first century, as extrapolated from Kondratieff and the early 1980s study of Korpinen (1981). The mostly *ex ante* extrapolated fourth cycle seems to fit very well with the developments in the world economy since the 1970s.

Kondratieff (ibid., pp. 64–80) presumed that before the beginning of the rising wave of each long cycle a number of profound changes in economic conditions take place, including technical innovations, monetary alterations and expansion of space for capitalist markets. Downward waves are also accompanied by long depressions in agriculture. Kondratieff was not alone in studying the long waves of the capitalist world economy. Famously, he was also followed by Joseph Schumpeter. By and large, Schumpeter (1939a; 1939b) agreed with many of Kondratieff's claims. Schumpeter (1939a, p. 220) suggested that the long cycles probably started in the last quarter of the seventeenth century. Like Kondratieff, Schumpeter (ibid., pp. 100–101) associated long wave cycles with the temporal rhythm of great technological innovations:

> First, . . . innovations do not remain isolated events, and are not evenly distributed in time, but on the contrary, they tend to cluster, to come about in bunches, simply because first some, and then most, firms follow in the wake of successful innovations; second, . . . innovations are not at any time

distributed over the whole economic system at random, but tend to concentrate in certain sectors and their surroundings.

The industrial revolution took place during the first wave. Steam power and weaving machines were adopted. The second wave was associated with the building of railways and the third with electricity and cars. The mass production of consumer durables and electronics began during the fourth wave. Some claim that the fifth wave has already started with the rapid development and expansion of the new information and communication technologies (Hämäläinen, 2003, pp. 80–90). Others anticipate that that may well happen with further development of intelligent and industrial robots, critical advances in the exploitation of renewable energy sources and in biotechnology (see e.g. Wagar, 1999, pp. 19–20).

The main problem with the studies on the long wave cycles has been the lack of clear accounts of those mechanisms that could be causally responsible for producing the outcome, namely synthetic time series indicating long wave cycles of economic development. Kondratieff himself believed that the fact that investments with true long-term effects (such as new factories, railways, channels, large land development projects, etc.) often get clustered accounts for the temporal rhythm of the capitalist world economy and fluctuations around the long-term growth trend. The upper turning point is explained in terms of shortage of capital and rising interest rates. On the other hand, Kondratieff claimed that a long decline of the price level and the accumulation of funds that can be loaned almost for free will eventually instigate a new wave of innovations and investments.

Schumpeter emphasized not only the historical uniqueness of each wave and the role of technological innovations. Elaborating upon Kondratieff's views, for Schumpeter the key to explaining cycles is his account of the role of money and banking. He proposed a theory according to which credit creation is, at least in significant part, directed to financing of innovations. Presupposing a highly specific historical-institutional setting of financial markets, Schumpeter (1939a, pp. 109–130) made controversial claims about bankers' rational foresight and capability to direct credit to profitable innovations, performing, as it were, the role of the rational (even if decentralized) planners of the capitalist system. Moreover, although Schumpeter ignored both the role of the uncertainty of the future and aggregate demand (the possibility of underconsumption), the core of his theory has been re-proposed recently:

> It is because there is available money looking for profit in the hands of non-producers that the new entrepreneurs can bring their ideas into commercial reality. It is here that the possibility of operating with borrowed money becomes a truly dynamic force. Financial capital will back the new entrepreneurs and it will be more likely to do so, in spite of the high risks, the more exhausted the possibilities are for investing in the accustomed directions. (Perez, 2002, p. 33)

Perez's neo-Schumpeterian account is, however, a major improvement upon Schumpeter at least in one respect. She takes into account the development of socio-economic inequalities that also result from each cluster of innovation and from the related speculative activities. Political struggles over the adequate institutional framework, also in order to ensure adequate aggregate demand, is very much part of her story of technological revolutions and financial capital.

Now, Kondratieff discussed also the occurrence of political violence in the nineteenth and early twentieth century Europe, Russia and North America. Although the most severe crises and depressions take place during a downward trend, 'as a rule, the periods of the rising waves of long cycles are considerably richer in big social upheavals and radical changes in the life of society (revolutions, wars) than are the periods of downward waves' (ibid., p. 70). Kondratieff acknowledged, however, that this is a loose empirical association. What is nonetheless noteworthy is that two out of three turning points in the twentieth century coincided with the world wars (also the first cycle turned at the time of the Napoleonic wars). The turning point of 1973–76 was relatively smooth and peaceful, however. Korpinen has pointed out that although this was a turning point in the fourth Kondratieff cycle, it did not resonate with shorter cycles as in the most severe economic crises. In 1981, he argued that the 'worst crisis is probably ahead of us, occurring at some point in the long downward wave, when the world economy is in recession' (Korpinen, 1981, p. 96).

Kondratieff's study indicates, however, that the relationship between economic developments, inequality and wars may be more complex than what we could presume on the basis of studies such as Nafziger and Auvinen (2003) only. Nafziger and Auvinen argue, on the basis of the systematic study of the late twentieth century violence in the global South, that humanitarian crises, catastrophes, genocides and wars are often preceded by an economic decline. It may be that not only depression but also certain kinds of growth may generate, inflame or trigger violent conflicts, particularly in the core areas of the world economy (Kondratieff excluded Latin America and the European colonies in Africa and Asia from his study). In particular, World War I came at the end of the third upward wave of 1890–1914. This concurs also with the basic claim of the so-called lateral pressure theory developed by Choucri and North (1975) and Ashley (1980).

However, there may be no contradiction between these two sets of hypotheses about the causal connections between economic growth or lack of growth and wars. The causal effects of many social processes are often delayed. According to Polanyi (1957/1944, pp. 264–266), the turning point for the nineteenth century era of long peace in the core areas of the world economy came in fact already the downward wave that lasted from 1870–75 to 1890. In particular, in 1875–80, significantly also as a response to the economic troubles of the day, the European great powers returned to the practices of imperial expansion of the past centuries. Thus, in the late nineteenth century, Africa was divided between the European colonial powers. The colonial control in the Middle East and Asia was deepened and extended. In 1876–1900, total colonial area expanded from 46.5 million square km to 72.9 million square km and colonial population from 314 million to 530 million people (Milios, 2001, p. 114). The great powers started also, again, to use power political means to support the interests of particular investors. The traditional champion of free trade, Britain, resorted to a system of imperial preferences, following the selected protectionism of its rivals, Germany and the US. Unilateralism and resort to force prevailed.

In the light of Kondratieff's cycles, it is possible to put forward a hypothesis that the late nineteenth century colonial expansion of markets, and the consequent availability of cheap raw materials, enabled the third upward wave that began around 1890. Of course, it was also based on new technical innovations such as steel, electricity, internal-combustion engine, cars and various machines. The growth of this era was accompanied by the rise of trade unions and social movements, which contributed to the rise of the real wages at least in many of the core countries. This in turn induced aggregate demand of goods and services at home, thereby contributing to further growth. Industrial growth was particularly strong in Germany and the US, which soon bypassed Britain in terms of production volumes.

With declining competitiveness, Britain began to rely more extensively on its empire and the system of imperial preferences. Others saw colonial possessions as equally important. The remaining non-colonized space was already occupied, however. A new science and practice of struggles over global territorial space was born, namely geo-politics.[4] The new neo-imperial and geo-political stories told and opinions adopted during the second downward wave constituted neo-imperial identities and also redefined the interests of the great powers. In the social context thus constituted, the unequal growth of the third upward wave led to the formation of new alliances and armament race between them. The shots of Sarajevo in summer 1914 triggered a consequent catastrophe that soon led also to Russian revolution and, later, to World War II and the Cold War as well. Is it possible that something similar could happen in the twenty-first century? Is it possible that—despite differences in historical contexts—a similar kind of pathological learning process may occur in response to a similar kind of economic troubles, setting the world onto a path towards a new major catastrophe?

Explaining the Long Cycles

A good analogy for Kondratieff's method might be to say that it is similar to Philips' famous wage–inflation trade-off—it is mainly trend spotting. As such, the identification of long waves in the capitalist world economy explains very little.

The long wave cycles are best understood as contrastive demi-regularities (or demi-regs) rather than universal invariances. Contrasts between different times and places often reveal relatively regular patterns in the way certain phenomena occur. Demi-regs are interesting first and foremost because they demand explanation. The essential question is whether it is possible to identify relatively enduring mechanisms that have causally produced the demi-reg we have detected. We also know that any demi-reg may at some historical point be transformed or cease to exist. Also this kind of change would require explanation (see Lawson, 1997, pp. 206–208).

The starting point must be the analysis of open systems with many simultaneous tendencies and complicated mechanisms. Social systems are not only open, they are also overlapping and, in parts, intra-related. The effects of various tendencies and mechanisms can be delayed, overlapping, mutually reinforcing and/or contradictory. Causal powers and processes can also be contradictory in the specific sense that they may lead to conflicts and learning. These may bring about the emergence or development of new modes of agency and transformation of social structures. Causally efficacious economic mechanisms are social, i.e. they depend on social practices and institutions and their internal and external relations. Changes of practices and institutions can transform these mechanisms or at least their effects. Moreover, it is not necessary that the same causal complexes would be responsible for the same rhythmic tendency, or the actual and empirically observed demi-reg, since different causes can bring about similar kinds of outcomes. Each wave of economic development is historically unique although some of the generative mechanisms may be inherent to capitalist market economy *per se* (as it evolved in the seventeenth and eighteenth centuries in Europe and the Americas).

From this perspective, how should we explain the long wave cycles in the capitalist world economy? In this section, I will very briefly outline a few basic hypotheses of an explanatory model that seems to fit with some of the relevant earlier explanatory models, and with available historical and empirical evidence concerning the fourth long cycle in particular (i.e. empirical evidence about the late twentieth century developments). A more systematic scrutiny of these hypotheses is beyond the scope of this paper but will appear in the book (Patomäki, forthcoming).

The Role of Economic Knowledge

Prevalent economic thinking can have real effects through economic policies and may, in part, be responsible for the phases of long cycles. Korpinen (1981, p. 14) has put forward an important hypothesis that monetarist, or more generally orthodox, economic policies tend to contribute to recession and deflation, and that Keynesian and monetarist policies occur in long cycles of learning and unlearning. However, Korpinen's point of departure ignores power both as transformative capacity and as relation of domination. More generally, we can posit a hypothesis that also because of the prevailing power relations based on private property, constitutive of capitalist relations of production and exchange, there is a tendency for the economic orthodoxy to assume prevalence in policy-making. Orthodoxy assumes that capitalist markets are self-correcting and in a state of equilibrium (or getting there) that is normally beneficial to all parties. Quantity theoretical thinking and modifications of monetarism and rational expectations theory are historical variations of economic orthodoxy. Only in specific circumstances can the countertendencies to orthodoxy become strong enough to make a real difference in policy-making.

Korpinen's hypothesis should thus be reinterpreted. In a capitalist market society, the general tendency towards the prevalence of orthodoxy becomes stronger when (1) the economic developments seem favourable in the world economy, i.e. when there is stable growth and high employment at least in the centres of the world economy and inflation is increasingly seen as the main problem; and/or when (2) the position of private capital becomes more secure in terms of structural power and/or political positioning. Once dominant, the orthodoxy starts to repress economic growth—in itself a tendency caused mostly by innovations and, also, commodification—through various mechanisms, efficacious in different world historical situations in different ways. However, the general tendency is towards gradually deepening deflation, that is, a downward phase involving under-consumption/overproduction, unemployment, declining prices, social problems and political reactions to them. This does not concern only the direct effects of orthodox monetary and fiscal policies—which vary historically and can sometimes be fused with other elements—but also the emergence, triggering, strengthening and releasing (e.g. by means of de- and re-regulation) of those mechanisms that are characteristic to capitalist market economy.

The Effects of Orthodoxy on Distribution of Incomes and Aggregate Demand

One typical consequence of orthodox policies is the concentration of incomes and wealth to relatively few while many others are either lagging increasingly behind or, particularly during a downward wave, are getting impoverished also in absolute terms. As Joan Robinson (1956, p. 78) has noted, a central paradox of capitalism is that 'each entrepreneur individually gains from a low real wage in terms of his own product, but all suffer from the limited market for commodities which a low real-wage entails'. The point is that workers are also consumers and their purchasing power creates demand for the goods and services the capitalist firms are selling. Moreover, we also know that the propensity to consume is usually (much) higher in lower income groups than among the wealthy. Thus, to the extent that the short-term wish of each and every individual capitalist employer is fulfilled (i.e. real labour costs are put down); to the extent that there is increasing unemployment; and/or to the extent there are growing socio-economic inequalities, the aggregate demand for mass products and services will decline. The result can be general under-consumption/overproduction in many if not most industries.

More precisely, what are those mechanisms that produce the outcome of growing inequalities? Obviously they can assume many different forms, from the structures of labour markets to the system of taxation or the characteristic functioning of global financial markets. A general hypothesis can be posited, however. A capitalist market society that is organized according to orthodox principles provides ample opportunities to translate the positions in relations of production, constituted by private property rights, into privately appropriated incomes and wealth. This is because the starting point of orthodoxy is that nothing should intervene in the 'free' operation of markets, including those structures and relations of power in labour markets and elsewhere that determine the distribution of profits and wages. Typically, orthodoxy also involves a Lockean sense of justice according to which the results of one's 'own labour'— including the products of labour hired by property owners—belong exclusively to oneself, i.e. the property owners, whether individual or corporate. Therefore the prevailing ethos is that privately appropriated wealth should be taxed and its use limited as little as possible. The property and wealth accumulated this way can also be used to raise and educate the next generation; and of course property is freely transferable and can be inherited. This kind of a historical-institutional context thus gives rise to the development and reproduction of relatively enduring socio-economic classes and growing disparities between them.

A trend towards increasing inequalities and thereby towards relative decline in aggregate demand ('under-consumption') would thus seem to be one of the main consequences of the prevalence of orthodoxy. This was also the fundamental explanation of e.g. J. A. Hobson (1988/1902) to the nineteenth century poverty, recessions and imperialism. Social problems and insufficient demand for products—and the corresponding excess capacity to produce—at home give rise to attempts to expand external markets and also export surplus labour to colonies. A number of early twentieth century theorists of business cycles and imperialism followed Hobson in this regard.

Uncertainty and the Marginal Productivity of Capital

Consumption explains business cycles only in part; the determination of investments is equally important. Unpredictability and uncertainty of future is a key to understanding many developments in market economy. When there is confidence in the future, people feel secure about consuming and investing. A crucial insight of Keynes was the notion that the development of financial markets changes the way capitalist market economy works. In developed money markets, it is possible to speculate about future and changes in interest and currency exchange rates. (Keynes, 1961/1936, p. 170) On the other hand, the marginal productivity of capital depends not only on the price of capital goods but also on expectations about future revenues. Rising prices, for instance, raise expectations about the future and thereby increase the marginal productivity of capital and investments. Investments in turn have multiplying effects on other economic activities (ibid., pp. 135–146).

Developed financial markets, where it is possible to buy and sell shares and other financial assets many times a day, imply the possibility of speculative investments. What is essential for speculative calculations is not the long-term productivity of capital goods but short-term changes in the prices of stocks and other financial assets and anticipation of others' expectations about changes in relative asset values (ibid., pp. 147–163). The development of financial markets makes the dynamics of savings, investments and interest rates more complicated and contradictory. When speculation in this sense prevails, financial markets become increasingly volatile and crisis-prone. Increased uncertainty and crises affect anticipations of the future and usually decrease the marginal productivity of capital and thereby investments. This has multiplying negative effects on other economic activities (although may, from a neo-Schumpeterian perspective, also release funds for risk investments in innovations).

Roughly in accordance with the neo-Schumpeterian account of historical phases, but giving finance much more autonomy, Minsky (1982, pp. 166–177) maintains that at times of long wave of growth and affluence, financial markets begin to develop in a more speculative and crisis-prone direction. Capitalism generates innovations also in finance, not only in production and exchange. New financial instruments and other innovations often presuppose de- and re-regulation. Consequently, there is a relation between the development of financial markets and the rise of orthodoxy to prevalence. Classical orthodoxy assumed that money is merely a good among other goods and therefore believes that the Smithian 'invisible hand' also guides free trade of money. Orthodoxy also assumes that real economy determines the prices of money and financial assets. In this fashion, the neoclassical orthodoxy has maintained that financial and other markets are either in a simultaneous (Pareto-optimal) equilibrium or moving towards such an equilibrium if there have been disturbances or movements of correction (Toporowski, 2002).

Minsky's (1982) model about the determination of investments explains why developed financial markets themselves tend to produce economic crisis, recessions and unemployment. Banks create money when they give loans against future revenues and profits. The monetary system is stable only as long as streams of revenue and profit enable firms to meet their financial liabilities (ibid., p. 22). Financial actors try to innovate new forms of profitable finance, which typically increase velocity of circulation and decrease liquidity. Many capital goods have been bought at least in part on credit. This makes their value dependent also on developments in financial markets, which in turn are contingent on actors' expectations about the future, commonness of speculative orientation and general degree of involvement in debt.

Speculative activities sensitize actors on alterations in expectations about the future while no-one can predict the future because the development of asset values is always uncertain in open systems and determined in significant part by actors' expectations and anticipations (ibid., pp. 59–69). The higher the liabilities in relation to revenues and liquidity, the more unstable the financial system becomes. Relatively small changes in interest rates or revenues may make some actors A insolvent and they can in turn endanger the solvency of those actors B who are expecting due payments from A. In the midst of mounting difficulties many have to opt for 'Ponzi finance', i.e. they have to take expensive short-term loans merely in order to meet their financial liabilities. Rapid rise in Ponzi finance indicates a crisis in the near future. Relatively small absolute changes in interest rates, streams of revenue and wealth can thus trigger a financial crisis (ibid., pp. 162–177). In other words, financial innovations and increasing involvement in debt make the financial system more chaotic.

The 'development' of financial markets takes capital and resources from other sectors of the economy, while increasing risks under uncertainty. Typically, at some point the distinction between speculative investments and swindle may be blurred and all sorts of scandals start to be increasingly common. For these and other reasons confidence in the continuation of the bubble may start to falter. Some may switch to speculating on decline and in some contexts these anticipations may become self-fulfilling. Small errors in calculations or unexpected changes can thereby make some financial actors quite easily insolvent (for instance, in the 1998 crisis the Long Term Capital Management, with the basic capital of US$4 billion, had created liabilities of US$200 billion-worth that it suddenly could not meet, thus risking the solvency of a number of banks and other major investors). To stress the basic point, in developed financial markets relatively minor problems or changes may trigger a major crisis (see Patomäki, 2001, Chap. 1; and for an analytical and very illuminating history of financial crises since the seventeenth century, Kindleberger, 2001).

Interaction of Tendencies and the Role of the State

The mechanisms created, strengthened or released by the orthodoxy often reinforce each other. For instance, under-consumption, co-caused by rising inequalities, compels firms to revise their expectations downwards. Depending on the particular geo-economic context, growing disparities

72   H. Patomäki

may thus decrease the marginal productivity of capital and thereby investments. Corporations which must operate on terms set in part by developed financial markets tend to become increasingly short-term oriented. Instead of planning, innovations and productive investments, it is often more important for firms to cut down their most immediate costs, particularly labour costs. Whether this means lower wages or more unemployment, the collective outcome is reduced aggregate demand for goods and services. This must be taken into account by firms when they adjust themselves to market developments. With lowered expectations, the marginal productivity of capital goes down and, with it, investments, with the standard multiplier effects.

Also the disturbances and uncertainties created by developed financial markets that tend to make the horizons of actors shorter can reduce the propensity to invest in such productive activities that would require long-term planning. Characteristically, financial markets also enable mechanisms that tend to concentrate wealth in the hands of relatively few, thereby contributing to the problem of under-consumption/overproduction. Financial crises have also direct effects on growth, employment and purchasing power. Since the late 1970s there have been more than 200 major financial crises, often involving substantial loss of output and employment. Combined banking sector and currency crisis is usually the most expensive type in terms of loss of output. The IMF (1998, p. 79) has estimated the loss of output to be in these cases, on average, 15% of national GDP. The Asian crisis led to the loss of 6% of the world GDP (UNDP, 1999, p. 2).

All this also has impacts on states' tax revenues and expenditure. When tax revenues go down, it is not easy to increase state expenditure, particularly if the prevalent orthodoxy requests states to follow balanced budgets, cut down taxes, eliminate price 'distortions', and commercialize as many activities as possible and transfer them to maximally 'liberalized' capitalist markets. Because states' expenditures constitute a major part of the world economy, this has obvious consequences for both aggregate demand and rising inequalities, reinforcing other tendencies. It seems that this is indeed the way the world economy has become locked-in in a long downward wave since the 1970s.

Concrete World Historical Processes since the 1960s

The mechanisms outlined above should now be put into a concrete world historical context (following the dialectical method of abstract and concrete moments of research). In the 1960s, the performance of the US economy declined also in terms of inflation, employment and rise of living standards. The US firms became less competitive compared to their competitors in Europe and Japan; the initial hegemonic position had turned, at least in some regards, into a burden. After 1965 it was clear that there was overproduction capacity in the US (Brenner, 2002, pp. 11–24). Minsky (1982) argues that by the mid-1960s a crisis-prone financial system had re-emerged in the US. The ratios of debt to income and of debt to liquid assets had risen to levels that had ruled prior to the Great Depression. 'As the financial system became more heavily weighted with layered private debts, the susceptibility of the financial structure to disturbances increased. With these disturbances, the economy moved to the turbulent regime that still rules' (ibid., p. xiii). Consequently, a series of financial crises erupted, the first one in 1966. However, the crash of 1929 has not been repeated, for two main reasons. Firstly, the US Federal Reserve had become a lender of last resort for other banks. Secondly, the big government that had evolved since the 1930s meant that the share of public expenditure of GDP had grown significantly. Government actions and automatic mechanisms of changes in expenditure had begun to make a difference. For instance, in the late 1960s the Vietnam War led to a large government deficit, functioning as a Keynesian-type stimulating fiscal policy.

The Americans could pay their bills—for military spending among others things—with IOUs ('I Owe You'), that is, by issuing bonds, notes and other forms of financial commitments (Strange, 1986, pp. 6–7). Unlike the others, the US did not need to export goods and services to pay its bills. In the 1950s and 1960s, the dollar expansion helped to revive world trade and even fund investments, particularly in Europe. Yet the parity to gold tied the hands of the US government. The accumulated dollar liabilities exceeded the large but declining gold reserves of the US already in 1958–59. The unpopular Vietnam War, financed largely through a further expansion of dollars and IOUs, aggravated the problem. Also, because of the constant surplus of the US allies, there emerged a shortage of gold. The dollar liabilities to foreigners exploded in the late 1960s (Walter, 1993, pp. 166–168).

In 1971 the Nixon administration dissolved the constraints stemming from this situation by unilaterally delinking dollar and gold. This link had been the basis of the Bretton Woods system. The US justified this move also in terms of orthodox economic theory. Famously, Milton Friedman (1953) maintained that floating rates are both more efficient and more in line with monetarism at home that was required to counter inflation (for a critical discussion, see Patomäki, 2001, pp. 223–231). This justification also served to give grounds for further demands to liberalize financial markets in other sectors and countries. This had both intended consequences (continuation of debt financing; reinforcement of US monetary autonomy and sovereignty; and boosting of US transnational corporations) and unintended consequences (speculative profits for US investors, while the costs of financial crises turned out to be covered by others) (for more details, see ibid., pp. 74–79).

It can be claimed that actions by the US have been roughly consistent with the under-consumption hypothesis of Hobson's theory of imperialism. Obviously there are historical differences. Whereas the past European empires expanded their markets and economic activities by colonizing overseas lands and regions, the US actions have taken place in a multilaterally organized global political economy that is exhaustively covered by sovereign states. Most of the Southern states—in Africa, the Middle East and Asia in particular—had become full members of the international society through the late twentieth century decolonization process that the US and the Soviet Union at the time supported (against the old European empires).

Nevertheless, it seems that in some important regards the US has behaved in a way similar to the nineteenth century European empires. Overproduction capacity and insufficient demand for US products at home and the increased competition in the economically successful Europe and Japan have led to attempts to expand markets for goods and transnational investments also by political and sometimes military means, particularly in the South. In the 1970s, the situation in the US worsened still when rising inequalities began to diminish the purchasing power of large segments of society. The construction of conditions for further economic expansion elsewhere was justified in terms of a particular universalism, namely the orthodox belief that 'free markets' is the best possible arrangement for everybody everywhere. From Ronald Reagan and Margaret Thatcher onwards, this has become the explicit ideology of reconstructing systems of global governance along neoliberal and US/UK-centric lines.

The US started to campaign for its increasingly narrow interests and vision in various fora. These interests were defined in terms of gaining free access for the US transnational corporations, banks and investments funds everywhere (trade, investment or whatever), on their own terms, and making their monopolistic gains as permanent and extensive as possible e.g. through intellectual property rights. The mechanisms of global financial markets have supported this aim in a number of ways. Global financial markets discipline states to follow orthodox recipes. They enable transnational purchases, buy-outs and mergers of corporations (means of production), i.e. facilitate non-territorial economic expansion. They also redirect a large part of global savings to the US, including into US Treasury bonds. In 2003, the net debt of the US federal state is almost US$3,000 billion and it needs more than a billion a day to fund its balance of payments deficit. Private debt in the US is about US$4,000 billion. Altogether the US debt is about a quarter of the world GDP and rising. The federal debt has been mostly used to fund private consumption (income transfers) or public consumption (military spending) (cf. Minsky, 1982, pp. xxiii–xxiv). Also private loans have often been taken to feed consumption rather than investments.

Actions of the US have been justified by representing particular interests as universal, also in terms of an inevitable process of 'globalization'. The conceptual framework for this has been provided by the economic orthodoxy. However, even in the most charitable possible interpretation (assuming away the undue monopolistic gains, the specific position of the dollar, and other US-favouring institutions of the world economy), this justification is based on the fallacy of composition. X may be rational choice for A in a specific historical situation, but if everyone does X simultaneously the collective outcome is counterfinal, i.e. contradicts the purpose of X (see Elster, 1978, pp. 96–122). The aim of replacing the wanting (i) domestic demand and (ii) savings/investments by exporting or moving activities elsewhere presupposes that there is effective demand, savings and productive investment opportunities elsewhere. This in turn presupposes confidence in the future economic developments, including anticipations of future demand for goods and services.

However, by reorganizing the economies and economic policies in many if not most countries on orthodox principles one has created a general tendency to deflation and recession almost everywhere. Moreover, free trade benefits mostly, or only, those countries where the technologically dynamic industries are located. Specialization in stagnating industries or, even worse, primary products means that one can only compete in terms of quantity and price, implying typically declining terms of trade (cf. Hämäläinen, 2003, pp. 3–32; Akyüz, 2003). Many countries in many parts of the world—in Latin America, sub-Saharan Africa, the Middle East, Central Asia and even Southeast Asia—have experienced economic decline or even partial collapse, instead of sustained per capita growth.

Orthodox economic policies co-cause increasing inequalities and imply attempts to cut down state expenditure. In a number of contexts of the late twentieth and early twenty-first century, however, this is more easily said than done. Growing impoverishment, unemployment, disparities and social problems tend to increase public expenditure particularly in those countries where a well-functioning welfare state once evolved. Consequently, the ratio of state expenditure to GDP may rise at first, even when welfare services and income transfers are drastically downsized (cf. Esping-Andersen, 1990, p. 19; Clayton and Pontusson, 1998). Because of this automatic Keynesian mechanism, the decrease of global aggregate demand has been gradual and contradictory, rather than assuming the form of a great crash. Moreover, central banks and the IMF have been acting as lenders of last resort—and also tightened financial regulations in some regards after each major crisis—and thus been able to prevent 1929 from happening again (at least for the time being).

Conclusions

It is impossible to preclude the possibility that a fifth Kondratieff cycle would begin at some point as a consequence of a combination of neo-imperial policies of securing cheap raw materials and energy and opening up new markets, military consumption, further commodification and partially autonomous technological innovations, possibly aided by mechanisms and processes that have been ignored in the explanatory model presented in this paper. Some followers of Schumpeter might also think that innovations—new technologies and new fields of economic activity—could play the key role in generating a new upward trend, particularly with the help of appropriate financial conditions. However, the tentative explanatory model of the geo-economic mechanisms and processes I have presented in this paper does not make this possibility look particularly likely.

At times, Kondratieff himself emphasized the role of massive—and at least partially publicly mobilized—investments such as construction of railways or channels or building of a system of basic education for the entire population in instigating a new upward phase. Perhaps a more thorough, long-term economic turn in the early twenty-first century would require analogical collective measures? Indeed, publicly co-mobilized or stimulated large-scale investments in a possibly new field of economic activities would increase aggregate demand and generate investments also in sectors linked to it. Both would have multiplier and cumulative effects on other economic activities. Global tax-and-transfer policies are also part and parcel of global Keynesianism. Some investments such as building an egalitarian system of basic public health and education for everybody on the planet would also increase the overall propensity to consume, and thereby total demand. Additional new fields include the exploitation of old and new renewable energy sources, information and communication technologies (including perhaps the development of a cheap and simple folk-computer and adequate public networking infrastructure for it), and sustainable biotechnology. A wave of new developments would also reverse the prevailing deflationary tendencies by inducing economic growth, and growth involves also some inflation. The new developments would also make the horizons of firms longer and raise positive expectations, thereby increasing the marginal productivity of capital.

However, it also seems that this shift would have to be accompanied by a more general reorientation of the prevalent economic policies. Monetary and fiscal policy—as well as social and industrial policy—must be compatible, and they must resonate, with the effects of the productive investments. In addition, the global financial system should be reformed thoroughly and its characteristic mechanisms re-regulated or removed. This is perhaps the core problem of global economic governance in the early twenty-first century. The problem is not only to mobilize large-scale investments—also globally—but to transform the mechanisms of the capitalist market economy in order to enable various heterodox economic policies to flourish.

Particularly in the 1980s and 1990s many of the key systems of global governance have been harnessed to the project of locking-in economic orthodoxy for good. Stephen Gill (1997) has coined the term 'new constitutionalism' to describe this project. New constitutionalism is a political and legal strategy to disconnect economic policies from democratic accountability and will-formation. The aim is to 'constitutionalize' the protection of absolute and exusive private property rights and the freedom of transnational traders and investors. This is achieved through regional and global multilateral institutions such as the EU and North American Free Trade Agreement (NAFTA); the Bretton Woods institutions; and the World Trade Organization (WTO). These treaties and institutions are more difficult to revise than many constitutions. Thereby they provide a solid and firm protection against all challenges to orthodoxy. One of the consequences of the neo-constitutional project is the difficulty of mobilizing public funding for the required massive investments.

In the early 2000s, it seems that on the initiative of the ever-stronger transnational management class, and under the leadership of the US, a worldwide framework of institutional arrangements has been created that prevents a turn to a new long upward phase in the world economy.

States are not equal in economic or political terms. Structures of production and exchange, as well as global financial markets, tend to favour actors based in particular states, while the consequent resources can be harnessed in international diplomacy and global governance to serve the particular interests of the powerful private actors and related states (see Braithwaite & Drahos, 2000; Patomäki & Teivainen, 2004, Chaps. 1–3).

The most powerful interests tend to prefer orthodox economic policies, universalizing their particular short-term interests, while this tends to be damaging for both the (world) economy as a whole and also for most parts of the world citizenry. Once again, in the early twenty-first century, the world economy is vacillating between zero per capita growth and deepening deflation and recession. Many signs point towards the latter. Of course, as I have emphasized, not all countries and regions are in exactly the same situation. A long downward wave may perhaps be compatible with relatively sustained growth in some countries such as China, for instance, at least as long as it is able to insulate itself from global financial markets and cultivates more heterodox arrangements at home. The downward wave is also compatible with short and weak booms in some other places, possibly also in the US, stimulated by the massive yet rather short-sighted debt-financing of military spending and private consumption of the wealthiest. This may stimulate economic growth for a while in some places.

The overall global picture is rather gloomy, however. Unilateral attempts to strengthen one's position by concessions from the others and further orthodox measures only serve to strengthen the tendencies towards steepening the collective downhill. At the same time, conflicts within and between states, as well as between regional groupings, may well escalate, threatening the existence of the post-World War II multilateral arrangements. What would be needed, instead, is a systematic revision of the institutions and formative contexts of the world economy. Unfortunately, in the absence of sufficiently strong political forces and/or countertendencies, a major catastrophe in the not-so-distant future seems a real possibility as well. From this insight, the next step is to articulate systematic scenarios on the possible and likely futures.

Notes

1   Due to restrictions on length, I must leave aside the more detailed developments as well as the role of commodification in economic growth (implying among other things that growth may also be impoverishing) or ecological consequences and constraints of growth (meaning that the activities generating growth may be detrimental to some parts or aspects of the biosphere which includes humanity). Also from a political point of view, what matters is not only the GDP or Gini coefficient figures but people's concrete experiences and understandings of the conditions of everyday life both in the immediately present contexts and in society at large.

2   Parity refers to the exchange rate between the currencies of two countries making the purchasing power of both currencies substantially equal. Purchasing power is the extent to which a given monetary unit can buy goods and services. Purchase power parity compares living standards in national economies independent of currency variations.

3   The number of people living on less than US$1 per day worldwide is said to have declined from 1,237 million in 1990 to 1,100 million in 2000. However, most of this reduction is accounted for by the changes in China (with some reduction also in East Asia and, possibly, in India). Elsewhere absolute poverty in this sense has been rising. The famous Millennium Development Goal, adopted by the UN Millennium Summit in September 2000, to halve, by the year 2015, the proportion of the world's people whose income is less than one dollar a day and the proportion of people who suffer from hunger and, by the same date, to halve the proportion of people who are unable to reach or to afford safe drinking water, thus seems fairly distant. Moreover, 'one dollar a day' also means different things in different social contexts. To a relatively self-sufficient farmer one dollar a day may be sufficient for many needs, but in a big city it is much harder to get by without money. Urbanization and increased commodification may thus imply that more money is needed to cover basic needs. Thus people may become poorer while there could be, in principle, positive development as measured by the UN.

4   Although Rudolph Kjellén introduced the term geo-politics only in 1916, Friedrich Ratzel had already developed the notion of *lebensraum* in the 1880s and Harold Mackinder his theories of the heartland in the very early twentieth century. As a concept that constituted many practices of governance, geo-politics is a characteristic product of this era.

References

Akyüz, Y., Ed. (2003) *Developing Countries and World Trade. Performance and Prospects* (London: Zed Books).

Ashley, R. (1980) *The Political Economy of War and Peace: The Sino-Soviet–American Triangle and the Modern Security Problematique* (London: Pinter).

Braithwaite, J. & Drahos, P. (2000) *Global Business Regulation* (Cambridge: Cambridge University Press).

Brenner, R. (2002) *The Boom and the Bubble. The US in the World Economy* (London: Verso).

Choucri, N. & North, R. C. (1975) *Nations in Conflict. National Growth and International Violence* (San Francisco: Freeman).

Clayton, R. & Pontusson, J. (1998) Welfare-state retrenchment revisited. Entitlement cuts, public sector restructuring, and inegalitarian waves in advanced capitalist countries, *World Politics*, 51(1), pp. 67–98.

Cornia, G. A. (2004) Inequality, growth and poverty: an overview of changes over the last two decades, in: G. A. Cornia (Ed) *Inequality, Growth and Poverty in an Era of Liberalization and Globalization*, pp. 3–25 (Oxford: Oxford University Press).

Cornia, G. A., Addison, T. & Kiiski, S. (2004) Income distribution changes and their impact in the post-Second World War period, in: G. A. Cornia (Ed) *Inequality, Growth and Poverty in an Era of Liberalization and Globalization*, pp. 26–54 (Oxford: Oxford University Press).

Elster, J. (1978) *Logic and Society. Contradictions and Possible Worlds* (Chichester: John Wiley & Sons).

Esping-Anderson, G. (1990) *The Three Worlds of Welfare Capitalism* (Cambridge: Polity).

Felix, D. (1995) Financial globalization versus free trade: the case for the Tobin tax, *UNCTAD Discussion Paper* No.108 (Geneva).

Freeman, A. (2002) The New World Order and the failure of globalization. Paper presented at the BISA-conference, London, 17 December 2002.

Freeman, A. (2003) Globalization: economic stagnation and divergence, in: A. Pettifor (Ed) *Real World Economic Outlook. The Legacy of Globalization: Debt and Deflation*, pp. 152–159 (Houndmills, Basingstoke: Palgrave).

Friedman, M. (1953) The case for flexible exchange rates, in: M. Friedman (Ed), *Essays in Positive Economics*, pp.157–203 (Chicago: University of Chicago Press).

Gill, S. (1997) Analysing new forms of authority: new constitutionalism, panopticism and market civilization. Paper presented at the conference 'Non-State Actors and Authority in the Global System', Warwick University, 31 October–1 November 1997.

Hobson, J. A. (1988/1902) *Imperialism: A Study*, 3rd edition (London: Unwin Hyman).

Hämäläinen, T. (2003) *National Competitiveness and Economic Growth. The Changing Determinants of Economic Performance in the World Economy* (Cheltenham: Edward Elgar).

IMF (1998) *World Economic Outlook* (Washington, DC: International Monetary Fund).

Keynes, J. M. (1961/1936) *The General Theory of Employment, Interest and Money* (London: MacMillan).

Kindleberger, C. (2001) *Manias, Panics and Crashes: A History of Financial Crashes* (London: John Wiley & Sons).

Kondratieff, N. (1984/1928) *The Long Wave Cycle*, Trans. G. Daniels (New York: Richardson & Snyder).

Korpinen, P. (1981) *Kriisit ja pitkät syklit* [Crises and Long Cycles] (Helsinki: TTT).

Lawson, T. (1997) *Economics and Reality* (London: Routledge).

Milios, J. (2001) Colonialism and imperialism: classic texts, in: P. O'Hara (Ed) *Encyclopedia of Political Economy*, pp. 113–116 (London: Routledge).

Minsky, H. P. (1982) *Can 'It' Happen Again? Essays on Instability and Finance* (Armonk, NY: M. E. Sharpe).

Nafziger, E. W. & Auvinen, J. (2003) *Economic Development, Inequality and War. Humanitarian Emergencies in Developing Countries* (Houndmills, Basingstoke: Palgrave MacMillan).

Patomäki, H. (2001) *Democratising Globalisation. The Leverage of the Tobin Tax* (London: Zed Books).

Patomäki, H. & Teivainen, T. (2004) *A Possible World. Democratic Transformation of Global Institutions* (London: Zed Books).

Patomäki, H. (forthcoming) *Global Economic Decline. Future Crises and Changes of Global Governance* (a manuscript in progress).

Perez, C. (2002) *Technological Revolutions and Financial Capital. The Dynamics of Bubbles and Golden Ages* (Cheltenham: Edward Elgar).

Polanyi, K. (1957/1944) *The Great Transformation. The Political and Economic Origins of Our Times* (Boston: Beacon Press).

Robinson, J. (1956) *The Accumulation of Capital* (London: MacMillan).

Schumpeter, J. (1939a) *Business Cycles. A Theoretical, Historical, and Statistical Analysis of the Capitalist Process, Volume 1* (London: McGraw-Hill).

Schumpeter, J. (1939b) *Business Cycles. A Theoretical, Historical, and Statistical Analysis of the Capitalist Process, Volume 2* (London: McGraw-Hill).

Strange, S. (1986) *Casino Capitalism* (Oxford: Blackwell).

Toporowski, J. (2002) Institutions and the development of critical theories of finance in the twentieth century, mimeo (London: South Bank University).

UNDP (1999) *Human Development Report 1999* (New York: Oxford University Press).

Wagar, W. W. (1999) *A Short History of Future*, 3rd edition (Chicago: University of Chicago Press).

Walter, A. (1993) *World Power and World Money*, revised edition (London: Harvester Wheatsheaf).

World Commission on the Social Dimension of Globalization (2004) *A Fair Globalization. Creating Opportunities for All* (Geneva: ILO).

Heikki Patomäki is a Professor of International Relations at the University of Helsinki and also the Research Director of NIGD, the Network Institute for Global Democratisation. Until summer 2003 he was a Professor of World Politics and Economy at the Nottingham Trent University, UK. His research interests include critical realism as a philosophy of social sciences; theories and issues of peace research and global political economy; and global democratization. Among his most recent books are *Democratising Globalisation: The Leverage of the Tobin Tax* (Zed Books, 2001); *After International Relations: Critical Realism and the (Re)Construction of World Politics* (Routledge, 2002); and *A Possible World: Democratic Transformation of Global Institutions* with Teivo Teivainen (Zed Books, 2004). At the moment, he is working on a book entitled *Global Economic Decline. Future Crises and Changes of Global Governance* as well as related methodologies of studying possible futures.

The Repositioning of Citizenship and Alienage: Emergent Subjects and Spaces for Politics*

SASKIA SASSEN

Most of the scholarship on citizenship has claimed a necessary connection to the national state. The transformations afoot today raise questions about this proposition insofar as they significantly alter those conditions which in the past fed that articulation between citizenship and the national state. The context for this possible alteration is defined by two major, partly interconnected conditions. One is the change in the position and institutional features of national states since the 1980s resulting from various types of globalization-linked policies. These range from economic privatization and deregulation to the increased prominence of the international human rights regime. The second is the emergence of multiple actors, groups, and communities partly strengthened by these transformations in the state and increasingly unwilling automatically to identify with a nation as represented by the state.

Addressing the question of citizenship against these transformations entails a specific stance. It is quite possible to posit that at the most abstract or formal level not much has changed over the last century in the essential features of citizenship. The theoretical ground from which I address the issue is that of the historicity and the embeddedness of both categories, citizenship and the national state, rather than their purely formal features. Each of these has been constructed in elaborate and formal ways. And each has evolved historically as a tightly packaged bundle of what were in fact often rather diverse elements. The dynamics at work today are destabilizing these particular bundlings and bringing to the fore the fact itself of that bundling and its particularity. Through their destabilizing effects, these dynamics are producing operational and rhetorical openings for the emergence of new types of political subjects and new spatialities for politics.

More broadly, the destabilizing of national state-centered hierarchies of legitimate power and allegiance has enabled a multiplication of non-formalized or only partly formalized political dynamics and actors. These signal a deterritorializing of citizenship practices and identities, and of discourses about loyalty and allegiance. Finally, specific transformations inside the national state have directly and indirectly altered particular features of the institution of citizenship. These transformations are not predicated necessarily on deterritorialization or locations for the institution outside the national state as is key to conceptions of postnational citizenship, and hence are usefully distinguished from current notions of postnational citizenship. I will refer to these as denationalized forms of citizenship.

Analytically, I seek to understand how various transformations entail continuities or discontinuities in the basic institutional form. That is to say, where do we see continuities in the formal bundle of rights at the heart of the institution and where do we see movement towards postnational and/or denationalized features of citizenship? And where might as yet informal citizenship practices engender formalizations of new types of rights? Particular attention goes to several specific issues that capture these features. One of these is the relationship between citizenship and nationality and the evolution of the latter towards something akin to 'effective' nationality rather than as 'allegiance' to one state or exclusively formal nationality. A later section examines the mix of distinct elements that actually make up the category of citizenship in today's highly developed countries. Far from being a unitary category or a mere legal status, these diverse elements can be contradictory. One of my assumptions here is that the destabilizing impact of globalization contributes to accentuate the distinctiveness of each of these elements. A case in point is the growing tension between the legal form and the normative project towards enhanced inclusion as various minorities and disadvantaged sectors gain visibility for their claim-making. Critical here is the failure in most countries to achieve 'equal' citizenship— that is, not just a formal status but an enabling condition.

The remaining sections begin to theorize these issues with a view towards specifying incipient and typically not formalized developments in the institution of citizenship. Informal practices and political subjects not quite fully recognized as such can nonetheless function as part of the political landscape. Undocumented immigrants who are long-term residents engage in practices that are the same as those of formally defined citizens in the routines of daily life; this produces an informal social contract between these undocumented immigrants and the community. Subjects who are by definition categorized as non-political, such as 'housewives', may actually have considerable political agency and be emergent political subjects. Insofar as citizenship is at least partly shaped by the conditions within which it is embedded, conditions that have today changed in certain very specific and also general ways, we may well be seeing a corresponding set of changes in the institution itself. These may not yet be formalized and some may never become fully formalized. Further, social constructions that mark individuals, such as race and ethnicity, may well become destabilized by these developments in both the institution of citizenship and the nation-state. Generally, the analysis in this paper suggests that we might see an unbounding of existing types of subjects, particularly dominant ones such as the citizen-subject, the alien, and the racialized subject.

A concluding section argues that many of these transformations in the broader context and in the institution itself become legible in today's large cities. Perhaps the most evolved type of site for these transformations is the global city.[1] In this process, the global city is reconfigured as a partly denationalized space that enables a partial reinvention of citizenship. This reinvention takes the institution away from questions of nationality narrowly defined and towards the enactment of a large array of particular interests, from protests against police brutality and globalization to sexual preference politics and house-squatting by anarchists. I interpret this as a move towards citizenship practices that revolve around claiming rights to the city. These are not exclusively or necessarily urban practices. But it is especially in large cities that we see simultaneously some of the most extreme inequalities as well as conditions enabling these citizenship practices. In global cities, these practices also contain the possibility of directly engaging strategic forms of power, a fact which I interpret as significant in a context where power is increasingly privatized, globalized, and elusive.

Citizenship and Nationality

In its narrowest definition citizenship describes the legal relationship between the individual and the polity. This relation can in principle assume many forms, in good part depending on the definition of the polity. Thus, in Europe this definition of the polity was originally the city, both in ancient and in medieval times. But it is the evolution of polities along the lines of state formation that gave citizenship in the west its full institutionalized and formalized character and that made nationality a key component of citizenship.

Today the terms citizenship and nationality both refer to the national state. In a technical legal sense, while essentially the same concept, each term reflects a different legal framework. Both identify the legal status of an individual in terms of state membership. But citizenship is largely confined to the national dimension, while nationality refers to the international legal dimension in the context of an interstate system. The legal status entails the specifics of whom the state recognizes as a citizen and the formal basis for the rights and responsibilities of the individual in relation to the state. International law affirms that each state may determine who will be considered a citizen of that state (see Hague Convention 1954). Domestic laws about who is a citizen vary significantly across states and so do the definitions of what it entails to be a citizen. Even within Europe, let alone worldwide, there are marked differences in how citizenship is articulated and hence how non-citizens are defined.

The aggressive nationalism and territorial competition among European states in the eighteenth, nineteenth and well into the twentieth centuries made the concept of dual nationality generally undesirable, incompatible with individual loyalties, and destabilizing of the international order. Absolute state authority over a territory and its nationals could not easily accommodate dual nationality. Indeed, we see the development of a series of mechanisms aimed at preventing or counteracting the common causes for dual nationality (Marrus, 1985). This negative perception of dual nationality continued into the first half of the twentieth century and well into the 1960s. There were no international accords on dual nationality. The main effort by the international system remained rooting out the causes of dual nationality by means of multi-lateral codification of the law on the subject (Rubenstein & Adler, 2000). It is probably the case that this particular form of the institution of citizenship, centered on exclusive allegiance, reached its highpoint in the twentieth century.

The major transformations of the 1980s and into the 21st century have once again brought conditions for a change in the institution of citizenship and its relation to nationality, and they have brought about changes in the legal content of nationality. Mostly minor formal and informal changes are beginning to dilute the particular formalization coming out of European history. The long lasting resistance to dual or multiple nationality is shifting towards a selective acceptance. According to some legal scholars (Spiro, 1997; Rubenstein & Adler, 2000), in the future dual and multiple nationality will become the norm. Today, we see growing numbers of people with dual nationality (Spiro, 1997). Insofar as the importance of nationality is a function of the central role of states in the international system, it is quite possible that a decline in the importance of this role and a proliferation of other actors will affect the value of nationality.

These transformations may give citizenship yet another set of features as it continues to respond to the conditions within which it is embedded (Sassen, 1996: Chap. 2). The nationalizing of the institution, which took place over the last several centuries, may today give way to a partial denationalizing. A fundamental dynamic in this regard is the growing articulation of national economies with the global economy and the associated pressures on states to be competitive. Crucial to current notions of competitive states is withdrawal from various spheres of citizenship entitlements, with the possibility of a corresponding dilution of loyalty to the state. Citizens' loyalty may in turn be less crucial to the state today than at a time of people-intensive and frequent warfare, with its need for loyal citizen-soldiers (Turner, 2000). Masses of troops today can be replaced by technologically intensive methods of warfare. Most importantly, in the highly developed world, warfare has become less significant partly due to economic globalization. Global firms and global markets do not want the rich countries to fight wars among themselves. The resistance to join the Bush Administration's call to war on Iraq illuminates this. The 'international' project of the most powerful actors on the world stage today is radically different from what it was in the nineteenth and first half of the twentieth centuries.

Many of the dynamics that built economies, polities, and societies in the nineteenth and twentieth centuries contained an articulation between the national scale and the growth of entitlements for citizens. During industrialization, class formation, class struggles, and the advantages of both employers and workers tended to scale at the national level and became identified with state-produced legislation and regulations, entitlements and obligations. The state came to be seen as a key to ensuring the well-being of significant portions of both the working class and the bourgeoisie. The development of welfare states in the twentieth century became a crucial institutional domain for granting entitlements to the poor and the disadvantaged. Today, the growing weight given to notions of the 'competitiveness' of states puts pressure on states to cut down on these entitlements. This in turn weakens the reciprocal relationship between the poor and the state (e.g. Munger, 2002). Finally, the growth of unemployment and the fact that many of the young are developing weak ties to the labor market, once thought of as a crucial mechanism for the socialization of young adults, will further weaken the loyalty and sense of reciprocity between these future adults and the state (Roulleau-Berger, 2002).

As these trends have come together towards the end of the twentieth century they are contributing to destabilize the meaning of citizenship as it was forged in the nineteenth and much of the twentieth century. Economic policies and technical developments we associate with economic globalization have strengthened the importance of cross-border dynamics and reduced that of borders. The associated emphasis on markets has brought into question the foundations of the welfare state. T. H. Marshall (1977 [1950]) and many others saw and continue to see the welfare state as an important ingredient of social citizenship. Today the assumptions of the dominant model of Marshallian citizenship have been severely diluted under the impact of globalization and the ascendance of the market as the preferred mechanism for addressing these social issues. For many critics, the reliance on markets to solve political and social problems is a savage attack on the principles of citizenship. Thus Peter Saunders (1993) argues that citizenship inscribed in the institutions of the welfare state is a buffer against the vagaries of the market and the inequalities of the class system.

The nature of citizenship has also been challenged by a proliferation of old issues that have gained new attention. Among the latter are the question of state membership of aboriginal communities, stateless people, and refugees (Sassen, 1999; Knop, 2002). All of these have important implications for human rights in relation to citizenship. These social changes in the role of the state, the impact of globalization on states, and the relationship between dominant and subordinate groups also have major implications for questions of identity. 'Is citizenship a useful concept for exploring the problems of belonging, identity and personality in the modern world?' (Shotter, 1993; Ong, 1999, Chaps. 1 & 4). Can such a radical change in the conditions for citizenship leave the institution itself unchanged?

Deconstructing Citizenship

Though often talked about as a single concept and experienced as a unitary institution, citizenship actually describes a number of discrete but related aspects in the relation between the individual and the polity. Current developments are bringing to light and accentuating the distinctiveness of these various aspects, from formal rights to practices and psychological dimensions (see Ong, 1996; Bosniak, 2000). They make legible the tension between citizenship as a formal legal status and as a normative project or an aspiration. The formal equality granted to all citizens rarely rests on the need for substantive equality in social and even political terms. In brief, current conditions have strengthened the emphasis on rights and aspirations that go beyond the formal legal definition of rights and obligations.

This is mirrored most recently in the reinvigoration of theoretical distinctions: communitarian and deliberative, republican and liberal, feminist, postnational and cosmopolitan notions of citizenship. Insofar as citizenship is a status which articulates legal rights and responsibilities, the mechanisms through which this articulation is shaped and implemented can be analytically distinguished from the status itself and so can the content of the rights. In the medieval cities so admired by Max Weber (1958), it was urban residents themselves who set up the structures through which to establish and thicken their rights in the space of the city. Today it is the national state that provides these mechanisms and it does so for national political space. But these mechanisms may well be changing once again given globalization, the associated changes in the national state, and the ascendance of human rights. In each of these major phases, the actual content and shape of the legal rights and obligations also changed.

Some of these issues can be illustrated through the evolution of equal citizenship over the last few decades. Equal citizenship is central to the modern institution of citizenship. The expansion of equality among citizens has shaped a good part of its evolution in the twentieth century. There is debate as to what brought about the expanded inclusions over this period, most notably the granting of the vote to women. For some (e.g. Karst, 2000) it is law itself—and national law—that has been crucial in promoting recognition of exclusions and measures for their elimination. For others (Young, 1990; Taylor, 1992) politics and identity have been essential because they provide the sense of solidarity necessary for the further development of modern citizenship in the nation-state. Either way, insofar as equality is based on membership, citizenship status forms the basis of an exclusive politics and identity (Walzer, 1985; Bosniak, 1996).

In a country such as the US, the principle of equal citizenship remains unfulfilled, even after the successful struggles and legal advances of the last five decades (Karst, 1997).[2] Groups defined by race, ethnicity, religion, sex, sexual orientation, and other 'identities', still face various exclusions from full participation in public life notwithstanding formal equality as citizens. Second, because full participation as a citizen rests on a material base (Marshall, 1977; Handler, 1995) poverty excludes large sectors of the population and the gap is widening. Feminist and race-critical scholarship have highlighted the failure of gender- and race-neutral conceptions of citizenship, such as legal status, to account for the differences of individuals within communities (Benhabib et al., 1995; Crenshaw et al., 1996; Delgado & Stefancic, 2001; Benhabib, 2002). In brief, legal citizenship does not always bring full and equal membership rights. Citizenship is affected by the position of different groups within a nation-state.

Yet it is precisely the position of these different groups that has engendered the practices and struggles that forced changes in the institution of citizenship itself. Thus Kenneth Karst (1997) observes that in the US it was national law that 'braided the strands of citizenship'—formal legal status, rights, belonging—into the principle of equal citizenship. This took place through a series of Supreme Court decisions and acts of Congress beginning with the Civil Rights Act of 1964. Karst emphasizes how important these constitutional and legislative instruments are, and that we cannot take citizenship for granted or be complacent about it.

There are two aspects here that matter for my argument. This history of interactions between differential positionings and expanded inclusions signals the possibility that the new conditions of inequality and difference evident today and the new types of claim-making they produce may well bring about further transformations in the institution. Citizenship is partly produced by the practices of the excluded. Secondly, by expanding the formal inclusionary aspect of citizenship, the national state contributed to create some of the conditions that eventually would facilitate key aspects of postnational citizenship. At the same time, insofar as the state itself has undergone significant transformation, notably the changes bundled under the notion of the competitive state, it may reduce the chances that state institutions will do the type of legislative and judiciary work that has led to expanded formal inclusions.

The consequence of these two developments may well be the absence of a lineal progression in the evolution of the institution. The expanding inclusions that we have seen in the US since the 1960s may have produced conditions which make possible forms of citizenship that follow a different trajectory. Furthermore, the pressures of globalization on national states may mean that claim-making will increasingly be directed at other institutions as well. This is already evident in a variety of instances. One example is the decision by first-nation people to go directly to the UN and claim direct representation in international fora, rather than going through the national state. It is also evident in the increasingly institutionalized framework of the international human rights regime and the emergent possibilities for bypassing unilateral state sovereignty.

As the importance of equality in citizenship has grown and become more visible, and as the role of national law in giving presence and voice to hitherto silenced minorities has grown, the tension between the formal status and the normative project of citizenship has also grown. For many, citizenship is becoming a normative project whereby social membership becomes increasingly comprehensive and open ended. Globalization and human rights are further enabling this tension and therewith furthering the elements of a new discourse on rights. These developments signal that the analytic terrain within which we need to place the question of rights, authority and obligations is shifting (Sassen, 1996, Chap. 2; Sassen, 2006). Some of these issues can be illustrated by two contrasting cases described below.

Towards Effective Nationality and Informal Citizenship

Unauthorized yet Recognized

Perhaps one of the more extreme instances of a condition akin to effective as opposed to formal nationality is what has been called the informal social contract that binds undocumented immigrants to their communities of residence (Schuck & Smith, 1985). Thus, unauthorized immigrants who demonstrate civic involvement, social deservedness, and national loyalty can argue that they merit legal residency. To make this brief examination more specific, I will focus on one case, undocumented immigrants in the US.

Individuals, even when undocumented immigrants, can move between the multiple meanings of citizenship. The daily practices by undocumented immigrants as part of their daily life in the community where they reside—such as raising a family, schooling children, holding a job—earn them citizenship claims in the US even as the formal status and, more narrowly, legalization may continue to evade them. There are dimensions of citizenship, such as strong community ties and participation in civic activities, which are being enacted informally through these practices. These practices produce an at least partial recognition of them as full social beings. In many countries around the world, including the US, long term undocumented residents often can gain legal residence if they can document the fact of this long term residence and 'good conduct'. US immigration law recognizes such informal participation as grounds for granting legal residency. For instance, prior to the new immigration law passed in 1996, individuals who could prove seven years of continuous presence, good moral character, and that deportation would be an extreme hardship, were eligible for suspension of deportation, and thus US residency. NACARA extended the eligibility of this suspension of deportation to some 300,000 Salvadorans and Guatemalans who were unauthorized residents in the US.[3]

The case of undocumented immigrants is, in many ways, a very particular and special illustration of a condition akin to 'effective' citizenship and nationality. One way of interpreting this dynamic in the light of the discussion in the preceding sections is to emphasize that it is the fact of the multiple dimensions of citizenship which engenders strategies for legitimizing informal or extra-statal forms of membership (Soysal, 1994; Coutin, 2000). The practices of these undocumented immigrants are a form of citizenship practices and their identities as members of a community of residence assume some of the features of citizenship identities. Supposedly this could hold even in the communitarian model where the community can decide on whom to admit and whom to exclude, but once admitted, proper civic practices earn full membership.

Further, the practices of migrants, even if undocumented, can contribute to recognition of their rights in countries of origin. During the 1981–92 civil war, Salvadoran migrants even though citizens of El Salvador were directly and indirectly excluded from El Salvador through political violence, enormous economic hardship, and direct persecution (Mahler, 1995). They could not enjoy their rights as citizens. After fleeing, many continued to provide support to their families and communities. Further, migrants' remittances became a key factor for El Salvador's economy—as they are for several countries around the world. The government of El Salvador actually began to support the emigrants' fight to get residency rights in the US, even joining US-based activist organizations in this effort. The Salvadoran government was thus supporting Salvadorans who were the formerly excluded enemy citizens—they needed those remittances to keep coming and they wanted the emigrants to stay out of the Salvadoran workforce given high unemployment. Thus the participation of these undocumented migrants in cross-border community, family, and political networks has contributed to increasing recognition of their legal and political rights as Salvadoran citizens (Coutin, 2000; Mahler, 1996).

According to Coutin (2000) and others, movements between membership and exclusion, and between different dimensions of citizenship, legitimacy and illegitimacy, may be as important as redefinitions of citizenship itself. Given scarce resources, the possibility of negotiating the different dimensions of citizenship may well represent an important enabling condition. Undocumented immigrants develop informal, covert, often extra-statal strategies and networks connecting them with communities in sending countries. Hometowns rely on their remittances and their information about jobs in the US. Sending remittances illegally by an unauthorized immigrant can be seen as an act of patriotism, and working as an undocumented immigrant can be seen as contributing to the host economy. Multiple interdependencies are thereby established and grounds for claims on the receiving and the originating country can conceivably also be established even when the immigrants are undocumented and laws are broken (Basch et al., 1994; Cordero-Guzmán et al., 2001).

Authorized yet Unrecognized

At perhaps the other extreme of undocumented immigrants whose practices allow them to become accepted as members of the political community is the case of those who are full citizens yet not recognized as political subjects through discrimination, cultural stereotyping, etc.

In an enormously insightful study of Japanese housewives, Robin LeBlanc (1999) finds precisely this combination. Being a housewife is basically a full-time occupation in Japan and restricts Japanese women's public life in many important ways, both practical and symbolical. A 'housewife' in Japan is a person whose very identity is customarily that of a particularistic, non-political actor. Yet, paradoxically, it is also a condition providing these women with a unique vehicle for other forms of public participation, where being a housewife is an advantage denied to those who might have the qualifications for higher level political life. LeBlanc documents how the housewife has an advantage in the world of local politics or the political life of a local area: she can be trusted precisely because she is a housewife; she can build networks with other housewives; hers is the image of desirable public concern and of a powerful—because believable—critic of mainstream politics.

There is something extremely important in this condition which is shared with women in other cultures and vis-à-vis different issues. For instance, and in a very different register, women emerged as a specific type of political actor during the brutal dictatorships of the 1970s and 1980s in several countries of Latin America. It was precisely their condition as mothers and wives that gave them the clarity and the courage to demand justice and to demand bread and to do so confronting armed soldiers and policemen. Mothers in the barrios of Santiago during Pinochet's dictatorship, the Mothers of the Plaza de Mayo in Buenos Aires, the mothers regularly demonstrating in front of the major prisons in El Salvador during the civil war—all were driven to political action by their despair at the loss of children and husbands and the struggle to provide food in their homes. And they were recognized as such.

Further, and in a very different type of situation, there is an interesting parallel between LeBlanc's capturing of the political in the condition of the housewife and a set of findings in some of the research on immigrant women in the US. There is growing evidence that immigrant women are more likely than immigrant men to emerge as actors in the public domain precisely because of their responsibilities in the household. Regular wage work and improved access to other public realms has an impact on their culturally specified subordinate role to men in the household. Immigrant women gain greater personal autonomy and independence while immigrant men lose ground compared to what was their condition in cultures of origin. Women gain more control over budgeting and other domestic decisions, and greater leverage in requesting help from men in domestic chores. Their responsibility for securing public services and other public resources for their families gives them a chance to become incorporated in the mainstream society—they are often the ones in the household who mediate in this process (e.g., Chinchilla & Hamilton, 2001). It is likely that some women benefit more than others from these circumstances; we need more research to establish the impact of class, education, and income on these gendered outcomes.

Besides the relatively greater empowerment of immigrant women in the household associated with waged employment, what matters here is their greater participation in the public sphere and their possible emergence as public actors. There are two arenas where immigrant women are active: institutions for public and private assistance, and the immigrant or ethnic community. The incorporation of women in the migration process strengthens the settlement likelihood and contributes to greater immigrant participation in their communities and vis-à-vis the state. For instance, Pierrette Hondagneu-Sotelo (1994) found immigrant women come to assume more active public and social roles, which further reinforces their status in the household and the settlement process. These immigrant women are more active in community building and community activism and they are positioned differently from men regarding the broader economy and the state. They are the ones that are likely to have to handle the legal vulnerability of their families in the process of seeking public and social services for their families. This greater participation by women suggests the possibility that they may emerge as more forceful and visible actors and make their role in the labor market more visible as well.[4]

These are dimensions of citizenship and citizenship practices that do not fit the indicators and categories of mainstream frameworks for understanding citizenship and political life. Women in the condition of housewives and mothers do not fit the categories and indicators used to capture participation in political life. Feminist scholarship in all the social sciences has had to deal with a set of similar or equivalent difficulties and tensions in its effort to constitute its subject or to reconfigure a subject that has been flattened. The theoretical and empirical distance that has to be bridged between the recognized world of politics and the as yet unmapped experience of citizenship of the housewife—not of women as such, but of women as housewives—is a distance we encounter in many types of inquiry. Bridging this distance requires specific forms of empirical research and of theorization.

Postnational or Denationalized?

From the perspective of nation-based citizenship theory, some of these transformations might be interpreted as a decline or devaluation of citizenship or, more favorably, as a displacement of citizenship in the face of other forms of collective organization and affiliation, as yet unnamed (Bosniak, 2000). Insofar as citizenship is theorized as necessarily national (e.g. Himmelfarb, 2001), by definition these new developments cannot be captured in the language of citizenship.[5] An alternative interpretation would be to suspend the national, as in postnational conceptions, and to posit that the issue of where citizenship is enacted is an empirical question (e.g. Soysal, 1994; Jacobson, 1996; Torres, 1998; Torres et al., 1999; Isin & Turner, 2002).

From where I look at these issues, there is a third possibility, beyond these two. It is that citizenship—even if situated in institutional settings that are 'national'—is a possibly changed institution if the meaning of the national itself has changed (Sasson, 2006, ch. 6). That is to say, insofar as globalization has changed certain features of the territorial and institutional organization of the political power and authority of the state, the institution of citizenship—its formal rights, its practices, its psychological dimension—has also been transformed even when it remains centered in the national state. I have argued, for instance, that this territorial and institutional transformation of state power and authority has produced operational, conceptual and rhetorical openings for nation-based subjects other than the national state to emerge as legitimate actors in international and global arenas that used to be exclusive to the state (see *Indiana Journal of Global Legal Studies*, 1996).

I distinguish what I would narrowly define as denationalized from postnational citizenship, the latter the term most commonly used and the only one used in the broader debate.[6] In my reading we are dealing with two distinct dynamics rather than only the emergence of locations for citizenship outside the frame of the national state. Their difference is a question of scope and institutional embeddedness. The understanding in the scholarship is that postnational citizenship is located partly outside the confines of the national. In considering denationalization, the focus moves on to the transformation of the national, including the national in its condition as foundational for citizenship. Thus it could be argued that postnationalism and denationalization represent two different trajectories. Both are viable, and they do not exclude each other.

The national, then, remains a referent in my work (e.g., Sassen, 2006). But, clearly, it is a referent of a specific sort: it is, after all, its change that becomes the key theoretical feature through which it enters my specification of changes in the institution of citizenship. Whether or not this devalues citizenship (Jacobson, 1996) is not immediately evident to me at this point. Citizenship has undergone many transformations in its history precisely because it is to variable extents embedded in the specifics of each of its eras.[7] Significant to my argument here is also the fact discussed earlier about the importance of national law in the process of expanding inclusions, inclusions which today are destabilizing older notions of citizenship. This pluralized meaning of citizenship, partly produced by the formal expansions of the legal status of citizenship and through the institutionalization of the human rights regime, is today contributing to explode the boundaries of that legal status even further.

First, and most importantly in my reading, is the strengthening, including the constitutionalizing, of civil rights which allow citizens to make claims against their states and allow them to invoke a measure of autonomy in the formal political arena that can be read as a lengthening distance between the formal apparatus of the state and the institution of citizenship. The implications, both political and theoretical, of this dimension are complex and in the making: we cannot tell what will be the practices and rhetorics that might be invented.

Secondly, I add to this the granting, by national states, of a whole range of 'rights' to foreign actors, largely and especially, economic actors—foreign firms, foreign investors, international markets, foreign business people (see Sassen, 1996: Chap. 2). Admittedly, this is not a common way of framing the issue. It comes out of my particular perspective about the impact of globalization and denationalization on the national state, including the impact on the relation between the state and its own citizens, and the state and foreign economic actors. I see this as a significant, though not much recognized, development in the history of claim-making. For me the question as to how citizens should handle these new concentrations of power and 'legitimacy' that attach to global firms and markets is a key to the future of democracy. My efforts to detect the extent to which the global is embedded and filtered through the national (e.g., the concept of the global city—Sassen, 2001; Bartlett, in process) is one way of understanding whether therein lies a possibility for citizens, still largely confined to national institutions, to demand accountability of global economic actors through national institutional channels, rather than having to wait for a 'global' state.

Citizenship in the Global City

The particular transformations in the understanding and theorization of citizenship discussed thus far bring us back to some of the earlier historical formations around questions of citizenship, most prominently the crucial role played by cities and civil society. The large city of today, most especially the global city, emerges as a strategic site for these new types of operations. It is one of the nexuses where the formation of new claims materializes and assumes concrete forms. The loss of power at the national level produces the possibility for new forms of power and politics at the subnational level. The national as container of social process and power is cracked. This cracked casing opens up possibilities for a geography of politics that links subnational spaces. Cities are foremost in this new geography. One question this engenders is how and whether we are seeing the formation of new types of politics that localize in these cities.

If we consider that large cities concentrate both the leading sectors of global capital and a growing share of disadvantaged populations—immigrants, many of the disadvantaged women, people of color generally, and, in the megacities of developing countries, masses of shanty dwellers—then we can see that cities have become a strategic terrain for a whole series of conflicts and contradictions. We can then think of cities also as one of the sites for the contradictions of the globalization of capital, even though, heeding Ira Katznelson's (1992) observation, the city cannot be reduced to this dynamic. Recovering cities along these lines means recovering the multiplicity of presences in this landscape. The large city of today has emerged as a strategic site for a whole range of new types of operations—political, economic, cultural, subjective (Drainville, 2004; Isin, 2000; Allen et al., 1999; Bridge & Watson, 2000).

While citizenship originated in cities and cities played an important role in its evolution, I do not think we can simply read some of these current developments as a return to that older historical condition. The significance of the city today as a setting for engendering new types of citizenship practices and new types of incompletely formalized political subjects does not derive from that history. Nor does current local city government have much to do with earlier notions of citizenship and democracy described for ancient and medieval cities in Europe (Isin, 2000, p. 7). It is, rather, more connected to what Henri Lefebvre (1991; 1995) was capturing when describing the city as oeuvre and hence the importance of agency. Where Lefebvre found this agency in the working class in the modern (Fordist) city, I find it in two strategic actors—global corporate capital and immigration—in today's global cities. Here I would like to return to the fact of the embeddedness of the institution of citizenship.

What is being engendered today in terms of citizenship practices in the global city is quite different from what it might have been in the medieval city of Weber. In the medieval city we see a set of practices that allowed the burghers to set up systems for owning and protecting property and to implement various immunities against despots of all sorts.[8] Today's citizenship practices have to do with the production of 'presence' of those without power and a politics that claims rights to the city. What the two situations share is the notion that through these practices new forms of citizenship are being constituted and that the city is a key site for this type of political work and is, indeed, partly constituted through these dynamics. After the long historical phase that saw the ascendance of the national state and the scaling of key economic dynamics at the national level, the city is once again today a scale for strategic economic and political dynamics.

In his effort to specify the ideal-typical features of what constitutes the city, Weber sought out a certain type of city—most prominently the cities of the late Middle Ages rather than the modern industrial cities of his time. Weber sought a kind of city that combined conditions and dynamics which forced its residents and leaders into creative, innovative responses and adaptations. Further, he posited that these changes produced in the context of the city signaled transformations that went beyond the city, and that could have a far reach in instituting often fundamental transformations. In that regard the city offered the possibility of understanding far-reaching changes that could—under certain conditions—eventually encompass society at large.

There are two aspects of Weber's *The City* (1958) that are of particular importance here. Weber sought to understand under what conditions cities can be positive and creative influences on people's lives. For Weber, cities are a set of social structures that encourage social individuality and innovation and hence are an instrument of historical change. There is in this intellectual project a deep sense of the historicity of these conditions. For Weber, modern urban life did not correspond to this positive and creative power of cities; Weber saw modern cities as dominated by large factories and office bureaucracies. My own reading of the Fordist city corresponds in many ways to Weber's in the sense that the strategic scale under Fordism is the national scale and cities lose significance. It is the large Fordist factory and the mines which emerge as key sites for the political work of the disadvantaged and those without power.

For Weber, it is particularly the cities of the late Middle Ages that combine the conditions that pushed urban residents, merchants, artisans and leaders to address them and deal with them. These transformations could make for epochal change beyond the city itself: Weber shows us how in many of these cities these struggles led to the creation of the elements of what we could call governance systems and citizenship. In this regard, struggles around political, economic, legal, cultural, issues which are centered in the realities of cities can become the catalysts for new transurban developments in all these institutional domains: markets, participatory governance, rights for members of the urban community regardless of lineage, judicial recourse, cultures of engagement and deliberation.

The particular analytic element I want to extricate from this aspect of Weber's understanding and theorization of the city is the historicity of those conditions that make cities strategic sites for the enactment of important transformations in multiple institutional domains. Elsewhere (Sassen, 2001) I have developed the argument that today a certain type of city—the global city—has emerged as a strategic site precisely for such innovations and transformations in multiple institutional domains. Several of the key components of economic globalization and digitization instantiate in this type of city and produce dislocations and destabilizations of existing institutional orders and legal, regulatory, and normative frames for handling urban conditions. It is the high level of concentration of these new dynamics in these cities that forces creative responses and innovations. There is, most probably, a threshold effect at work here.

The historicity of this process rests in the fact that under Keynesian policies, particularly the Fordist contract, and the dominance of mass manufacturing as the organizing economic dynamic, cities had lost strategic functions and were not the site for creative institutional innovations. The strategic sites were the large factory and the whole process of mass manufacturing and mass consumer markets, and, secondly, the national government where regulatory frameworks were developed and the Fordist contract instituted. The factory and the government were the strategic sites where the crucial dynamics producing the major institutional innovations of the epoch were located.

With globalization and digitization—and all the specific elements they entail—global cities emerge as such strategic sites. While the strategic transformations are sharply concentrated in global cities, many of the transformations are also enacted, besides being diffused, in cities at lower orders of national urban hierarchies. Furthermore, in my reading, particular institutions of the state also are such strategic sites even as there is an overall shrinking of state authority through deregulation and privatization (e.g., Body-Gendrot, 1999; Wacquant, 2004).

A second analytic element I want to extricate from Weber's The City is the particular type of embeddedness of the transformations he describes and renders as ideal-typical features. This is not an embeddedness in what we might think of as deep structures because the latter are precisely the ones that are being dislocated or changed and are creating openings for new fundamental arrangements to emerge. The embeddedness is, rather, in very specific conditions, opportunities, constraints, needs, interactions, contestations, interests. The aspect that matters here is the complexity, detail, and social thickness of the particular conditions and the dynamics he identifies as enabling change and innovation. This complexity and thickness also produces ambiguities in the meaning of the changes and innovations. It is not always clear whether they are positive—where we might interpret positive as meaning the creation or strengthening of some element, even if very partial or minor, of participatory democracy in the city—and in what timeframe their positiveness would become evident. In those cities of the late Middle Ages he saw as being what the city is about, he finds contradictory and multivalent innovations. He dissects these innovations to understand what they can produce or launch.

The argument I derive from this particular type of embeddedness of change and innovation is that current conditions in global cities are creating not only new structurations of power but also operational and rhetorical openings for new types of political actors which may have been submerged, invisible, or without voice. A key element of the argument here is that the localization of strategic components of globalization in these cities means that the disadvantaged can engage the new forms of globalized corporate power, and secondly that the growing numbers and diversity of the disadvantaged in these cities under these conditions assumes a distinctive 'presence'. This entails a distinction between powerlessness and invisibility or impotence. The disadvantaged in global cities can gain 'presence' in their engagement with power but also vis-à-vis each other. This is different from the 1950s–1970s period in the US, for instance, when white flight and the significant departure of major corporate headquarters left cities hollowed out and the disadvantaged in a condition of abandonment. Today, the localization of the global creates a set of objective conditions of engagement. This can be seen, for example, in the struggles against gentrification—which encroaches on minority and disadvantaged neighborhoods and led to growing numbers of homeless beginning in the 1980s—and the struggles for the rights of the homeless, or also in demonstrations against police brutalizing minority people. These struggles are different from the ghetto uprisings of the 1960s, which were short, intense eruptions confined to the ghettos and causing most of the damage in the neighborhoods of the disadvantaged themselves. In these ghetto uprisings there was no engagement with power.

The conditions that today mark the possibility of cities as strategic sites are basically two, and both capture major transformations that are destabilizing older systems organizing territory and politics. One of these is the re-scaling of what are the strategic territories that articulate the new political-economic system. The other is the partial unbundling or at least weakening of the national as container of social process due to the variety of dynamics encompassed by globalization and digitization. The consequences for cities of these two conditions are many: what matters here is that cities emerge as strategic sites for major economic processes and for new types of political actors. Insofar as citizenship is embedded and in turn marked by its embeddedness, these new conditions may well signal the possibility of new forms of citizenship practices and identities.

There is something to be captured here—a distinction between powerlessness and the condition of being an actor even though lacking power. I use the term presence to name this condition. In the context of a strategic space such as the global city, the types of disadvantaged people described here are not simply marginal; they acquire presence in a broader political process that escapes the boundaries of the formal polity. This presence signals the possibility of a politics. What this politics will be will depend on the specific projects and practices of various communities. Insofar as the sense of membership of these communities is not subsumed under the national, it may well signal the possibility of a politics that, while transnational, is actually centered in concrete localities.

Notes

This text is based on a keynote lecture from 7 March 2002 conference of the *Berkeley Journal of Sociology*, 'Race and Ethnicity in a Global Context' at the University of California, Berkeley. It was published in 2002 in the *Berkeley Journal of Sociology*, Volume 46, pp. 4–26 under the title 'The Repositioning of Citizenship: Emergent Subjects and Spaces for Politics'.

1   For the full treatment of my concept of the global city, see the updated second edition of *The Global City: New York, London, Tokyo* (Sassen, 2001).
2   In Kenneth Karst's interpretation of US law, aliens are 'constitutionally entitled to most of the guarantees of equal citizenship, and the Supreme Court has accepted this idea to a modest degree' (Karst, 2000, p. 599; see also fn. 20 where he cites cases). Karst also notes that the Supreme Court has not carried this development nearly as far as he might wish.
3   NACARA is the 1997 Nicaraguan Adjustment and Central American Relief Act. It created an amnesty for 300,000 Salvadorans and Guatemalans to apply for suspension of deportation. This is an immigration remedy that had been eliminated by the Illegal Immigration Reform and Immigrant Responsibility Act in 1996 (see Coutin, 2000).
4   For the limits of this process see, e.g., Parreñas, 2001.
5   Thus for Karst 'In the US today, citizenship is inextricable from a complex legal framework that includes a widely accepted body of substantive law, strong law-making institutions, and law-enforcing institutions capable of performing their task' (2000, p. 600). Not recognizing the centrality of the law is, for Karst, a big mistake. Postnational citizenship lacks an institutional framework that can protect the substantive values of citizenship. Karst does acknowledge the possibility of rabid nationalism and the exclusion of aliens when legal status is made central.
6   Bosniak (2000) uses denationalized interchangeably with postnational. I do not.
7   In this regard, I have emphasized as significant (1996, Chap. 2) the introduction in the new constitutions of South Africa, Brazil, Argentina, and the Central European countries, of a provision that qualifies what had been an unqualified right—if democratically elected—of the sovereign to be the exclusive representative of its people in international fora.
8   Only in Russia—where the walled city did not evolve as a center of urban immunities and liberties—does the meaning of citizen diverge from concepts of civil society and cities, and belong to the state, not the city (Weber, 1958).

References

Allen, J., Massey, D. & Pryke, M., Eds (1999) Unsettling Cities (London: Routledge).

Basch, L., Glick Schiller, N. & Blanc-Szanton, C. (1994) *Nations Unbound: Transnational Projects, Postcolonial Predicaments, and Deterritorialized Nation-States* (Langhorne, PA: Gordon & Breach).

Bartlett, A. (forthcoming) Political Subjectivity in the Global City (Ph.D. Dissertation, Department of Sociology, University of Chicago).

Benhabib, S. (2002) *Democractic Equality and Cultural Diversity: Political Identities in the Global Era* (Princeton, NJ: Princeton University Press).

Benhabib, S., Butler, J., Cornell, D. & Fraser, N. (1995) *Feminist Contentions: A Philosophical Exchange* (New York: Routledge).

Body-Gendrot, S. (1999) *The Social Control of Cities* (London: Blackwell).

Bosniak, L. (1996) 'Nativism' the concept: some reflections, in: J. Perea (Ed) *Immigrants Out! The New Nativism and the Anti-Immigrant Impulse in the United States* (New York: NYU Press).

Bosnaik, L. (2000) Citizenship denationalized, *Indiana Journal of Global Legal Studies*, 7(2), pp. 447–509.

Bridge, G. & Watson, S., Eds (2000) *A Companion to the City* (Oxford, UK: Blackwell).

Chinchilla, N. & Hamilton, N. (2001) *Seeking Community in the Global City: Salvadorans and Guatemalans in Los Angeles* (Philadelphia, PA: Temple University Press).

Cordero-Guzmán, H. R., Smith, R. C. & Grosfoguel, R., Eds (2001) *Migration, Transnationalization, and Race in a Changing New York* (Philadelphia, PA: Temple University Press).

Coutin, S. B. (2000) Denationalization, inclusion, and exclusion: negotiating the boundaries of belonging, *Indiana Journal of Global Legal Studies*, 7(2), pp. 585–594.

Crenshaw, K., Gotanda, N., Peller, G. & Thomas, K., Eds (1996) *Critical Race Theory: The Key Writings that Formed the Movement* (New York: New Press).

Delgado, R. & Stefancic, J., Eds (2001) *Critical Race Theory: The Cutting Edge* (Philadelphia, PA: Temple University Press).

Drainville, A. (2004) *Contesting Globalization: Space and Place in the World Economy* (London: Routledge).

Hague Convention (1954) Available at http://exchanges.state.gov/education/culprop/hague.html

Handler, J. (1995) *The Poverty of Welfare Reform* (New Haven, CT: Yale University Press).

Himmelfarb, G. (2001) *One Nation, Two Cultures: A Searching Examination of American Society in the Aftermath of Our Cultural Revolution* (New York: Vintage Books).

Hondagneu-Sotelo, P. (1994) *Gendered Transitions: Mexican Experiences of Immigration* (Berkeley, CA: University of California Press).

Indiana Journal of Global Legal Studies (1996) Special Issue: Feminism and globalization: the impact of the global economy on women and feminist theory, 4(1).

Isin, E. (2000) Introduction: democracy, citizenship and the city, pp. 1–22 in E. Isin (Ed) *Democracy, Citizenship and the Global City* (New York: Routledge).

Isin, E. & Turner, B. S., Eds (2002) *Handbook of Citizenship Studies* (London, Thousand Oaks, CA: Sage).

Jacobson, D. (1996) *Rights Across Borders: Immigration and the Decline of Citizenship* (Baltimore, MD: Johns Hopkins Press).

Karst, K. (1997) The coming crisis of work in constitutional perspective, *Cornell Law Review*, 82(3), pp. 523–571.

Karst, K. (2000) Citizenship, law, and the American nation, *Indiana Journal of Global Legal Studies*, 7(2), pp. 595–601.

Katznelson, I. (1992) *Marxism and the City* (Oxford: Clarendon).

Knop, K. (2002) *Diversity and Self-Determination in International Law* (Cambridge, UK: Cambridge University Press).

LeBlanc, R. (1999) *Bicycle Citizens: The Political World of the Japanese Housewife* (Berkeley, CA: University of California Press).

Lefebvre, H. (1991) *The Production of Space* (Cambridge, MA: Blackwell).

Lefebvre, H. (1995) *Writing on Cities* (Cambridge, MA: Blackwell).

Mahler, S. (1995) *American Dreaming: Immigrant Life on the Margins* (Princeton, NJ: Princeton University Press).

Marrus, M. R. (1985) *The Unwanted: European Refugees in the Twentieth Century* (New York: Oxford University Press).

Marshall, T. H. & Lipset, S. M. (1977[1950]) *Class, Citizenship, and Social Development* (Chicago, IL: University of Chicago Press).

Munger, F., Ed (2002) *Laboring Under the Line* (New York: Russell Sage Foundation).

Ong, A. (1996) Strategic sisterhood or sisters in solidarity? Questions of communitarianism and citizenship in Asia, *Indiana Journal of Global Legal Studies*, 4(1), pp. 107–135.

Ong, A. (1999) *Flexible Citizenship: The Cultural Logics of Transnationality* (Durham, NC: Duke University Press).

Portes, A. (1996). Global villagers: the rise of transnational communities, *American Prospect*, 7(25), pp. 74–77.

Parreñas, R. S. (2001) *Servants of Globalization: Women, Migration and Domestic Work* (Stanford, CA: Stanford University Press).

Roulleau-Berger, L., Ed (2002) *Youth and Work in the Postindustrial Cities of North America and Europe* (Leiden, Netherlands: Brill).

Rubenstein, K. & Adler, D. (2000) International citizenship: the future of nationality in a globalized world, *Indiana Journal of Global Legal Studies*, 7(2), pp. 519–548.

Sassen, S. (1996) *Losing Control? Sovereignty in an Age of Globalization* (New York: Columbia University Press).

Sassen, S. (1999) *Guests and Aliens* (New York: New Press).

Sassen, S. (2001) *The Global City: New York, London, Tokyo*, 2nd edition (Princeton, NJ: Princeton University Press).

Sassen, S. (2006) *Denationalization: Territory, Authority, and Rights in a Global Digital Age* (Princeton, NJ: Princeton University Press).

Saunders, P. (1993) Citizenship in a liberal society, pp. 57–90 in B. Turner (Ed) *Citizenship and Social Theory* (London: Sage).

Schuck, P. & Smith, R. (1985) *Citizenship without Consent: Illegal Aliens in the American Polity* (New Haven, CT: Yale University Press).

Shotter, J. (1993) Psychology and citizenship: identity and belonging, pp. 115–138 in B. Turner (Ed) *Citizenship and Social Theory* (London: Sage).

Soysal, Y. N. (1994) *Limits of Citizenship: Migrants and Postnational Membership in Europe* (Chicago, IL: University of Chicago Press).

Spiro, P. (1997) Dual nationality and the meaning of citizenship, *Emory Law Review*, 46(4), pp. 1412–1485.

Taylor, C. (1992) The politics of recognition, pp. 25–74 in C. Taylor & A. Gutmann (Eds) *Multiculturalism: Examining the Politics of Recognition* (Princeton, NJ: Princeton University Press).

Torres, M. de los Angeles. (1998) Transnational political and cultural identities: crossing theoretical borders, pp. 169–182 in F. Bonilla, E. Mélendez, R. Morales & M. de los Á. Torres (Eds) *Borderless Borders* (Philadelphia, PA: Temple University Press).

Torres, R. D., Inda, J. X. & Miron, L. F. (1999) *Race, Identity, and Citizenship* (Oxford: Blackwell).

Turner, B. (2000) Cosmopolitan virtue: loyalty and the city, pp. 129–147 in E. Isin (Ed) *Democracy, Citizenship and the Global City* (New York, NY: Routledge).

Wacquant, L. (2004) Ghetto, pp. 129–147 in N. J. Smelser and P. B. Baltes (Eds) *International Encyclopedia of the Social and Behavioral Sciences* (London: Pergamon Press, rev. ed).

Walzer, M. (1985) *Spheres of Justice: A Defense of Pluralism and Equality* (New York: Basic Books).

Weber, M. (1958) *The City* (New York: Free Press).

Young, I. M. (1990) *Justice and the Politics of Difference* (Princeton, NJ: Princeton University Press).

At the Global Crossroads: The End of the Washington Consensus and the Rise of Global Social Democracy?

DAVID HELD

Introduction

Immanuel Kant wrote over two hundred years ago that we are 'unavoidably side by side'. A violent challenge to law and justice in one place has consequences for many other places and can be experienced everywhere. While he dwelt on these matters at length, he could not have known how profound his concerns would become.

Since Kant, our mutual interconnectedness and vulnerability have grown rapidly. We no longer live, if we ever did, in a world of discrete national communities. Instead, we live in a world of what I like to call 'overlapping communities of fate' where the trajectories of countries are deeply enmeshed with each other. In our world, it is not only the violent exception that links people together across borders; the very nature of everyday problems and processes joins people in multiple ways.

The story of our increasingly global order—'globalization'—is not a singular one. Globalization is not just economic; for it also involves growing aspirations for international law and justice. From the United Nations to the European Union, from changes to the laws of war to the entrenchment of human rights, from the emergence of international environmental regimes to the foundation of the International Criminal Court, there is also another narrative being told—a narrative which seeks to reframe human activity and entrench it in law, rights and responsibilities.

Many of these developments were framed against the background of formidable threats to humankind—above all, Nazism, fascism and the Holocaust. Those involved in them affirmed the importance of universal principles, human rights and the rule of law in the face of strong temptations to simply put up the shutters and defend the position of only some countries and nations. They rejected the view of national and moral particularists that belonging to a given community limits and determines the moral worth of individuals and the nature of their freedom, and they defended the irreducible moral status of each and every person. The principles of equal respect, equal concern and the priority of the vital needs of all human beings are not principles for some remote utopia; they are at the centre of significant post-Second World War legal and political developments.

A Clear Moment of Choice

The international community has reached a clear moment of choice. It is still possible to build on the achievements of the post-Second World War era. Alternatively, we can participate (actively or passively) in their erosion or dismantling. The signs are not good; for the post-war multilateral order is now threatened by the intersection of a number of crises. I shall emphasize four. Each one of these is a serious matter; taken together, they constitute the severest test.

First, the collapse of the trade talks at Cancún raised the possibility of a major challenge to the world trading system. At the same time, a large growth in bilateral trade arrangements and preferential trading agreements singled out some nation-states for favoured treatment by others. If the growth in bilateral agreements were to continue, there would be a real danger that the Doha trade round would collapse, or produce derisory results. Recent trade negotiations have made progress on phasing out agricultural subsidies, but there is no clear timetable attached to the implementation of many of the key points. There are many risks involved, but perhaps the most serious risk is to the world's poorest countries. They cannot alone overcome the handicaps of a world trading system marked by rigged rules and double standards. If the world's poorest countries (along with middle income nations) are to find a secure access point into the global economic order, they require a free and fair footing so to do. The slow progress of trade talks signals that they may not reach this point.

Second, little progress has been made towards achieving the millennium goals—the moral consciousness of the international community. The millennium goals set down minimum standards to be achieved in relation to poverty reduction, health, educational provision, the combating of HIV/AIDS, malaria and other diseases, environmental sustainability and so on. Progress towards these targets has been lamentably slow, and there is evidence that they will be missed by a very wide margin. In fact, there is evidence that there may have been no point in setting these targets at all, so far are we from attaining them in many parts of the world.

Third, little, if any, progress has been made in creating a sustainable framework for the management of global warming. The British chief scientist, Sir David King, has recently warned that 'climate change is the most serious problem we are facing today, more serious than the threat of terrorism'. Irrespective of whether one finds this characterization accurate, it is the case that global warming has the capacity to wreak havoc on the world's diverse species, biosystems, and socio-economic fabric. Violent storms will become more frequent, water access a battle ground, and the mass movement of desperate people more common. The overwhelming body of scientific opinion now maintains that global warming constitutes a serious threat not in the long term, but in the here and now. The failure of the international community to generate a sound framework for managing global warming is one of the most serious indications of the problems facing the multilateral order.

Fourth, the multilateral order has been weakened by the fall-out from the war in Iraq, as the report of Kofi Annan's High Level Panel clearly indicates. The value of the UN system has been called into question, the legitimacy of the Security Council has been challenged, and the working practices of multilateral institutions have been eroded. Post-Iraq, the weaknesses of the UN system have been exposed, the arrogance of the great powers has been dramatized, international law and legitimacy have been disorganized, and the prospects for combating global terrorism seem no better, if not worse.

Interconnectedness, Integration and Justice

The world we are in is highly interconnected, but it is far from integrated or just. By this I mean that the economic, political, social and environmental fortunes of countries are increasingly enmeshed, but that all too many nations do not share values or a commitment to remedying the position of the least well-off, most impoverished and most at risk.

The interconnectedness of countries can readily be measured by mapping the ways in which trade, communication, pollutants, violence, among many other factors, flow across borders and lock the well-being of countries into common patterns. Social integration can be measured by the extent to which countries share frameworks not just of communications but of cultural ideas, symbols and values. While the latter frequently diverge, the twentieth century gave rise to a grand meta-framework of values—those embodied in the international human rights regime. For the first time in history this provided a sense of the proper limits of the diversity of human associations. Yet, obviously enough, it is far from fully subscribed to and far from fully embedded in many parts of the world. By contrast, a global commitment to justice might be indicated by a sustained concern to ameliorate the radical asymmetries of life chances that pervade the world and by addressing the harm inflicted by these on people against their will and without their consent. However, we see no systematic and effective effort in this direction. The failure of the international community to get anywhere close to achieving the millennium goals is a case in point. In short, while there is a high degree of interconnectedness in the world, social integration is shallower and a commitment to social justice pitifully thin.

Why? Two reasons above all others will be focused on here: the old Washington Consensus, and the new Washington security agenda. These two hugely powerful policy programmes have profoundly shaped our age—and have profoundly weakened our public institutions, nationally and globally. Only by understanding their failures and limitations can we move beyond them to recover a democratic, responsive politics at all levels of public life.

Economics

The Washington Consensus

The Washington Consensus can be defined in relation to an economic agenda which is focused typically on free trade, capital market liberalization, flexible exchange rates, market-determined interest rates, the deregulation of markets, the transfer of assets from the public to the private sector, the tight focus of public expenditure on well-directed social targets, balanced budgets, tax reform, secure property rights and the protection of intellectual property rights (see Table 1). It has been the economic orthodoxy for a significant period of the last 20 years in leading OECD countries, and in the international financial institutions. It has been prescribed, in particular, by the IMF and World Bank as the policy basis for developing countries.

The 'Washington Consensus' was first set out authoritatively by John Williamson (1990). While Williamson (see 2003) endorsed most of the policies listed above, he did not advocate free capital mobility. Williamson's original formulation drew together a policy agenda which he thought most people in the late 1980s and early 1990s in the policy making circles of Washington DC—the treasury, the World Bank and the IMF—would agree were appropriate for developing countries. Subsequently, the term acquired a very particular right-wing connotation as it became linked to the economic agenda of Ronald Reagan and Margaret Thatcher, with their emphasis on free capital movements, monetarism and a minimal state that accepts no responsibility for correcting income inequalities or managing serious externalities. There were important overlaps between the original Williamson programme and the neoliberal agenda, including macroeconomic discipline, a free market economy, privatization and free trade. Today Williamson distances himself from the neoliberal sense of the Washington Consensus, although he accepts that this version of the Consensus, with its endorsement of capital account liberalization, did become the dominant orthodoxy in the 1990s. I use the term Washington Consensus in this latter sense.

Critics charge that the measures of the Washington Consensus are bound up with US geopolitics, that all too often they are preached by the US to the rest of the world but not practised

Table 1. The original and augmented Washington Consensus

The original Washington Consensus
- Fiscal discipline
- Reorientation of public expenditures
- Tax reform
- Financial liberalization
- Unified and competitive exchange rates
- Trade liberalization
- Openness to DFI
- Privatization
- Deregulation
- Secure property rights

The augmented Washington Consensus: the original list plus:
- Legal/political reform
- Regulatory institutions
- Anti-corruption
- Labour market flexibility
- WTO agreements
- Financial codes and standards
- 'Prudent' capital-account opening
- Non-intermediate exchange rate regimes
- Social safety nets
- Poverty reduction

Source: Rodrik (2001), p. 51.

by it, and that they are deeply destructive of the social cohesion of the poorest countries. Interestingly, Williamson holds that while aspects of this may be true about the neoliberal version, his policy recommendations are sensible principles of economic practice whoever recommends and deploys them, and that they leave open the question of the progressivity of the tax system (see Williamson, 1993; 2003). Two points will be at issue here. First, while some of the policies of the Washington Consensus may be reasonable in their own terms, others are not and, taken together, they represent too narrow a set of policies to help create sustained growth and equitable development. Second, the Washington Consensus underplays the role of government, a strong public sector, and the development of multilateral governance, with serious consequences for the capacity of public institutions to solve critical problems, national and global.

The Washington Consensus and Development

The relationships between the Washington Consensus, economic liberalization and development has been extensively examined (see, for example, Mosley, 2000; Chang, 2002). The focus has been on the way the Washington Consensus has been implemented through loans (and debt rescheduling) that require developing countries to undergo 'structural adjustment'—the alignment of their economies to the requirements of the core policies—and on the subsequent results. In this context, some very serious issues have arisen which need to be confronted. They have been summarized pithily by Branko Milanovic (2003, p. 679) in the form of three questions:

1. how to explain why after sustained involvement and many structural adjustment loans, and as many IMF Stand-bys, African GDP per capita has not budged from its level of 20 years ago. Moreover, in 24 African countries, GDP per capita is less than in 1975, and in 12 countries even below its 1960s level;
2. how to explain the recurrence of Latin crises, in countries such as Argentina, that months prior to the outbreak of the crisis are being praised as model reformers;
3. how to explain that . . . 'pupils' among the transition countries (Moldova, Georgia, Kyrghyz Republic, Armenia), after setting out in 1991 with no debt at all, and following all the prescriptions of the IFIs, find themselves 10 years later with their GDPs halved and in need of debt-forgiveness.

Something is clearly awry. The dominant economic orthodoxies have not succeeded in many parts of the developing world; they have failed to generate sustained economic growth, poverty reduction and fair outcomes.

The Washington Consensus prescriptions can be misleading and damaging. It has been found that one of the key global factors impacting on the capacity of the poorest countries to develop is not tariff liberalization, but capital liberalization (see Garrett, forthcoming). The neoliberal Washington Consensus recommends both. Tariff liberalization has been broadly beneficial for low income countries. By contrast, rapid capital liberalization can be a recipe, in the absence of prudential regulation and sound domestic capital markets, 'for volatility, unpredictability and booms and busts in capital flows' (ibid.). Countries that have rapidly opened their capital accounts have performed significantly less well (in terms of economic growth and income inequality) than countries that have maintained tight control on capital movements and cut tariffs (see Bhagwati, 2004).

Both the crises in East Asia in the late 1990s and the recent recessions in Latin America show, Joseph Stiglitz (2004, p. 25) affirms, that 'premature capital market liberalisation can result in economic volatility, increasing poverty, and the destruction of the middle classes'. And a recent study by economists at the IMF itself finds that 'there is no strong, robust and uniform support for the theoretical argument that financial globalization per se delivers a higher rate of economic growth' and, more troubling, that 'countries in the early stages of financial integration have been exposed to significant risks in terms of higher volatility of both output and consumption' (2003, pp. 6, 7). Yet the Bush administration is still leading the way in demanding a tough form of such liberalization through international financial institutions and bilateral trade agreements. The governing capacities of developing countries can be seriously eroded as a result.[1]

Moreover, the experience of China and India—along with Japan, South Korea and Taiwan in earlier times—shows that countries do not have to adopt, first and foremost, liberal trade and/or capital policies in order to benefit from enhanced trade, to grow faster, and to develop an industrial infrastructure able to produce an increasing proportion of national consumption. All these countries, as Robert Wade (2003a) has recently noted, have experienced relatively fast growth behind protective barriers, growth which fuelled rapid trade expansion, focused on capital and intermediate goods. As each of these countries has become richer, it has tended to liberalize its trade policy.

Accordingly, it is a misunderstanding to say that trade liberalization per se has fuelled economic growth in China and India; rather, it is the case that these countries developed relatively quickly behind protective barriers, before they liberalized their trade. If it is the case that these countries, and others like them, did not straightforwardly develop as a result of trade liberalization, and if it is the case that some of the poorest countries of the world are worse off as a result of an excessive haste with respect to global capital market integration, then the case is strengthened for applying the precautionary principle to global economic integration and resisting the developmental agenda of the Washington Consensus.

Internal and External Economic Integration

While economic protectionism should be rejected as a general strategy (with its attendant risks of creating a vicious circle of trade disputes and economic conflicts), there is much evidence to suggest that a country's *internal* economic integration—the development of its human capital, of its economic infrastructure and robust national market institutions, and the replacement of imports with national production where feasible—needs to be stimulated initially by state-led economic and industrial policy. The evidence indicates that higher internal economic integration can help generate the conditions in which a country can benefit from higher *external* integration (Wade, 2003a). The development of state regulatory capacity, a sound public domain and the ability to focus investment on job creating sectors in competitive and productive areas is more important than the single-minded pursuit of integration into world markets. This finding should not come as a surprise since nearly all of today's developed countries initiated their growth behind tariff barriers, and only lowered these once their economies were relatively robust. They did not begin their development by rapidly opening their economies to foreign trade, capital flows and investment, as recommended by the Washington Consensus.

The argument above should not be taken as a simple endorsement of state-centric development and of the progressive nature of state interventionism, just because the latter runs counter to the Washington Consensus. Rather, the argument here is that the Washington Consensus has eroded the ability to formulate and implement sound public policy and has damaged political capacity. Moreover, public-sector objectives can be delivered by a diversity of actors, public and private. The wider development of civil society—trade unions, citizen groups, NGOs and so on—is indispensable to a robust programme of national development, although there can, of course, be conflicts between economic development and the strengthening of civil society. All societies need significant measures of autonomy to work out their own ways of managing this conflict.

There is, in fact, no single route or set of policy prescriptions to economic development; knowledge of local conditions, experimentation with suitable domestic institutions and agencies and the nurturing of internal economic integration need to be combined with sound macro-economic policy and some elements of external market integration. The most successful recent cases of development—East Asia, China, India—have managed to find ways of taking advantage of the opportunities offered by world markets—cheaper products, exports, technology and capital—while entrenching domestic incentives for investment and institution building. As Dani Rodrik (2001, p. 22) has succinctly put it:

> Market incentives, macroeconomic stability, and sound institutions are key to economic development. But these requirements can be generated in a number of different ways—by making the best use of existing capabilities in light of resources and other constraints. There is no single model of a successful transition to a high growth path. Each country has to figure out its own investment strategy.

Asymmetries of global market access are a pressing development problem, including selective protectionism, tariff barriers in the developed and developing world, European and American subsidies in agriculture and textiles and so on. But an exclusive focus on these can distort development strategies. Development thinking has to shift from a dogged focus on 'market access' to a more complex mindset (see Rodrik, 2001). Developing nations need policy space to exercise institutional innovations that depart from the old orthodoxies of the World Bank, IMF and WTO. Concomitantly, organizations like the WTO need to move their agenda away from a narrow set of policies concerned with market creation and supervision to a broader range of policies which encourage different national economic systems to flourish within a fair and equitable rule-based global market order.

The Washington Consensus and the Limits of the Public Domain

The thrust of the Washington Consensus is to enhance economic liberalization, develop a neoliberal form of economic globalization and to adapt the public domain—local, national and global—to market leading institutions and processes. It thus bears a heavy burden of responsibility for the common political resistance or unwillingness to address significant areas of market failure, including:

- the problem of externalities, for example the environmental degradation caused by current forms of economic growth;
- the inadequate development of *non*-market social factors, which alone can provide an effective balance between 'competition' and 'cooperation', and thus ensure an adequate supply of essential 'public goods' such as education, effective transportation and sound health;
- the tendency towards the 'concentration' and 'centralization' of economic life, marked by patterns of oligopoly and monopoly;
- the propensity to 'short-termism' in investment strategy as fund holders and investment bankers operate policies aimed at maximizing immediate income return and dividend results;
- and the underemployment or unemployment of productive resources in the context of the demonstrable existence of urgent and unmet need.

Leaving markets to resolve alone problems of resource generation and allocation misses the deep roots of many economic and political difficulties; for instance, the vast asymmetries of life chances within and between nation-states which are a source of considerable conflict; the erosion of the economic fortune of some countries in sectors like agriculture and textiles while these sectors enjoy protection and assistance in others; the emergence of global financial flows which can rapidly destabilize national economies; and the development of serious transnational problems involving the global commons. Moreover, to the extent that pushing back the boundaries of state action or weakening governing capacities means increasing the scope of market forces, and cutting back on services which have offered protection to the vulnerable, the difficulties faced by the poorest and the least powerful—north, south, east and west—are exacerbated. The rise of 'security' issues to the top of the political agenda reflects, in part, the need to contain the outcomes which such policies provoke.

The Washington Consensus has, in sum, weakened the ability to govern—locally, nationally and globally—and it has eroded the capacity to provide urgent public goods. Economic freedom is championed at the expense of social justice and environmental sustainability, with long-term damage to both. And it has confused economic freedom and economic effectiveness.

Amending the Washington Consensus

The Washington Consensus has come under assault from many sides in recent years, from special domestic lobbies demanding protection for certain economic sectors (agriculture, textiles, steel) to the anti-globalization, environmental and social justice movements. The poor results and performance of the Washington Consensus itself have invoked deep unease and criticism. Disappointing economic growth and increasing insecurity in many parts of Latin America, economic stagnation or decline in many sub-Saharan countries, the Asian financial crisis and the stark difficulties experienced in some of the transition economies has led to a call to replace or broaden the policy range of the Washington Consensus. Within the IMF, World Bank and other leading international organizations there has been an attempt to respond to criticism by broadening the Consensus to encompass a concern with state capacity, poverty reduction and social safety nets. As a result, attention has slowly shifted from an exclusive emphasis on liberalization and privatization to a preoccupation with the institutional underpinnings of successful market activity (see Table 1). The new agenda still champions large parts of the old agenda, but adds governance and anti-corruption measures, legal and administrative reform, financial regulation, labour market flexibility and the importance of social safety nets.

To the extent that a country's public institutions are a crucial determinant of its long term development—and they are clearly very important—the new emphasis is helpful and welcome. But, as Rodrik (2001, p. 12) has emphasized, 'the institutional basis for a market economy is not uniquely determined. There is no single mapping between a well-functioning market and the *form* of non-market institutions required to sustain it.' The new agenda gives excessive weight to Anglo-American conceptions of the proper type of economic and political institutions such as flexible labour markets and financial regulation. In addition, the whole agenda is shaped by what is thought of as the necessary institutions to ensure external economic integration, e.g. the introduction of WTO rules and standards. Moreover, the new agenda provides no clear guidance on how to prioritize institutional change and gives little recognition to the length of time it has taken to create such developments in countries where it is well advanced. After all, nearly all the industrial countries which have nurtured these reforms did so over very substantial time periods (Chang, 2002).

Revitalizing Social Democracy

In contrast to the narrow scope and vision of the Washington Consensus, the nature and form of a free and fair global economy can, I believe, be articulated through the lens of social democratic concepts and values. Traditionally, social democrats have sought to deploy the democratic institutions of individual countries on behalf of a particular project; a compromise between the powers of capital, labour and the state which seeks to encourage the development of market institutions, private property and the pursuit of profit within a regulatory framework that guarantees not just the civil and political liberties of citizens, but also the social conditions necessary for people to enjoy their formal rights. Social democrats rightly accepted that markets are central to generating economic well-being, but recognized that in the absence of appropriate regulation they suffer serious flaws, especially the generation of unwanted risks for their citizens and an unequal distribution of those risks, and the creation of negative externalities and corrosive inequalities.

In the post-Second World War period, in particular, many Western countries sought to reconcile the efficiency of markets with the values of social community (which markets themselves presuppose) in order to develop and grow. The nature of the balance struck took different forms in different countries, reflecting different national political traditions: in the US, the New Deal, and in Europe, social democracy or the social market economy. Yet however this balance was exactly conceived, governments had a key role to play in enacting and managing this programme: moderating the volatility of transaction flows, managing demand levels and providing social investments, safety nets and adjustment assistance (see Ruggie, 2003).

Although for a few decades after the Second World War it seemed that a satisfactory balance could be achieved between self-government, social solidarity and international economic openness—at least for the majority of Western countries, and for the majority of their citizens—it now appears that this balance is much harder to sustain. The mobility of capital, goods, people, ideas and pollutants increasingly challenges the capacity of individual governments to sustain their own social and political compromises within delimited borders. New problems are posed by the increasing divergence between the extensive spatial reach of economic and social activity, and the traditional state-based mechanisms of political control. Moreover, these problems cannot be resolved within the framework of the Washington Consensus, old or new. Equipped with its policies, governance at all levels has too often been simply disarmed or naively reshaped.

While the values of social democracy—the rule of law, political equality, democratic politics, social justice, social solidarity and economic efficiency—are of enduring significance, the key challenge today is to elaborate their meaning, and to re-examine the conditions of their entrenchment, against the background of the changing global constellation of politics and economics. In the current era, social democracy must be defended and elaborated not just at the level of the nation-state, but at regional and global levels as well. The provision of public goods can no longer be equated with state-provided goods alone. Diverse state and non-state actors shape and contribute to their provision—and they need to do so if some of the most profound challenges of globalization are to be met. Moreover, some core public goods have to be provided regionally and globally if they are to be provided at all. From the establishment of fair trade rules and financial stability to the fight against hunger and environmental degradation, the emphasis is on finding durable modes of international and transnational cooperation and collaboration.

With this in mind, the project of social democracy has to be reconceived to include the promotion of the rule of law at the international level; greater transparency, accountability and democracy in global governance; a deeper commitment to social justice in the pursuit of a more equitable distribution of life chances; the protection and reinvention of community at diverse levels; and the regulation of the global economy through the public management of global trade and financial flows, and the engagement of leading stakeholders in corporate governance. These guiding orientations set the politics of what I call 'global social democracy' apart from the pursuit of the Washington Consensus—and, for that matter, from the aims of those pitched against globalization in all its forms.

Open Markets and Strong Governance

If social democracy at the level of the nation-state means being tough in pursuit of free markets while insisting on a framework of shared values and common institutional practices, at the global level it means pursuing an economic agenda which calibrates the freeing of markets with poverty reduction programmes and the immediate protection of the vulnerable— north, south, east and west. This agenda must be pursued while ensuring that different countries have the freedom they need to experiment with their own investment strategies and resources.

Economic growth can provide a powerful impetus to the achievement of human development targets. But it does not necessarily achieve these targets; unregulated economic development which simply follows the existing rules and entrenched interests of the global economy falls short of managed economic change geared to the prosperity of all. Economic development needs to be conceived as a means to an end, not an end in itself. Understood accordingly, it should be recognized that while international trade has huge potential for helping the least well-off countries to lift themselves out of poverty, and for enhancing the welfare and well-being of all nation-states, the current rules of global trade are heavily structured to protect the interests of the well-off and are heavily structured against the interests of the poorest countries as well as middle income ones (see Oxfam, 2002; Moore, 2003; Wade, 2003b).

Thus, while free trade is an admirable objective for progressives in principle, it cannot be pursued without attention to the power asymmetries of the global economy and to the poorest in the low and middle income countries who are extremely vulnerable to the initial phasing in of external market integration (especially of capital market liberalization), and who have few resources, if any, to fall back on during times of economic transformation (see Legrain, 2002; Garrett, forthcoming). A similar thing can be said, of course, for many people in wealthier societies. While they are not exposed to the unequal rules, double standards and inequalities of the global economic order in a parallel way to developing countries, if they lose their jobs or have to settle for lower wages they are also vulnerable in times of major economic shifts.

It is thus crucial to any social democratic agenda for free markets that it addresses simultaneously the needs of the vulnerable wherever they are. For the poorest countries this will mean that development policies must be directed to challenge the asymmetries of access to the global market, to ensure the sequencing of global market integration, particularly of capital markets, to ensure long-term investment in health care, human capital and physical infrastructure, to build a robust public sector, and to develop transparent, accountable political institutions. In developed countries this will mean the continued enhancement of strong, accountable political institutions to help mediate and manage the economic forces of globalization, and the provision of, among other things, high levels of social protection and generous safety nets, alongside sustained investment in lifelong learning and skills acquisition (cf. Swank, 2002). What follows here is complex and challenging for every country. But what is striking is that this range of policies has all too often not been pursued. This seems more a matter of psychology and political choice, and less a matter related to any fundamental obstacles in the nature of the economic organization of human affairs.

A more detailed social democratic agenda for economic globalization and global economic governance follows. Each element would make a significant contribution to the creation of a level playing field in the global economy; together, they would help reshape the economic system in a manner that is both free and fair. The agenda includes:

- salvaging the Doha trade round, and ensuring it is a development round that brings serious benefits to the world's poorest countries and to middle income ones;
- reforming TRIPS to ensure it is compatible with public health and welfare and offers flexibility for poor countries to decide when, and in what sectors, they want to use patent protection;
- recognizing that for many developing countries phasing in their integration into global markets, and only pursuing this agenda after the necessary domestic political and economic reforms are in place, is far more important than the pursuit of open borders alone;
- building on organizations like the WTO legal advisory centre to expand the capacity of developing countries to engage productively in the institutions of governance of the world economy;
- setting a clear timetable for governments to reach the UN 0.7% GNP/overseas aid target, and raising it to 1% in due course, to ensure the minimum flow of resources for investment in the internal integration of the world's poorest countries;
- supporting further reductions in the international debt burden of heavily indebted poor countries, linking debt cancellation, for instance, to education and the provision of financial incentives for poor children to attend school;
- creating a fair international migration regime that can regulate flows of people in a way that is economically beneficial and socially sustainable for developing as well as developed countries;
- improving cooperation among international financial institutions and other international donors, thus consolidating the development and policy-making efforts of the international community within the UN;
- opening up international financial institutions to enhance developing countries' involvement by addressing their under-representation in existing governance structures, and expanding their role in, among other places, the Financial Stability Forum (FSF) and the Basel Committee;
- building global networks and institutions focused on poverty and welfare, to act as counterweights and countervailing powers to the market driving IGOs (the WTO, IMF and World Bank);
- instituting a substantial international review of the functioning of the Bretton Woods institutions, created more than 50 years ago and now operating in an economic context that has drastically changed.

Do we have the resources to put such a programme into effect? Concern has already been expressed about whether the political resources exist; the interlocking crises of the multilateral order are evidence of a lack of political will to confront some of the most pressing global threats. But at least it cannot be said, somewhat paradoxically, that we lack the economic resources for such a programme. A few telling examples make the point. The UN budget is $1.25 billion plus the necessary finance for peacekeeping per annum. Against this, US citizens spend over $8 billion per annum on cosmetics, $27 billion per annum on confectionery, $70 billion per annum on alcohol and over $560 billion per annum on cars. (All these figures are from the late 1990s and so are likely to be much higher now.) Further telling examples from the EU include $11 billion per annum spent on ice-cream, $150 billion per annum spent on cigarettes and alcohol and, from the EU and the US together, over $17 billion per annum on pet food. What do we require to make a substantial difference to the basic well-being of the world's poorest? Again, telling statistics are available. Required would be $6 billion per annum on basic education; $9 billion per annum for water and sanitation; $12 billion per annum for the reproductive health of women; and $13 billion per annum for basic health and nutrition. These figures are substantial but, when judged against major consumption expenditure in the US and EU, they are not excessive demands.

Moreover, if all the OECD agricultural subsidies were removed and spent on the world's poorest peoples this would release some $300 billion per annum. In addition, it can be noted that a half percentage point shift in the allocation of global GDP would release over $300 billion per annum. Clearly, it is not the right question to ask whether the economic resources exist to put in place reforms that might aid the world's poorest and least well-off. The question really is about how we allocate available resources, to whose benefit and to what end. It is not a question of whether there are adequate economic resources, it is a question of how we choose to spend them—whether we choose to meet the challenges of the social democratic agenda, summarized in Table 2.

Security

9/11, the War in Iraq and the Further Attack on Multilateralism

If 9/11 was not a defining moment in human history, it certainly was for today's generations. The terrorist attack on the World Trade Center and the Pentagon was an atrocity of extraordinary proportions. Yet, after 9/11, the US and its major allies could have decided that the most important things to do were to strengthen international law in the face of global terrorist threats, and to enhance the role of multilateral institutions. They could have decided it was important that no single power or group should act as judge, jury and executioner. They could have decided that global hotspots like the Middle East which feed global terrorism should be the main priority. They could have decided that the disjuncture between economic globalization and social justice needed more urgent attention. And they could have decided to be tough on terrorism and tough on the conditions which lead people to imagine that Al-Qaeda and similar groups are agents of justice in the modern world. But they have systematically failed to decide any of these things. In general, the world after 9/11 has become more polarized and international law weaker. The systematic political weaknesses of the Washington Consensus have been compounded by the new Washington security doctrines.

The rush to war against Iraq in 2003 gave priority to a narrow security agenda which is at the heart of the new American security doctrine of unilateral and pre-emptive war. This agenda contradicts most of the core tenets of international politics and international agreements

Table 2. The social democratic agenda

Domestic
- Sound macroeconomic policy
- Nurturing of political/legal reform
- Creation of robust public sector
- State-led economic and investment strategy, enjoying sufficient development space to experiment with different policies
- Sequencing of global market integration
- Priority investment in human and social capital
- Public capital expenditure on infrastructure
- Poverty reduction and social safety nets
- Strengthening civil society

Global
- Salvaging Doha
- Cancellation of unsustainable debt
- Reform of TRIPS
- Creation of fair regime for transnational migration
- Expand negotiating capacity of developing countries at IFIs
- Increase developing country participation in the running of IFIs
- Establish new financial flows and facilities for investment in human capital and internal country integration
- Reform of UN system to enhance accountability and effectiveness of poverty reduction, welfare and environmental programmes

---

since 1945 (Ikenberry, 2002). It throws aside respect for open political negotiations among states, as it does the core doctrine of deterrence and stable relations among major powers (the balance of power). We have to come to terms not only with the reality that a single country enjoys military supremacy to an unprecedented extent in world history, but also with the fact that it can use that supremacy to respond unilaterally to perceived threats (which may be neither actual nor imminent), and that it will brook no rival.

The new doctrine has many serious implications (Hoffmann, 2003). Among these are a return to an old realist understanding of international relations as, in the last analysis, a 'war of all against all', in which states rightly pursue their national interests unencumbered by attempts to establish internationally recognized limits (self-defence, collective security) on their ambitions. But if this 'freedom' is (dangerously) granted to the US, why not also to Russia, China, India, Pakistan, North Korea and so on? It cannot be consistently argued that all states bar one should accept limits on their self-defined goals. The flaws of international law and the UN Charter can either be addressed, or taken as an excuse for further weakening international institutions and legal arrangements.

Narrow vs. Broad Security Agendas

Since 9/11 there has been a growing divergence between the American-led security agenda, on the one side, and the development, welfare and human rights agenda, on the other. The difference can be put simply by adapting Tony Blair's famous slogan on crime: 'tough on crime and tough on the causes of crime'. In global political terms this means being tough on security threats and tough on the conditions which breed them. This broader agenda requires three things of governments and international institutions—all currently missing (Held & Kaldor, 2001).

First, there must be a commitment to the rule of law and the development of multilateral institutions—not the prosecution of war on its own. Civilians of all faiths and nationalities need protection. Terrorists and all those who systematically violate the sanctity of life and human rights must be brought before an international criminal court that commands cross-national support. This does not preclude internationally sanctioned military action to arrest suspects, dismantle terrorist networks and deal with aggressive rogue states—far from it. But such action should always be understood as a robust form of international law enforcement, above all as a way, as Mary Kaldor (1998) has most clearly put it, of protecting civilians and bringing suspects to trial. In short, if justice is to be dispensed impartially, no power can act as judge, jury and executioner. What is needed is momentum towards global, not American or Russian or Chinese or British or French, justice. We must act together to sustain and strengthen a world based on common rules (Solana, 2003).

Second, a sustained effort has to be undertaken to generate new forms of global political legitimacy for international institutions involved in security and peace-making. This must include the condemnation of systematic human rights violations wherever they occur, and the establishment of new forms of political and economic accountability. This cannot be equated with an occasional or one-off effort to create a new momentum for peace and the protection of human rights, as is all too typical.

And, finally, there must be a head-on acknowledgement that the ethical and justice issues posed by the global polarization of wealth, income and power, and with them the huge asymmetries of life chances, cannot be left to markets to resolve, as already argued. Those who are poorest and most vulnerable, linked into geopolitical situations where their economic and political claims have been neglected for generations, may provide fertile ground for terrorist recruiters. The project of economic globalization has to be connected to manifest principles of social justice; the latter need to frame global market activity. Global social democracy must replace, in sum, the Washington Consensus.

Today, the attempt to develop international law, to enhance the capacity of international institutions for peacekeeping and peace-making, and to build bridges between economic globalization and the priorities of social justice is threatened not just by the dangers posed by extensive terrorist networks, but also by some deeply misguided responses to them. The new security agenda of the American neoconservatives, alongside the National Security doctrine of the current American administration (published in September 2002), arrogates to the United States the global role of setting standards, weighing risks, assessing threats and meting out justice. It breaks with the fundamental premises of the post-1945 world order with its commitment to deterrence, stable relations among major powers and the development of multilateral institutions to address common problems (Ikenberry, 2002, pp. 44f). It regards formerly held strategic views and diplomatic positions as largely obsolete. In short, it heralds the triumph of a narrowly focused security agenda.

Of course, terrorist crimes of the kind witnessed on 9/11 and on many occasions since (in Chechnya, Saudi Arabia, Pakistan, Morocco, Spain and elsewhere) may often be the work of the simply deranged and the fanatical and so there can be no guarantee that a more just and institutionally stable world will be a more peaceful one in all respects. But if we turn our back on this project, there is no hope of ameliorating the social basis of disadvantage often experienced in the poorest and most dislocated countries. Gross injustices, linked to a sense of hopelessness born of generations of neglect, feed anger and hostility. Popular support against terrorism depends upon convincing people that there is a legal and peaceful way of addressing their grievances. Without this sense of confidence in public institutions and processes, the defeat of terrorism becomes a hugely difficult task, if it can be achieved at all.

What is to be Done?

Clearly, agendas differ and are deeply contested. But there are a number of very pressing issues which need to be addressed if we are to salvage the achievements of the post-Holocaust world and build on them in a manner that provides not just security in the narrowest sense (protection from the immediate threat of coercive power and violence), but security in the broadest sense (protection for all those whose lives are vulnerable for whatever reason—economic, political, environmental and so on). Elsewhere, I have sought to set these out at length (Held, 2004). Here I will simply list some of the steps which could be taken to help implement a human security agenda at the heart of discussion in many parts of the world today ('old Europe', Latin America, Africa and Asia). These include:

- relinking the security and human rights agenda in international law—the two sides of international humanitarian law which, together, specify grave and systematic abuse of human security and well-being, and the minimum conditions required for the development of human agency;
- reforming UN Security Council procedures to improve the specification of, and legitimacy of, credible reasons for, credible threshold tests for, and credible promises in relation to, armed intervention in the affairs of a state—the objective being to link these directly to a set of conditions which would constitute a severe threat to peace, and/or a threat to the minimum conditions for the well-being of human agency, sufficient to justify the use of force;
- recognizing the necessity to dislodge and amend the now outmoded 1945 geopolitical settlement as the basis of decision-making in the Security Council, and to extend representation to all regions on a fair and equal footing;
- expanding the remit of the Security Council, or creating a parallel Social and Economic Security Council, to examine and, where necessary, intervene in the full gamut of human crises—physical, social, biological, environmental—which can threaten human agency;
- founding a World Environmental Organization to promote the implementation of existing environmental agreements and treaties, whose main mission would be to ensure that the development of world trading and financial systems are compatible with the sustainable use of the world's resources;
- understanding that 'representation' and 'taxation' presuppose each other; that is, that effective, transparent and accountable global governance requires reliable income streams, from aid to new financial facilities (as proposed by Gordon Brown) and, in due course, new tax revenues (for example, based on GNP, energy usage or financial market turnover).

In order to reconnect the security and human rights agenda and to bring them together into a coherent framework of law, it would be necessary to hold an international or global legal convention. Rather than set out a blueprint of what the results of such a convention should be, it is important to stress the significance of a legitimate process that reviews the security and human rights sides of international law and seeks to reconnect them in a global legal framework. One demonstrable result of such an initiative could be new procedures at the UN to specify the set of conditions which would constitute a threat to the peace and the well-being of humankind sufficient to justify the use of force. The question is often put in the form: do we need to amend the UN Charter to create new triggers for war or armed intervention in the affairs of another country?

Humanitarian Armed Intervention

A number of compelling accounts have emerged recently which seek to justify humanitarian armed intervention in exceptional circumstances. One prominent account comes from the Canadian-sponsored International Commission on Intervention and State Sovereignty (see Evans, 2003). The Commission's Report emphasizes the importance of a responsibility to protect people in the face of large-scale loss of life or ethnic cleansing. And it links this responsibility to additional principles which concern the use of proportional means in the face of a severe test to human well-being, the last resort use of military power, among other considerations. A second account has been offered by Anne-Marie Slaughter (2003). She focuses on three factors which, when present all at once, might justify armed humanitarian intervention: possession of weapons of mass destruction; grave and systematic human rights abuses; and aggressive intent with regard to other nations. Finally, Kenneth Roth of Human Rights Watch has recently argued that humanitarian intervention could be justified if it is an intervention of last resort; if it is motivated by humanitarian concerns; if it is guided by, and maximizes, compliance with international humanitarian law; if it is likely to achieve more good than bad; and if it can be legitimated via the UN Security Council (Roth, 2004).

Pressing additional questions arise when considering this matter and these include how one weighs the balance of the different factors involved, how one creates a framework that can be applied to all countries (and not just to those perceived as a threat by the West) and how one creates a new threshold test for legitimate use of force. All the positions which emerge in this regard need to be tested against the views and judgements of peoples from around the world—hence, a global legal convention—and not just against the views of those from the most powerful nation-states, if any new solution is to be durable and legitimate in the long run.

Moreover, we need to bear in mind that no modern theory of the nature and scope of the legitimate use of power within a state runs together the roles of judge, jury and executioner. Yet this is precisely what we have allowed to happen in the global order today. We need new bodies at the global level for weighing evidence, making recommendations, testing options and so on. These need to be separate and distinct bodies which embody a separation of powers at the global level. If one is in favour of the grounds that might legitimate humanitarian intervention one also needs to ask who is going to make these decisions and under what conditions. The weight of argument points in favour of taking seriously the necessity to protect peoples under extreme circumstances, and it also points in the direction of amending the institutional structures which pass judgement over these pressing matters. These structures need to be open, accountable and representative. Without suitable reform, our global institutions will be forever burdened by the mantle of partiality and illegitimacy. Table 3 summarizes the main reforms that are necessary if a new human security doctrine is to be achieved—and juxtaposes it with the Washington Security framework.

A New Global Covenant?

This agenda is not over-ambitious. The story of our increasingly global order is not a singular one. Globalization is not a one-dimensional phenomenon: it has helped generate vast new opportunities as well as risks. Moreover, the achievements of the post-Holocaust world—the

Table 3. The Washington and Human Security Doctrines

The Washington Security Doctrine
- Hegemonic
- Order through dominance
- 'Flexible multilateralism' or unilateralism where necessary
- Pre-emptive and preventive use of force
- Security focus: geopolitical and, secondarily, geoeconomic
- Collective organization where pragmatic (UN, NATO), otherwise reliance on US military and political power
- Leadership: the US and its allies
- Aims: making world safe for freedom and democracy; globalizing American rules and justice

The Human Security Doctrine
- Multilateralism and common rules
- Order through law and social justice
- Enhance multilateral, collective security
- Last resort use of internationally sanctioned force to uphold international humanitarian law
- Security focus: relinking security and human rights agendas; protecting all those facing threats to life, whether political, social, economic or environmental
- Strengthen global governance: reform UN Security Council; create Economic and Social Security Council; democratize UN
- Leadership: develop a worldwide dialogue to define new global covenant
- Aims: making world safe for humanity; global justice and impartial rules

---

consolidation of international law, multilateralism, the EU and other forms of supranational regionalism—can and need to be built upon.

A coalition could emerge to push this agenda further, comprising: European countries with strong liberal and social democratic traditions; liberal groups in the US polity which support multilateralism and the rule of law in international affairs; developing countries struggling for freer and fairer trade rules in the world economic order; non-governmental organizations, from Amnesty International to Oxfam, campaigning for a more just, democratic and equitable world order; transnational social movements contesting the nature and form of contemporary globalization; and those economic forces that desire a more stable and managed global economic order (Held & McGrew, 2002).

Europe could have a special role in advancing the cause of global social democracy (McGrew, 2002). As the home of both social democracy and an historic experiment in governance beyond the state, Europe has direct experience in considering the appropriate designs for more effective and accountable suprastate governance. It offers novel ways of thinking about governance beyond the state which encourage a (relatively) more democratic—as opposed to more neoliberal—vision of global governance. Of course, this is not to suggest that the EU should broker a crude anti-US coalition of transnational and international forces. On the contrary, it is crucial to recognize the complexity of US domestic politics and the existence of progressive social, political and economic forces seeking to advance a rather different kind of world order from that championed by the administrations of George W. Bush and by the Republican right of the political spectrum more broadly (Nye, 2002). Any European political strategy to promote a broad-based coalition for a new global covenant must seek to enlist the support of these progressive forces within the US polity, while it must resist within its own camp the voices calling for the exclusive re-emergence of national identities, ethnic purity and protectionism. An extended struggle will be required to create a new global covenant, a struggle that will last long after the unilateral mistakes of Bush—in trade, aid, the environment and security—are put right.

Acknowledgements

I would like to thank Robert Wade, Jonathan Perraton and Mathias Koenig-Archibugi for helpful criticism of earlier drafts of this essay. I would also like to thank Dani Rodrik for permission to use Table 1.

Note

1   This is not to say that developing countries do not need access to capital flows (public or private). They do, and especially during trade liberalization as initially imports tend to rise faster than exports. At present, private capital flows are both too low and too volatile.

References

Bhagwati, J. (2004) *In Defense of Globalisation* (Oxford: Oxford University Press).
Chang, H.-J. (2002) *Kicking Away the Ladder: Development Strategy in Historical Perspective* (London: Anthem).
Evans, G. (2003) The responsibility to protect: when it's right to fight, *Progressive Politics*, 2(2).
Garrett, G. (forthcoming) Globalization and inequality, *Perspectives on Politics*.
Held, D. and Kaldor, M. (2001) What hope for the future? Available at http://www.lse.ac.u/depts/global/maryheld.htm.
Held, D. & McGrew, A. (2002) *Globalization/Anti-Globalization* (Cambridge: Polity).
Held, D. (2004) *Global Covenant: The Social Democratic Alternative to the Washington Consensus* (Cambridge: Polity).
Hoffmann, S. (2003) America goes backward, *New York Review of Books*, 12 June.
Ikenberry, G. J. (2002) America's imperial ambition, *Foreign Affairs*, September–October.
Kaldor, M. (1998) *New and Old Wars* (Cambridge: Polity).
Legrain, P. (2002) *The Open World* (London: Abacus).
McGrew, A. (2002) Between two worlds: Europe in a globalizing era, *Government and Opposition*, 37(3).
Milanovic, B. (2003) Two faces of globalization: against globalization as we know it, *World Development*, 31(4).
Moore, M. (2003) *A World without Walls* (Cambridge: Cambridge University Press).
Mosley, P. (2000) Globalisation, economic policy and convergence, *World Economy*, 23(5).
Nye, J. (2002) *The Paradox of American Power* (Oxford: Oxford University Press).
Oxfam (2002) *Rigged Rules and Double Standards* (Oxford: Oxfam).
Prasad, E. S. et al. (2003) Effects of financial globalization on developing countries. Available at http://www.imf.org/external/pubs/nft/op/220/index.htm.
Rodrik, D. (2001) The global governance of trade as if development really mattered. Available at http://www.undp.org/bdp.
Roth, K. (2004) What price military intervention?, *Global Agenda*, January 2004.
Ruggie, J. (2003) Taking embedded liberalism global: the corporate connection, in pp. 93–129 D. Held & M. Koenig-Archibugi (Eds) *Taming Globalization* (Cambridge: Polity).
Slaughter, A.-M. (2003) A chance to reshape the UN, *Washington Post*, 13 April.
Solana, J. (2003) The future of transatlantic relations, *Progressive Politics*, 2(2).
Stiglitz, J. (2004) Distant voices, *The Guardian*, 12 March.
Swank, D. (2002) *Global Capital, Political Institutions, and Policy Change in Developed Welfare States* (Cambridge: Cambridge University Press).
Wade, R. (2003a) The disturbing rise in poverty and inequality, in D. Held & M. Koenig-Archibugi (Eds) *Taming Globalization* (Cambridge: Polity).
Wade, R. (2003b) What strategies are viable for developing countries today? The WTO and the shrinkage of development space, *Review of International Political Economy*, 10(4), pp. 18–46.
Williamson, J. (1990) *Latin American Adjustment: How Much has Happened?* (Washington, DC: Institute for International Economics).
Williamson, J. (1993) Democracy and the 'Washington consensus', *World Development*, 21(8).
Williamson, J. (2003) The Washington consensus and beyond, *Economic and Political Weekly*, 38(15).

David Held is Graham Wallas Professor of Political Science, London School of Economics. He was educated in Britain, France, Germany and the United States. He has held numerous Visiting Appointments in the US, Australia, Canada and Spain, among other places. In the last five years he has lectured regularly on questions of democracy, international justice and globalization to audiences in many countries. David Held's main research interests include rethinking democracy at transnational and international levels and the study of globalization and global governance. He has strong interests both in political theory and in the more empirical dimensions of political analysis. Among his recent books are: *Global Transformations: Politics, Economics and Culture*, co-author (Polity and Stanford University Press, 1999); *Globalization/ Anti-Globalization*, co-author (Polity, 2002); and *Global Covenant* (Polity, 2004).

Globalization, Cosmopolitanism, and the Kantian Revival: Commentary on David Held's 'At the Global Crossroads'

JAMES H. MITTELMAN

David Held is in the vanguard of the effort to elaborate cosmopolitan ethics and to apply these norms in an era marked by globalizing processes. A senior scholar, he writes elegantly and envisages ways in which an agenda for global social democracy could help steer world order. Held's bold and critical evaluation of the ethics of neoliberalism as well as his presentation of an alternative project contribute mightily to the discussion about ameliorating the problems of globalization. The explanatory payoff is impressive, as are the identification of mid- to long-range goals and the enunciation of major principles.

For Held, the bedrock of cosmopolitanism is Immanuel Kant's view of the quest for perpetual peace. Formulated in the eighteenth century, Kant's seminal ideas about giving up lawless freedom, staving off new wars, and gradually realizing a universal order transcended his time and are an inspiration in the contemporary era. But why is Held's analysis rooted in Kant and not other cosmopolitan philosophers instead of or in addition to him? If Held wants to invoke Kant, it would be worth bringing in the notion that there are multiple cosmopolitan foundations for action, including those that grant less autonomy to the ethical sphere and seek to meld norms and material power.

For example, Kant and Marx had more in common than is often acknowledged in the Kantian revival. Both Kant and Marx knew that struggles between self-interested groups were the stuff of history and believed that the state could be ultimately submerged in a peaceful world order. The one more ideational than the other, the two thinkers were cosmopolitans who sought the means to curb bitter antagonisms that afflict society and that are used to sanctify war. These renowned theorists understood the perils of outbreaks of war as a way to build lasting peace, later enshrined in slogans such as 'the war to end all wars'.

To be sure, Held is a prolific author whose penetrating writing on globalization, cosmopolitanism, and world order appears in many venues. These works are distinguished by the sheer logic of argumentation, the power of forceful reasoning. Held, who is at his best as a political philosopher, clings to Kant in launching his analysis of 'the global crossroads' and 'the end of the Washington consensus'; but why not invoke both varied sources and diverse forms of cosmopolitanism? Rather than make this move, Held proceeds by constructing long lists of bulleted points. Allowing his own preference for an elliptical style—and, as noted, there is an overall eloquence to the presentation—it appears that the lists amount to the institutionalization of everything. But is there a risk of over-institutionalizing? And what are the limits to liberal reformism?

While a theoretical mélange of liberalism and cosmopolitanism may have merit, are there alternative avenues of inquiry? One might begin with Fernand Braudel's insight about the value of adopting different observation points and thus seek to avoid a Eurocentric perspective on world order. Self-reflexive research proceeds from an acknowledgment of one's own standpoint. This is the way to try to identify illusions, or as Terry Eagleton (2004, p. 135; emphasis original) deftly puts it: '[Y]ou can only know how the situation is if you are in a *position* to know'. To the extent that Held attempts to free himself of illusions, the result is a conundrum, for he is too mechanical in building a model—an architecture of cosmopolitan democracy.

Throughout this modeling, there is a problem of voice, as reflected in the bulk of the references that Held provides. His model does not mesh well with the experience of people in the thick of underdevelopment. While he seeks to push his prior scholarly work more fully into the field of development, and, to his credit, recognizes the blending of security and development, the discourse represents certain domains of knowledge and experience and silences others. In terms of cosmopolitan ethics, there are discourses in the developing world that respond directly to globalization: they are not part of the Kantian revival, nor are they incompatible with it.

To illustrate, in southern Africa, especially in its most marginalized zones, the discourses among impoverished peasants and unemployed workers center on survival; and among employed city dwellers, including the educated, also on national unity and the need for reconciliation in post-conflict societies. Cosmopolitan ethics drawn from Kant do not enter these discourses. Rather, indigenous epistemologies are in some measure associated with historical forms of pan-movements, such as Pan-Africanism. An indigenous cosmopolitanism, namely, the spirit of *ubuntu* (an epistemology that emanates from southern Africa, with emphasis on community and solidarity), may be found at the grassroots and in official pronouncements, reflected in the broadcast media. *Ubuntu* is also manifest as a transnational social movement, and has a literature associated with it (Ngcoya, in progress). My point is that to come to grips with cosmopolitanism, it is necessary to adopt a decentered cosmopolitan perspective that is lacking in a Eurocentric cosmopolitanism.

Closely related is the problem of agency in Held's call for cosmopolitanism. His limp formulation 'diverse state and non-state actors' does not begin to address the basic questions: Who would be the torchbearers of cosmopolitan democracy? What is the constellation of social forces that is accelerating, or would propel, a move in this direction? Just who they are and how they will achieve their aims, Held does not tell the reader. If the agents are not identified, then one cannot know how they are joined to the muscular structures of globalization in the quest for a more equitable world order. If the balance of social forces is not grasped, how can one theorize about a just order?

The question, too, is: How are organic intellectuals connected to social forces? Beyond the insights of theorists such as Weber and Gramsci, what role does and should the intelligentsia play in effecting a cosmopolitan shift? If intellectuals are inserted directly in the process—witness the World Economic Forum and the World Social Forum—one would like

Held to speak to their responsibilities. What are the obligations of academic educators and scholar-activists? In Held's corpus, yearning for the good life is invested in those with superior capacities of awareness, the ability to project cosmopolitan values and norms. Full stop. So, too, in the nineteenth century, European intellectuals offered *la mission civilisatrice*, a set of values and norms, for non-Europeans, purportedly transferring a higher philosophy.

As agents, the marginalized portrayed in Held's account should not be represented as mere victims. Rather, some of them are actively involved in resistance to neoliberal globalization. Absent in Held's investigation of the erosion of the Washington Consensus is the vector of resistance politics. This observation point, one from the bottom, would provide a more complete picture. This position would also help to rectify Held's language—'must be', 'needs to be', and 'has to be'—that betrays wishful thinking without grounding. Indeed, the distance from everyday experience is too great. Held has not sought to forge the links.

A means to make the connections between Held's blueprint and the real production of ethics would be to mine published research on curricula in the schools and students' attitudes concerning globalizing processes. What is actually being taught about world-order values, and how is it changing in various educational systems? Is the trend to adopt Western corporatist prototypes lock, stock, and barrel, or to modify them by generating new configurations that encompass local and, in some cases, religious values (Stromquist & Monkman, 2000)? Do young people increasingly identify as global citizens, or are cosmopolitan norms ever more threatening? In fact, researchers, some of them in faculties and departments of education, are examining these issues, as seen, for instance, in the journal *Globalisation, Societies and Education*. This mode of inquiry helps to decipher whether cosmopolitan moral principles are being embraced or represent a pipedream.

When all is said and done, a normative approach is tantalizing and stimulates the political imagination. So, too, seeing the world through Held's rose-tinted glasses counters pessimistic outlooks on world order: he provides an important corrective to the dim images of the conflicts and inequalities prevalent today. But unalloyed principles derived from Western political philosophy are not an adequate prescription. Proceeding from multiple observation points, drawing from different stations on the hierarchy of power and wealth, listening to the voices of the marginalized, and embodying lived practices are the ways to refocus a cosmopolitan lens.

References

Eagleton, T. (2004) *After Theory* (London: Penguin).
Ngcoya, M. (in progress) *Ubuntu*: globalization, accommodation, and contestation in Southern Africa, Ph.D. dissertation, American University, Washington, DC.
Stromquist, N. P. & Monkman, K. (Eds) (2000) *Globalization and Education: Integration and Contestation across Cultures* (Lanham, MD: Rowman & Littlefield).

James H. Mittelman is professor in the School of International Service, American University, Washington, DC. His books include *The Globalization Syndrome: Transformation and Resistance* (Princeton University Press, 2000) and *Whither Globalization? The Vortex of Knowledge and Ideology* (Routledge, 2004). He is vice-president-elect of the International Studies Association.

Tasks of a Global Civil Society: Held, Habermas and Democratic Legitimacy beyond the Nation-State

ADAM LUPEL

Introduction

On 15 February 2003 across North America, Europe, the Middle East, Asia and Australia as many as 30 million people took to city streets to express opposition to the planned invasion of Iraq (Koch, 2003). It seemed an extraordinary moment for global civil society, perhaps for the first time living up to its name. The anti-war movement appeared to accomplish in a day what four years of transnational activism against neo-liberal globalization could not. It brought together constituencies from East and West, North and South into a broad-based movement with a common clear objective: stop the US-led drive for war. The next weeks saw what was perhaps a Pyrrhic victory for global civil society. The protests no doubt contributed to the Bush Administration's defeat in the UN Security Council. But in the end they also contributed to the heightened sense that the United Nations and global civil society were impotent next to the hegemonic power of the United States. President Bush made clear the US would follow its own course no matter what global public opinion.

My concern here is not with the intricacies of the recent rounds of high-stakes diplomacy, nor with the hard realities of the continuing conflict in Iraq, but rather with what these events reveal about the state of politics in the international sphere. Global public opinion, as best it could be determined, was overwhelmingly opposed to the war, and yet by most accounts war seemed inevitable from the very start. For all the advances in international communications and the spread of international law in the twentieth century, there remains no institutional mechanism to effectively channel the transnational communicative power of an emerging global civil society.

The recent events highlight a question already raised by processes of neo-liberal globalization: In an increasingly globalized world, where political, military, social, financial and environmental policies have transnational effects, how do we address the need for an invigorated transnational capacity for democratically legitimate collective action? This paper addresses the potential of transnational politics in the context of an incomplete process of globalization, where politics is understood as the capacity to make collectively binding decisions to constitute, steer, and at times transform the governing social, economic and legal institutions that influence our lives.

Although its precise definition continues to be subject to debate, references to the phenomenon of 'globalization' remain prevalent, notwithstanding those who have foreseen its demise in the American return to realist geo-politics (see e.g. Touraine, 2003; Wallerstein, 2004). For could one imagine more global media events than the 'war on terror' and the occupation of Iraq? The world is literally watching and reacting almost daily.

For many, emerging processes of globalization signal a threat to the viability of democratic practice. Globalization 'describe[s] a process, not an end-state' (Habermas, 2001a, p. 66). It 'implies, first and foremost, a *stretching* of social, political and economic activities across frontiers such that events, decisions and activities in one region of the world can come to have significance for individuals and communities in distant regions of the globe' (Held et al., 1999, p. 15). Whether one understands 'globalization' exclusively through the lens of neo-liberal capitalism, or through a broader view of grand historical and cultural processes spanning centuries, it has become increasingly clear that recent technological, economic, political and cultural developments challenge the capacity of the nation-state to function in relative autonomy. States do indeed still matter: they continue to wield powerful mechanisms capable of contributing to the shape of the social and economic contexts within their borders. Yet the model of the sovereign state independent from external authority is under increasing pressure; and the consistent capacity to draw clear distinctions between the domestic and the foreign is becoming increasingly difficult to maintain.

Clearly the nation-state shows no signs of disappearing completely.[1] And there is nothing about the expansion and acceleration of cultural, political and economic activities crisscrossing national and regional borders that is inherently incompatible with democratic practice. Yet, as the domain of governance transcends the reach of national institutions, the space for effective popular political input narrows. Thus, in order for processes of globalization to continue without resulting in a corresponding loss of the collective capacity to make legitimately binding decisions, new mechanisms of democratic politics need to be developed.

This article addresses three forms of transnational politics that could serve to broaden democratic legitimacy beyond the nation-state: (i) *cosmopolitan democracy*, (ii) *democratic regionalism*, and (iii) *democratic network governance*. Part one begins by examining David Held's important contributions to the project of rethinking liberal and social democracy in the context of globalization. I argue if cosmopolitan democracy is to meet the challenges of globalization and address the need for transnational forms of democratic politics, it must be able to illuminate the substantial political obstacles to the democratization of transnational power. It must be able to articulate the forms of politics necessary to chart the course from globalizing present to cosmopolitan future. Parts two and three examine two forms of politics seeking to chart such a middle course: Part two examines democratic regionalism through Jürgen Habermas 'postnational constellation', and part three examines democratic network governance through the concept of 'global civil society'. I will argue that each model—cosmopolitan democracy, democratic regionalism, and democratic network governance—encounters a tension between the particular contexts of democratic legitimacy and the universalism demanded of a transnational or even global political culture.

The *Cosmopolitics* of David Held

Cosmopolitan Democracy

Perhaps no theorist has taken up the project of rethinking the practice of popular sovereignty in the context of globalization as thoroughly as David Held. In addition to contributions in democratic theory he has also contributed to some of the most comprehensive empirical studies of globalization as a historical, political, economic and cultural phenomenon (Held et al., 1999). In his theory of cosmopolitan democracy David Held articulates a comprehensive global system of governance. He lays out the institutional and normative basis for a common structure of action that would in theory cover the entire globe in a decentralized but integrated political and legal system.

Held's concerns regarding globalization and the nation-state fall into three general categories. First, Held argues that the regulatory capacity of the state is being transformed—and in many cases reduced—by expanding political, economic, military and cultural connections across borders. Second, he argues such connections create chain reactions in political and economic institutions that transcend national borders. Decisions made at a distance have a profound effect on the political and economic development of nation-states; and as a result domestic constituencies experience a narrowing of the passage through which they may steer the course of government. And, third, processes of globalization transform political identities in myriad ways causing regional, sub-regional or local groups to reevaluate the representative capacity of their central governments (Held, 1995, pp. 99–136).

For Held, the solution lies in the gradual institution of a cosmopolitan polity that would one day cover the globe. Most recently he has described this as a 'global social democracy' (Held, 2004). Holding the system together would be a 'cosmopolitan democratic law' which would provide a 'common structure of action', protecting people's rights and securing the conditions for the possibility of democratic participation at a variety of levels. The political order conceived by Held is complex and burdensome. However, Held argues the seeds of cosmopolitan democracy have already been planted in the post-war regime of international institutions and the Universal Declaration of Human Rights. The task is thus to develop them further, to follow them through to their logical fulfillment. And he argues this becomes necessary if we wish to maintain the practice of democratic governance in the context of globalization (Held, 1995, pp. 219–286; Held, 2004).

Starting with a reform of the UN system, Held envisions the establishment of a Global Parliament and a globally interconnected legal system. A 'Boundary Court' would have to be established when disputes of jurisdiction (local, national, regional, cosmopolitan) needed resolution; and an effective international military force would have to be organized, diminishing the reliance on a national hegemonic military power like the United States (Held, 1995, p. 279). While the nation-state in some form would remain, according to Held, in such a cosmopolitan order the *sovereign* nation-state 'would in due course, "wither away"' (Held, 1995, p. 233).

Assuming such a comprehensive and progressive order could be realized and not collapse under its own weight, it could potentially solve many of the problems concerning the lost capacities of the nation-state. One can only speculate. However, serious questions arise when considering the conceptual ramifications of Held's project, independent from the practicality of its institutional architecture. For example, how could such a comprehensive polity incorporate the many levels of solidarity and identity that necessarily remain within the cosmopolitan system? How does Held make room for a variety of processes of collective self-determination? After all, his project is not simply to reinvigorate the capacity of government, but to understand how processes of democratic legitimation may be extended beyond the nation-state. If, as Held says, 'the idea of democracy derives its power and significance ... from the idea of self-determination' (Held, 1995, p. 145), how are we to understand the maintenance of this idea in the context of globalization? Held's answer lies in the principle of democratic autonomy and its implicit commitment to cosmopolitan law.

A Global Political Society?

At its core, democracy entails a commitment to the notion of self-determination. It implies the idea that people ought to have the freedom to choose the type of society in which they live; and they ought to be free to contribute to the steering of the political structures that govern their lives and work. The project of constituting a single legal structure to encompass the globe raises a variety of questions concerning the freedom of local or national self-determination. From a broadly communitarian or multiculturalist perspective, cosmopolitan democracy appears to lack the capacity to incorporate diverse political practices and traditions. It is charged with misunderstanding the importance of identity to the foundations of political obligation and solidarity; or with being too abstract or disconnected from the social structures of local contexts (Kymlicka, 2001; Calhoun, 2002; Thompson, 1998; Castiglione & Bellamy, 1998).

Yet, clearly cosmopolitan democracy could not seriously require homogeneity on a global scale. In fact, based on the principle of democratic autonomy, Held understands the individual in relation to community and, as such, he argues for a reinvigorated local politics as well as a comprehensive cosmopolitan law. In the liberal tradition, a commitment to self-determination presupposes the normativity of individual autonomy. Simply put, it states that individuals 'should be free and equal in the determination of the conditions of their own lives' (Held, 1995, p. 147). However, given that individuals always live in groups or among other individuals, the principle needs to be qualified: People ought to be free in so far as they do not violate the rights of others—liberty is not license. Thus for Held the principle of 'democratic autonomy' is not the right of atomistic individuals to greedily pursue self-interest without constraint; but rather it is a 'structural principle of self-determination where "the self" is part of the collectivity or "the majority"'. It is 'autonomy within the constraints of community' (Held, 1995, p. 156).

Held is thus aware that there is no emerging 'common global pool of memories' to constitute a single global political community. We may depend, he insists, on the 'persistence of a plurality of frames of political meaning' (Held, 1995, p. 125). In fact he argues that cosmopolitan democracy opens up the possibility for a reinvigorated participatory politics in the local sphere (Held, 1995, pp. 235, 278). Held envisions cosmopolitan democracy to be a system of overlapping authorities and divided loyalties (Held, 1995, p. 137).

There is nothing inherent to a community-based interpretation of political authority that is necessarily antithetical to the recognition of the normative and practical benefits of extending the rule of law to the transnational domain. Possessing a primary political attachment to one's own community does not signify an *ipso facto* rejection of general normative commitments to human rights and representative democracy. Rather it signifies that such commitments must be understood as rooted and substantiated in specific social contexts that inform and motivate people's various levels of commitment to the pursuit of transnational democratic politics. In fact, a consideration of globalization stemming from this insight could encourage the project of cosmopolitanism, as more and more communities come into regular contact, intertwine, and learn from one another, expanding the awareness of diverse ways of life.

According to Held, in a cosmopolitan democracy individuals would remain rooted in their local communities, but political participation would also be structured along national, regional and even global lines. Admittedly, this would likely result in boundary conflicts regarding what issue is to be settled where. At the very least, it would demand a rigorous system for determining the jurisdiction of particular issues. For example, distinguishing a national issue from a regional one would be an important and often difficult task.[2] According to Held, the key to keeping this system from descending into a chaotic medievalism would be a general commitment to a 'cosmopolitan model of democratic autonomy' (Held, 1995, p. 140). In order to avoid the predominance of centrifugal forces, each level of the system would have to remain compatible with the overall cosmopolitan model.

In this sense, it does in fact remain unclear how much latitude each local collectivity would in fact possess for distinguishing itself from the general political structure of the cosmopolitan whole. Yet, according to Held, this should not restrict local self-determination. In fact, he argues, in relation to the current context it would liberate self-determination. Held claims that a commitment to democratic autonomy embedded in a cosmopolitan legal structure is a *necessary* condition of collective self-determination in the context of globalization. The claim being if we choose democracy in the context of globalization we must choose some form of 'cosmopolitan democracy'. If we could assume that a form of liberal democracy indeed would be the world's choice, I would be inclined to accept a version of this claim. Yet Held does not adequately address the problem of articulating the proper *constitutive authority* for such an order. He does not adequately theorize what it would mean to legitimately constitute such an order, given the fact many would not freely choose it.

Held's cosmopolitan democracy is designed to maximize self-determination; but in the absence of a pre-existing consensus, the institutional reform necessary to constitute such a system would tend to require coercive means. And a top-down systemic reform executed on an unwilling base could have volatile consequences. While Held clearly recognizes the persistence of pluralism, his model requires convergence upon a global overlapping consensus: the development of a common political culture.

The normative core of a cosmopolitan democratic order is firmly rooted in the liberal tradition. Those who find this tradition distasteful will tend to oppose Held's cosmopolitan democracy. Those who resist the language of autonomy and self-determination may resist the cosmopolitan democratic project altogether. This is true not simply for some non-Western traditions, but for tendencies within the West as well. Indeed, Held suggests that at their core the Rousseauian and Marxist traditions—not to mention conservative Judeo-Christian traditions—do not entail commitments to the principle of autonomy (Held, 1995, p. 149).

To what extent does Held presuppose convergence into a global political society? He makes clear that he does not see globalization inevitably leading toward a 'world society', a single integrated global community (Held et al., 1999, p. 28). However, he remains dependent on a thinner notion of political society. Cosmopolitan governance depends upon a fundamental agreement over the need to regulate association by democratically legitimate law on a global scale. Currently, none of the principal actors in the international arena—not states, peoples, or capital—would participate in such an agreement. None have an immediate interest in the transnational democratization of power (Wendt, 1999).

For example, a new level of regulation and oversight is antithetical to the libertarian instincts of capital, the driving force behind neo-liberal ideology. While capital benefits from international legal agreements guaranteeing property relations and processes of exchange, it opposes regulatory procedures that might restrict labor or trade policies in the name of social interests. States, as the major actors in the international arena, have a strong interest in maintaining their *de jure* sovereignty; sovereign status remains the foundation of state identity and agency in the international arena. This is never to be given up lightly. And perhaps most troublesome for the cosmopolitan vision, while individuals are set to benefit the most from cosmopolitan democratic law, *peoples* are often the most reactionary forces regarding notions of world community and transnational solidarity. Popular opinion is often more nationalistic and parochial than that of political, social and economic elites.

Recently, Held has argued that a coalition of European social democrats, liberal Americans, and developing countries seeking fair trade and debt relief, allied with powerful NGOs, could provide the impulse to push the international agenda toward a 'global social democracy' (Held, 2004). In this spirit he has striven to provide detailed policy recommendations for the project of reforming global governance in the direction of a more social democratic future. Doing so in accessible terms, he has provided an invaluable service for the practitioners of global policy; and we can only hope they give him the attention he is due. Nevertheless, while the formation of such a powerful coalition for cosmopolitan social democracy is certainly within the realm of possibility, after even the most cursory survey of the contemporary scene, one would be hard-pressed to call it likely. Held is admittedly an optimist.

The conditions for the establishment of a common political culture on a global scale do not yet exist. While this must not spell doom for the project of cosmopolitan democracy as a normative ideal, it does raise tough questions concerning the constitution of the global political culture necessary to legitimately institute a system of cosmopolitan democratic law. How does the system incorporate groups that reject its normative appeal? This is more than a practical or institutional question. The acceleration of globalization and the spread of cosmopolitan ideals have witnessed a concomitant rise in reactionary and extremist activism. To institute cosmopolitan law without a broad-based supportive politics is to invite violent, energetic counter-action.[3] Held is at his best when he theorizes either the global reality of contemporary affairs or the ideal of a cosmopolitan future. But it is the road between that is the most challenging and vital. For Held, the short-term project is to reform the international system according to its inherent principles, which, he argues, logically lead toward cosmopolitan social democracy. However, he does not provide an adequate explanation of the politics entailed in achieving this end in the context of vigorous dissent and extreme asymmetries of power.

Jürgen Habermas' recent work on the 'postnational constellation' in some ways provides such a bridge between globalizing present and cosmopolitan future. Similar to Held, Habermas perceives the nation-state under siege in the context of globalization. However, unlike Held, Habermas stops short of articulating the design for a consolidated cosmopolitan system. And yet, I argue, he encounters similar problems regarding the particular context of democratic politics and the legitimate constitution of cosmopolitan governance.

The Politics of Regionalism: Habermas [4]

Post-national Citizenship

One way to imagine the middle course between a retreat to national isolationism and the rush to global integration is the pursuit of regional structures of governance. The accelerated integration of separate nation-states into new political and economic units on a regional scale may be read as a particular response to the exigencies of globalization. Habermas offers a theory of a democratized European Union in these terms. His version of the post-national constellation presents a form of *regionalism* as an attempt to demonstrate how democratic politics might be reconfigured to regain power lost to transnational economic and political actors. *Regionalism* is thus understood as a political project that is more than the gradual integration of a large, previously divided territory. It is a response to political and economic developments that threaten to spin out of control, by attempting to provide for the first time an effective infrastructure for the governance of the transnational sphere. And in this sense *regionalism* can be generalized to represent a normative project for the articulation of a new global order.

Habermas invites us to understand European regional politics as *post*-national; it clearly seeks to transcend long-standing ethnic or linguistic divisions: the French and Germans, the Spanish and British, the Czechs and Poles all to share a common citizenship. Yet the cultivation of a post-national or transnational common citizenship must entail more than the democratic reform of regional institutions. As Habermas has previously indicated, the relationship between nationalism and modern democratic practice has long been intertwined (Habermas, 1998, Chap. 4). Thus history would suggest achieving post-national citizenship could not entail simply substituting democratic identity for national identity.

The history of the liberal democratic nation-state is characterized by a tension between republicanism and nationalism—between the ideals of universal citizenship and the historical, cultural context in which such ideals take root. And, according to Habermas, the fate of democracy depends upon which tendency predominates (Habermas, 1998, Chap. 4). Democratic citizenship articulates more than a legal status for Habermas; it provides the foundation of a shared political culture that can serve the purpose of social integration often provided for by ethnocentric nationalism. In order for the democratic integration of a regional polity to be successful it must be able to cultivate a common political culture among an extremely diverse array of peoples. Habermas argues that in a liberal democratic nation-state political culture may arise from a rational consensus over the general principles of legitimate democratic practice. Basic constitutional rights and principles can serve as a 'fixed point of reference' around which a '"constitutional patriotism" may develop, politically integrating people from a variety of world-views' (Habermas, 1998, p. 225; see also Habermas, 1989). To the extent that the legal definition of citizenship is based upon the notion of universal equality before the law, these basic rights and principles remain independent from the identity of any particular group. Conceptually speaking, there is no reason why this could not function similarly at the regional or continental level.

However, while the principles of *universal* legal equality may transcend national divisions in a regional polity, to become operational they must be situated within a *particular* historical context. According to Habermas, in a complex, multicultural, value-pluralist world, basic political rights and principles pertain to those that 'citizens must confer on one another if they want to legitimately regulate their interactions and life contexts by means of positive law' (Habermas, 1996, p. 122). However, the basic categories of positive and negative rights are in Habermas' terms, 'unsaturated'; they lack the substance of particular historical, political or social concerns. And, as a result, they cannot become the 'driving force' behind the project of democratic political integration 'until they are situated in the historical context of the history of a nation of citizens' (Habermas, 1996, p. 499). And for Habermas this is equally true for democratic integration on the regional scale.

Arguing in favor of a European constitution, Habermas suggests the prerequisites for success go beyond the abstract allegiance to broad principles to the 'interest in and affective attachment to a particular ethos: in other words, the attraction of a specific way of life' (Habermas, 2001b, p. 8). Regional political integration thus depends not only on a shared commitment to the values of liberal democratic practice but on a shared historical experience which may provide a common backdrop for the interpretation of basic constitutional principles and to a specific shared way of life. Sharing the values of liberal democratic practice is not the same as sharing a 'specific way of life'. While both are committed to liberal democracy, for example, there are notoriously sharp distinctions between the broadly speaking American and the broadly speaking European ethos.

According to Habermas, the nations of Europe already share a certain historical horizon based in the shared experiences of modernization and violent upheaval. After centuries of conflict—between religions and between nations—culminating in two disastrous international wars, Europe has come to share a common tendency toward toleration, 'the overcoming of particularisms ... and the institutionalization of disputes' (Habermas, 2001a, p. 103). Thus it is not only that the European nations share a geographic and therefore historical contiguity, but that, according to Habermas, they have lived a shared history that particularly prepares them for regional political integration.

While Habermas is thus optimistic about the solidarity producing effects of a common European history, there are many reasons to be less sanguine. For many, it is precisely the variety of the European experience that calls into question the viability of political integration on the regional scale. This is becoming all the more apparent with the most recent round of EU expansion to include former Communist bloc countries. How will the different state traditions and historical experiences of the North and the South, or the East and West affect the cultivation of a common regional political culture in Europe? And ultimately where does the European border lie? Why is Turkey potentially in while Russia is out? As the debates surrounding 'the Draft Treaty establishing a Constitution for Europe' would suggest, such questions are not easily answered.

Yet, in spite of the variety of political traditions across the continent, according to Habermas, the course of European history reflects a general process of modernization that forms a common value horizon, providing the shared context for the interpretation and application of basic constitutional rights and principles, making possible the development of a common political culture across the diverse peoples of Europe. He argues, the experiences of European history 'have shaped the normative self-understanding of European modernity into an egalitarian universalism that can ease the transition to postnational democracy's demanding contexts of mutual recognition' (Habermas, 2001a, p. 103).

Regional political integration requires an expansion of civil solidarity beyond the nation-state; and the basis of this solidarity is a shared political culture that can only succeed within the common horizon of a shared course of history and a sense of common fate. While regional political integration does not require homogenization, it does require the cultivation of a regional political identity that 'goes beyond mere legal classification' (Calhoun, 2002a). According to Habermas' own terms, European political integration depends upon a territorially based political identity situated in a shared history. In the sense that the shared history occurs on the regional level, and entails solidarity among a variety of ethnic groups, it is understood as *post*-national. Yet one could equally discuss this in terms of an 'extended nationalism', or a regional civic-nationalism.[5]

Habermas tends to equate nationalism with ethnonationalism (Calhoun, 2002a, note 17; see also, Calhoun, 2002b, p. 279). Yet 'constitutional patriotism' in another manner of speaking is the civic-nationalism inspired by the principles of liberal-democracy at work in a multicultural polity. While ethnonationalism places the basis for political membership in a collective identity existentially prior to state institutions, civic-nationalism understands the origins of political membership as inseparable from legal rights and institutions. Membership in the nation is defined by equal status before the law without necessary reference to ethnic, cultural, or religious identity of any kind.

A democratized European Union would be animated by a spirit of 'extended nationalism' in that its integration would depend upon a territorially based political identity, situated in a shared history, and cultivated by the constitution of a political process that enabled a continental collective capacity to make legitimately binding decisions. As should be clear, situated in a particular history, the regional polity does not transcend the relationship between universal citizenship and political particularity: the tension between the two remains.

Cosmopolitan Governance

For Habermas, the democratized regional polity is concerned with reinvigorating the democratic capacity to govern in the context of globalization. Integral to the project of democratic regionalism is the potential for transnational coordination between regional polities, civil society actors, and international organizations. The consolidation of regional polities, for Habermas, represents the possibility of providing an effective, democratically legitimate infrastructure to the international system for the first time. However, the extent to which a regional democratic polity could be integrated into a comprehensive cosmopolitan system in Habermas terms remains open to question.

Like many before him,[6] Habermas is skeptical about the normative justifiability and practical feasibility of a comprehensive World State. He argues that an international system composed of regional polities, global civil society actors, and international organizations such as the UN would be preferable and more likely to succeed than a more comprehensive and integrated cosmopolitan democracy like the one proposed by David Held (1995). Habermas proposes a system of cosmopolitan *harmonization* rather than administrative institutional *consolidation* (Habermas, 2002, p. 232).

However, Habermas clearly seeks an international system regulated by more than the inconsistencies of transnational power politics and generalized commitments to human rights.

In reflecting on Kant's *Perpetual Peace* with 'the benefit of two hundred years' hindsight', Habermas argues that cosmopolitan law must carry the threat of sanction. It must have the coercive power to bind state governments in the interest of protecting the legal rights of individuals as free and equal world citizens without reference to particular national belonging (Habermas, 1998, pp. 179–181). At its best, for Habermas, the present is a transition period between the Westphalian system of nation-states and a future de-centered cosmopolitan legal order characterized by the broad acceptance of human rights and a transnational commitment to social justice (Habermas, 1998, p. 183). Democratic regional polities offer the best practical stepping-stones to this cosmopolitan future.

Yet a serious problem arises in Habermas's is model: achieving cosmopolitan legal harmony necessitates convergence upon a political identity he suggests lacks the ethical-political foundations necessary to produce democratic legitimacy. For, '[e]ven a world-wide consensus on human rights could not serve as the basis for a strong equivalent to the *civic* solidarity that emerged in the framework of the nation-state' (Habermas, 2001a, p.108).

Habermas envisions a system where processes of democratic political identity-formation remain tied to national and regional historical experience. Yet it is unclear, in Habermas's own terms, how cosmopolitan law would be able to gain democratic legitimacy, given that world citizenship cannot constitute the requisite sense of civic solidarity, something he recognizes is necessary even in the discourse model of the regional polity. For Habermas, 'constitutional patriotism' may serve to reconcile the universality of cosmopolitan right and the particularity of popular sovereignty. Yet 'constitutional patriotism' proves to be either too strong or too weak to succeed at the global level. Either it strongly binds a political community together around vigorous particular interpretations of abstract constitutional rights at the cost of cosmopolitan identification, or its content remains at such a level of generality that it allows for cosmopolitan identification but fails to produce the 'ethic of solidarity' on the domestic level necessary for the production of democratic legitimacy (see Fine & Smith, 2003).

Thus the development of an enforceable cosmopolitan legal order out of an emerging post-Westphalian system of nation-states, regional polities, international institutions, and global civil society actors, entails a more radical leap than Habermas is willing to concede. The project of cosmopolitan democracy is subject to a serious conceptual problem: democratic legitimacy depends upon the cultivation of a common political culture and the solidarity that arises from it. Yet the conditions for the constitution of such a culture are incompatible with a global domain of cosmopolitan governance. The historic tension between the ideal of universal citizenship and the necessarily particular contexts in which it becomes situated is only exacerbated when extended to the transnational sphere.

Networks and the Tasks of Global Civil Society

The Ambivalence of Networks

David Held diagnoses the threat to traditional forms of democratic politics posed by processes of globalization, and he articulates a normative and institutional vision of cosmopolitan democracy as a response to that threat. However, he does not adequately theorize a form of politics that may legitimately constitute such a system. We are left with the impression that cosmopolitan democracy is an elite project constituted from the top down (Cochran, 2002). Habermas, on the other hand, offers a form of democratic regional politics as the best practical stepping-stone between globalizing present and cosmopolitan future. Yet the stone path falls one step short: the ethical foundations of popular sovereignty and democratic legitimacy remain unable to extend the final distance to a globalized system of law. Might then a form of de-centered global civil society and democratic network governance provide the tools to bridge the gap?

Cosmopolitan democracy and democratic regionalism are strategies to regain lost capacities for collective self-government by establishing new levels of political integration, either on the regional or global scale. Theories of global *network governance* on the other hand attempt to elude the tensions inherent to projects of integration by operating under the assumption that social and political institutions must adapt to an environment of increasingly de-centered authority (Held & McGrew, 2002). Theorists of global governance reject the traditional state-centered view of international relations and global politics. They argue that in the last quarter of the twentieth century the world witnessed a proliferation of centers of authority whose sources are neither the individual nation-state nor the state-based treaties of international law. Instead they develop out of interest-based functional networks that either bypass or establish equal partnerships with government in the international sphere. For example, the International Accounting Standards Committee since 1973 has set international accountancy standards independent from state regulation. And since 1998 the G7, the IMF and the World Bank have officially recognized the Committee's authority (Woods, 2002, p. 31).

In contrast to the hierarchical model of state authority, the model of global governance is based on the horizontal form of the 'network'. While the contributing factors to the decline of state capacities are many, as James Rosenau argues, 'one of the most important of these has been the shifting balance between hierarchical and network forms of organization' (Rosenau, 2002, p. 77). Manual Castells pioneering work in this field is instructive: simply put, 'a network is a set of interconnected nodes' (Castells, 2000, p. 501). The character of the individual node depends upon the specific network: a currency trader's office in London is a node in the global financial market; a local gathering of A.N.S.W.E.R. coalition, a node in the international anti-war movement; an Al-Qaeda cell in Spain, a node in the global terrorism network.

This manner of de-centering transnational practice away from the nation-state has clearly been amplified and accelerated by the recent revolution in information and communication technology. Most importantly the development of the world-wide-web has vastly improved the capacity of networks to coordinate action, disseminate information, and recruit new members. In the information age of the Internet and satellite communications, networks have the capacity to all but transcend distance completely. For the academic in the course of organizing a conference or editing a book, a colleague overseas that checks his email regularly is ironically 'closer' than the Emeritus Professor down the hall who still refuses to 'get connected'. Distance in the information age, Castells argues, ranges from zero, between any two nodes on the same network, to the infinite distance to a point outside of a given network. In this way, political action and authority based in the network form is *deterritorialized*. Distance or proximity becomes detached from territorial space, thus undermining the paradigm of the state, categorically organized around the geographic limits of 'national territory'.

The network form clearly raises the ability of non-state actors to accumulate political power. But does this signify a redistribution of power to the historically powerless? Is it a form of transnational democratization? Can we speak of it as a form of transnational popular sovereignty in the same way we discussed cosmopolitan politics or democratic regionalism? The movement against the war in Iraq indeed established 'chains of equivalence'[7] across a broad swath of humanity, creating a potent political solidarity where there was none previously. And yet, while network-based governance does perhaps carry such a potential for inclusion, it does not necessarily do so. For example, one can observe an emerging pattern in which the governance of technical issues is given over to networks of experts. Ngaire Woods argues that an emerging form of 'Technocratic Network Governance' devolves regulatory procedures away from traditionally representative institutions and processes of transparency into the inaccessible, jargon-filled boardrooms of technical elite rule. In such cases, legitimacy becomes detached from democratic procedure. The technical quality of results comes to matter more than the status of 'democratic inputs' (Woods, 2002, p. 34). Thus, network forms while non-hierarchical are not necessarily inclusive; they may serve as tools of exclusion as easily as they can provide avenues for the proliferation of political participation; they are in effect normatively ambivalent.

Global Civil Society

Recent years have witnessed the accelerated evolution of a complex system of de-centered transnational regulation and rule making on a near global scale. This system includes states, international organizations, treaty regimes, security relationships, transnational networks, private agencies, public–private partnerships, financial institutions and more. Serving an important function in an increasingly interconnected world, however, this complex of mechanisms and organizations lacks a coherent structure for the consideration of democratic will-formation. That is to say, global governance suffers from a clear democratic deficit. As David Held and Anthony McGrew have argued, 'global governance is said to be distorted in so far as it promotes the interests of the most powerful states and global social forces, and restricts the realization of greater global social justice and human security' (Held & McGrew, 2002, p. 13).

If network governance is only potentially a democratic form of transnational politics, how do we distinguish its democratic form from its exclusionary cousin? May we specify 'global civil society' as the democratic form of network-based global governance? While the meaning of the term 'civil society' has shifted over time, in the post-cold war world it has come largely to signify the sphere of 'social interaction', independent from the state and the market, encompassing formal and informal associations, non-governmental organizations (NGOs), social movements, and other processes of public communication (Cohen & Arato, 1992; Kaldor, 2003).

Concomitant with processes of globalization and the spread of information technology, civil society in this sense has transcended national and regional borders. The 1990s witnessed the vast growth in the number of transnational social movements, NGOs and international citizen networks, for the first time contributing to the sense that a truly global civil society was in the making. Such movements and organizations contributed to the growing emphasis on human rights and social justice in the international agenda in the late 1990s. At times they have proven to be genuinely effective in changing international policy, for example, in the case of the campaign against landmines (Glasius & Kaldor, 2002). The strong presence of civil society organizations at the large global forums of the 1990s such as the Rio Earth Summit or the Beijing conference on Women and Development, and the subsequent advent of the annual World Social Forum, have also elevated the presence and influence of such actors on the global stage.

However, does this then mean that the continued spread of civil society organizations represents the democratization of global governance? Some have argued that the central role played by civil society organizations in the Ottawa Convention Banning Landmines served for the first time to democratize the process of international legislation (Anderson, 2000). Could perhaps a vibrant global civil society provide the necessary democratic legitimacy to a de-centered form of global governance? Could it extend the conditions for the constitution of democratic governance all the way out to the global domain?

A strong version of the civil society argument suggests that a vibrant, diverse global civil society could democratize global governance, independent of reform at the level of states or international law. James Rosenau has argued that the more global civil society becomes populated with a variety of social movements, NGOs and international institutions the more global governance will in fact exhibit 'democratic tendencies'. Empowered by the information and communication revolution, such grassroots networks and social movements can provide a counterbalance to transnational 'technical networks' that support or reproduce the agenda of entrenched interests. As global civil society becomes more populated with a diversity of movements and organizations making specific demands on specific institutions and articulating previously excluded political perspectives, the more receptive to popular concerns and the more transparent the mechanisms of global governance will become (Rosenau, 1998). Similarly, John Dryzek argues that in the absence of global government, transnational democratization is achievable at the discursive level through the capacity of global civil society to control the terms of debate. He argues that the 'network form can play a key part in establishing deliberative democratic control over the terms of political discourse and so the operation of governance in the international system' (Dryzek, 1999, p. 48).

However, this represents a very ideal view of the position and potential of global civil society. In many respects, global civil society is extremely limited and often does not live up to its normative expectations. Global civil society organizations are often Eurocentric, frequently co-opted by powerful interests, and of questionable representative status. The claim that in international affairs the mere presence of global civil society organizations represents a democratization of the international domain must be treated with extreme caution. Global civil society must itself be on object of critique.

For one thing, global civil society institutions arise out of the same political economy as other international institutions. Thus you find the same inequalities reproduced in civil society institutions as elsewhere (Chandhoke, 2002). For example, civil society resources are much higher in the OECD countries, thus tipping the scale of influence heavily in their favor. In fact, predictably, the only city outside of Europe or America in the top ten centers for international NGOs is Tokyo (*Global Civil Society*, 2002, p. 6, Table 1.1). Furthermore, clearly not every civil society organization directly or indirectly promotes values consistent with liberal or social democracy. What about associations promoting extreme sectarian or fundamentalist causes? Consideration certainly must be given to what Simone Chambers and Jeff Kopstein have called 'bad civil society' (Chambers & Kopstein, 2001).

A more moderate form of the global civil society argument understands its role within the context of domestic reform and international agreement. It argues that civil society has an important role in bringing issues of global concern to the top of the international agenda. For example, civil society played a vital role in providing the momentum for the creation of the International Criminal Court (Kaldor, 2003, pp. 131–132) and, as previously mentioned, it was integral to the Ottawa Convention Banning Landmines. Furthermore, Margaret Keck and Kathryn Sikkink have described what they call the 'boomerang pattern', when a social movement or NGO finds its own government unresponsive to its demands, and thus turns to the international community for help. Usually this takes the form of stimulating what Keck and Sikkink call 'transnational advocacy networks' which petition foreign states and third-party intergovernmental organizations to pressure the violating government to change. This has proven highly effective in the past, for example in the case of the anti-apartheid movement (Keck &

Sikkink, 1998, pp. 12–28). In this sense, the participation of civil society organizations in the process of international legislation, previously restricted to states, is understood as a major factor in democratizing the constitution of global governance.

Yet, again, if taken as a general rule, this position entails considerable idealization. For one, as indicated, civil society institutions can be gradually co-opted by powerful interests. The international environmental movement is a case in point. After the Rio Earth Summit in 1992 the environmental movement gained tremendous influence. Green parties joined coalition governments in Europe and corporations hired environmental advisors. Yet in July of 2001 when the parties to the UN Framework Convention on Climate Change met in Bonn they systematically rolled back the commitments made in Rio in 1992. And global civil society organizations such as Greenpeace and Friends of the Earth International were left to applaud as historic an agreement they would have found completely unacceptable only ten years earlier (Kaldor, 2003, pp. 7–9).

There are also questions concerning the representative status of civil society institutions. Who do they in fact speak for? And how do they set their agendas? NGOs at the global level can be very large complex organizations highly removed from any basic social or political community. Their only true constituency, so to speak, is their member base, people who send in a check from time to time—a financial contribution being the only form of participation expected from the general public—their policies often the product of specialized professionals and not public deliberation. Furthermore, often those people most in need of articulating their requirements outside of state institutions live in hostile political environments that restrict peaceful protest and free association, making the functioning of civil society associations all but impossible.

Thus in order for the sum effect of global civil society to be the democratization of global governance, it must exist within a framework of normative rules and egalitarian institutions that ensures equal access to all and compensates for broad differentials of power. Organizations and movements from around the world must have the capacity and freedom to articulate their diverse interests, as they simultaneously cultivate the sense of global interdependence necessary to address issues of common concern for the entire planet. However, then we must ask, how would this framework be constituted? And, in such case, have we not thus come full circle? In the interest of democratic legitimacy, the constitution of global governance must incorporate the input of civil society. And yet civil society, in order to live up to its normative expectations, requires an already existing framework of governance to provide the relatively level and inclusive playing field necessary to establish its conditions of possibility.

Democratic legitimacy remains tied to particular contexts of interest and historical perspective. Transnational democratic legitimacy even for a de-centered global civil society depends upon the cultivation of a minimal common frame of action, necessary to avoid the perception that transnational politics benefit only powerful states at the expense of the weak—a charge at times leveled against environmental or human rights accords. Global civil society is perhaps caught in an infinite regress: it must play a constitutive role in cultivating the recognition of a common planetary project for the democratization of global governance; but this awareness must in some sense already be present in order to produce the 'democratic tendencies' necessary for it to gain legitimacy. Global civil society must construct its own conditions of possibility. It is the ship at sea, still under construction.

Conclusion

New forms of global governance and transnational legal structures are now emerging in a de-centered 'evolutionary process'.[8] The question is how to instill this process with democratic legitimacy. Is it possible for a form of democratic practice to take part in the constitution of the emerging forms of global governance? Can the collective capacity to steer the social, political and economic institutions that affect our lives be reinvigorated on a transnational scale? Cosmopolitan democracy, democratic regionalism, and democratic network governance represent three forms of politics that attempt just that.

In the context of globalization no form of politics may be thought of in isolation: Regionalism must be thought of in the context of the broader world order; cosmopolitanism implies transformations at the local, national, and regional levels. And global networks are enabled or hindered depending upon the character of national and international politics as they traverse national and regional boundaries. I have argued that each model of transnational politics encounters a tension between the particular contexts of democratic legitimacy and the universalism demanded of a political culture that can address the myriad issues in need of transnational governance revealed by our increasingly global interdependence.

While interdependence is on the rise, the universal recognition of a planetary common good remains an elusive goal, to say the very least. More than expressing the unity of humanity, the rise of global civil society highlights the complexity and asymmetry of the world. Global civil society does not constitute a single *proto*-world-community; it is complex, stratified, and endlessly diverse. Yet this need not present an impassable obstacle to the democratization of global governance. For *pace* Rousseau, popular sovereignty has seldom concerned the governance of unified societies but rather struggles for power in divided societies (Morgan, 1988).

Habermas has suggested the unity between the particular context-embedded democratic will and the abstract, universal rule of law 'can only develop in the dimension of time' (Habermas, 2001c, p. 768). If we can understand the constitution of transnational democracy as an ongoing, tradition-building process based in local, national and regional democratic projects, perhaps over time the tension between the particularity of democratic legitimacy and the universality of cosmopolitanism could be reconciled. Yet again this depends upon a growing awareness of global interdependence, the cultivation of the perception that we are in effect all 'in the same boat'.

This is not simply a matter of determining which comes first: transnational solidarity or cosmopolitan institutions, but rather of the long-term politics and open-ended processes of democratizing international institutions and political culture simultaneously. It is a matter of the interrelation between institutional innovation and the cultivation of democratic norms. The world is now indeed a community of shared risks—environmental disaster, international terror and crime, nuclear proliferation, the interrelation of financial markets, all have transnational effects. A transnational politics must build bridges across borders to address these problems. Such a transnational politics must achieve real results for a wide range of humanity; a globalization of heightened inequality is doomed to disaster. Raising awareness to that effect is perhaps the most important role for global civil society today. Only such a politics could establish the conditions for the legitimate constitution of a democratic global governance.

Notes

1   In fact as many have argued the post-cold war era has witnessed a reinvigoration of nationalism rather than its transcendence (see e.g. Brubaker, 1996).

2   In fact some have argued that this would gravitate extraordinary power in the hands of cosmopolitan judges. Risking a form of global 'judicial imperialism', see Scheuerman, 2002; Zolo, 2000, pp. 79–80.

3   In addition, without broad support, the shift away from a system of sovereign states toward a system of global law carries the risk of domination by a single power: 'empire'. Thus Jean L. Cohen (2004), for example, argues the key is to pursue cosmopolitan justice while simultaneously maintaining the historical commitment to the 'sovereign equality' of states.

4   An extended version of this discussion appears in Lupel (2004).

5   Dudley Seers in discussing the political economy of the European Union describes the future of Europe in these terms (Seers, 1983; see also Hettne, 2000).

6   Most notably Kant, in his famous essay 'To Perpetual Peace', argued for a federation of nations or a 'league of peace (foedus pacificum)' rather than a 'World republic' (Kant, 1983 [1795], p. 117).

7   This is the terminology of Ernesto Laclau (see Laclau & Mouffe, 1985; Laclau, 1996).

8   On the 'evolutionary process' of constitution-making see Arato (2000, p. 235).

References

Anderson, K. (2000) The Ottawa convention banning landmines, the role of international non-governmental organizations and the idea of international civil society, *European Journal of International Law*, 11(1), pp. 91–120.

Arato, A. (2000) *Civil Society, Constitution, and Legitimacy* (New York: Rowman & Littlefield).

Brubaker, R. (1996) *Nationalism Reframed* (Cambridge: Cambridge University Press).

Calhoun, C. (2002a) The class consciousness of frequent travelers: towards a critique of actually existing cosmopolitanism, *South Atlantic Quarterly*, 101 (Fall), pp. 869–897.

Calhoun, C. (2002b) Constitutional patriotism and the public sphere: interests, identity, and solidarity in the integration of Europe, pp. 275–312 in P. De Grief and C. Cronin (Eds) *Global Justice and Transnational Politics* (Cambridge, MA: The MIT Press).

Castells, M. (2000) *The Rise of the Network Society*, 2nd edition (Oxford: Blackwell Publishers).

Castiglione, D. & Bellamy, R. (1998) Between cosmopolis and community, pp. 152–178 in D. Archibugi, D. Held and M. Köhler (Eds) *Re-imagining Political Community* (Cambridge: Polity Press).

Chambers, S. & Kopstein, J. (2001) Bad civil society, *Political Theory*, 29(6), pp. 837–865.

Chandhoke, N. (2002) The limits of global civil society, pp. 35–54 in Glasius, M., Kaldor, M. and Anheir, H. (Eds) *Global Civil Society* (Oxford: Oxford University Press).

Cochran, M. (2002) A democratic critique of cosmopolitan democracy: pragmatism from the bottom-up, *European Journal of International Relations*, 8(4), pp. 517–548.

Cohen, J. L. (2004) Whose sovereignty? Empire versus international law, *Ethics and International Affairs* (December), pp. 1–24.

Cohen, J. & Arato, A. (1992) *Civil Society and Political Theory* (Cambridge, MA: MIT Press).

Dryzek, J. S. (1999) Transnational democracy, *Journal of Political Philosophy*, 7(1), pp. 30–51.

Fine, R. & Smith, W. (2003) Jürgen Habermas's theory of cosmopolitanism, *Constellations*, 10(4), pp. 469–487.

Glasius, M. & Kaldor, M. (2002) The state of global civil society: before and after September 11, pp. 3–34 in Glasius, M., Kaldor, M. and Anheir, H. (Eds) *Global Civil Society* (Oxford: Oxford University Press).

Habermas, J. (1989) *The New Conservatism: Cultural Criticism and the Historians' Debate*, Trans. S. W. Nicholsen (Cambridge, MA: MIT Press).

Habermas, J. (1996) *Between Facts and Norms: Contributions to a Discourse Theory of Law and Democracy*, Trans. W. Rehg (Cambridge, MA: MIT Press).

Habermas, J. (1998) *The Inclusion of the Other*, C. Cronin & P. De Greiff (Eds) (Cambridge, MA: The MIT Press).

Habermas, J. (2001a) *The Postnational Constellation*, Ed. & Trans. Max Pensky (Cambridge, MA: MIT Press).

Habermas, J. (2001b) Why Europe needs a constitution, *New Left Review*, 11 (September/October), pp. 5–26.

Habermas, J. (2001c) Constitutional democracy: a paradoxical union of contradictory principles?, *Political Theory*, 29(6), pp. 766–781.

Habermas, J. (2002) The European nation-state and the pressures of globalization, pp. 217–234 in P. De Grief and C. Cronin (Eds) *Global Justice and Transnational Politics* (Cambridge, MA: MIT Press).

Held, D. (1995) *Democracy and the Global Order: From the Modern State to Cosmopolitan Governance* (Cambridge: Polity Press).

Held, D. (2004) *Global Covenant: The Social Democratic Alternative to the Washington Consensus* (Cambridge: Polity Press).

Held, D. & McGrew, A., Eds (2002) *Governing Globalization* (Cambridge: Polity Press).

Held, D., McGrew, A., Goldblatt, D. & Perraton, J. (1999) *Global Transformations: Politics, Economics and Culture* (Cambridge: Polity Press).

Hettne, B. (2000) Global market versus regionalism, in: D. Held & A. McGrew (Ed.) *The Global Transformations Reader*, pp. 156–166 (Cambridge: Polity Press).

Kaldor, M. (2003) *Global Civil Society: An Answer to War* (Oxford: Polity).

Kant, I. (1983[1795]) 'To Perpetual Peace: A Philosophical Sketch', in *Perpetual Peace and Other Essays*, Trans. Ted Humphrey (Cambridge: Hackett Publishing Co.).

Keck, M. E. & Sikkink, K. (1998) *Activists Beyond Borders* (Ithaca, NY: Cornell University Press).

Koch, C. (2003) *2/15: The Day the World Said No to War* (Oakland: AK Press).

Kymlicka, W. (2001) *Politics in the Vernacular* (Oxford: Oxford University Press).

Laclau, E. (1996) *Emancipation(s)* (London: Verso).

Laclau, E. & Mouffe, C. (1985) *Hegemony and Socialist Strategy* (London: Verso).

Lupel, A. (2004) Regionalism and globalization: post-nation or extended nation?, *Polity*, 36(2), pp. 153–174.

Morgan, E. S. (1988) *Inventing the People: The Rise of Popular Sovereignty in England and America* (New York: W. W. Norton and Co.).

Rosenau, J. (1998) Governance and democracy in a globalizing world, pp. 28–57 in D. Archibugi, D. Held & M. Köhler (Eds) *Reimagining Political Community* (Cambridge: Polity Press).

Rosenau, J. N. (2002) Governance in a new global order, pp. 70–86 in D. Held & A. McGrew (Eds) *Governing Globalization* (Cambridge: Polity Press).

Scheuerman, W. E. (2002) Cosmopolitan democracy and the rule of law, *Ratio Juris*, 15, pp. 439–457.

Seers, D. (1983) *The Political Economy of Nationalism* (Oxford: Oxford University Press).

Thompson, J. (1998) Community identity and world citizenship, pp. 179–197 in D. Archibugi, D. Held & M. Köhler (Eds) *Reimagining Political Community* (Cambridge: Polity Press).

Touraine, A. (2003) *Constellations*, 10(3).

Wallerstein, I. (2004) *Alternatives: The U.S. Confronts the World* (London: Paradigm Publishers).

Wendt, A. (1999) A comment on Held's cosmopolitanism, pp. 127–133 in I. Shapiro and C. Hacker-Cordón (Eds) *Democracy's Edges* (Cambridge: Cambridge University Press).

Woods, N. (2002) Global governance and the role of institutions, pp. 25–45 in D. Held & A. McGrew (Eds) *Governing Globalization* (Cambridge: Polity Press).

Zolo, D. (2000) The lords of peace: from the holy alliance to the new international criminal tribunals, pp. 73–86 in B. Holden (Ed.) *Global Democracy* (New York: Routledge).

Adam Lupel is a Ph.D. Candidate in Political Theory at the Graduate Faculty of the New School for Social Research and the Managing Editor of *Constellations: An International Journal of Critical and Democratic Theory*. He is currently completing a dissertation on globalization and the concept of popular sovereignty. His work has appeared previously in *Polity, Constellations*, and *Critical Sociology*.

The Changing Face of Anti-Globalization Politics: Two (and a Half) Tales of Globalization and Anti-Globalization

RAY KIELY

Transnational Capitalism and Seattle

Various theories have attempted to argue that we have moved into a new phase of globalized capitalism. These include the theory of post-imperialism (Becker et al., 1987), the theory of the transnational capitalist class (Sklair, 1991; 2001) and the theory of Empire (Hardt & Negri,

2000). The broad argument of these theories is that 'global corporations function to promote the integration of diverse national interests on a new transnational basis' (Becker & Sklar, 1987, p. 6). Robinson and Harris (2000, p. 20; also Sklair, 2001) argue that the transnational capitalist class is both cause and product of globalizing processes, and that as the circuit of capital becomes globalized 'so too do classes, political processes, states and cultural ideological processes'. The development of a transnational capitalist class therefore transcends the old imperialist division of the world. Conflict and competition exist, but between companies rather than states, and even when the latter exists it is subordinate to capitalist cooperation beyond the nation-state (Harris, 2003a, pp. 69, 71). Competition therefore reflects divisions within the transnational capitalist class, rather than inter-state conflict (Robinson, 2001/02, p. 507). Instead, it is argued that the nation-state is 'neither retaining its primacy nor disappearing but becoming transformed and absorbed into a TNS (transnational state)' (Robinson, 2002, p. 210).

This emerging transnational state is composed of international institutions like the World Bank, International Monetary Fund (IMF) and Bank of International Settlements, the European Union, the World Trade Organisation (WTO) and the North American Free Trade Agreement (NAFTA). Nation-states continue to carry out important functions, but these have been increasingly transnationalized, as macroeconomic policy becomes increasingly focused on appropriate fiscal, monetary, trade and investment policies that allow for the intensification of transnationalization. Thus, welfare and developmental states have been transformed into neo-liberal states (Robinson, 2001a, pp. 182–191).

In this approach, US (economic) hegemony is said to be declining, and being replaced by a nascent transnational hegemony exercised through supranational structures (Robinson, 2002, p. 210), which as yet are too weak to provide the functions necessary for the reproduction of global capitalism. The United States has taken the lead in the promotion of a global capitalist agenda, but this has involved an agenda that promotes the interests of the transnational capitalist class, rather than those of the United States (Robinson, 2001b, p. 228). There are conflicts within the US state apparatus and the capitalist class, which are essentially between international hegemonists who want to reassert US hegemony through military power, and transnational globalists who want to expand capitalist hegemony beyond any particular nation-state (Harris, 2002, p. 3).

A not dissimilar theory is associated with the work of Hardt and Negri (2000). They argue that US hegemony has been replaced by a deterritorialized apparatus of power, which they call Empire. For Hardt and Negri (2000, p. xiv), '[i]mperialism is over. No nation will be world leader in the way modern European nations were'. Therefore, '[w]hat used to be conflict or competition among several imperialist powers has in important respects been replaced by the idea of a single power that overdetermines them all, structures them in a unitary way and treats them under one common notion of right that is decidedly postcolonial and postimperialist' (Hardt & Negri, 2000, p. 9). This is the new system of Empire, comprised of a three-tier pyramid: the US and G7 are at the apex, representing the monarchy; transnational companies and some nation-states represent the aristocracy; and a number of institutions and organizations such as the UN General Assembly and NGOs represent 'democracy' (Hardt & Negri, 2000, Chap. 3.5). Against these hierarchies is the transnational multitude, that represents a genuinely global democratic counter-power to Empire. For Hardt and Negri, Empire may be progressive compared to the system of national imperialist capitalisms, as capitalism was progressive compared to feudalism, but it still represents exploitation. But this is exploitation that transcends nation-states, with the implication that contemporary progressive resistance 'opposes any national solutions and seeks instead a democratic globalization' and organizes 'in horizontal networks [which] tend to cluster at the non-sovereign pole' (Hardt, 2002, pp. 114, 116). Hardt's position is thus in stark contrast to those who argue that nation-states continue to be the main organizers of the world capitalist system, and that therefore resistance should continue to focus on nation-states (Halperin & Laxer, 2003).

Critique 1: The Specifics of Seattle

This final point concerning global resistance is problematic. Many social movements, particularly in the South, are mass movements that simply have too many members and supporters for organization to be based on informal networking (Kiely, 2005, Chap. 7). The informal, non-hierarchical structure of tiny organizations like the Ruckus Society in the US is a far cry from the mass support of the MST (Landless Workers Movement) in Brazil (Mertes, 2002, pp. 106–107). Moreover, such movements continue to place demands on their 'own' nation-states, even if they also attempt to win broader international support. This point does not make such movements narrowly nationalist or Leninist, but neither does it makes them purely globalist or anarchist.

It is also far from clear that a pure strategy of 'going global' will promote an unambiguously progressive politics. In the case of organized labour, there has been some pressure to globalize labour demands through pressure placed on international organizations such as the WTO. This strategy differs from that proposed by Hardt and Negri, who essentially reject all existing institutions and celebrate the spontaneous resistance of the multitude. But there is also some similarity in that both strategies are based on transnationalizing resistance. In recent years, fearing a loss of jobs for North American workers as capital relocates to low-cost areas, the American Federation of Labour-Congress of Industrial Organisations (AFL-CIO) has called for labour clauses in international trade agreements. The AFL-CIO's official protest at the WTO talks in Seattle in 1999 was based on this premise, as was the subsequent launch of the Campaign for Global Fairness. This campaign called for strengthened international solidarity between workers (AFL-CIO, 2000). In this account, there is said to be a very real basis for labour solidarity, as a transnational bourgeoisie exploits a transnational proletariat, irrespective of particular location (Robinson & Harris, 2000, p. 23). Indeed, Burbach and Robinson (1999, pp. 27–28) argue that '[w]orldwide convergence, through the global restructuring of capitalism, means that the geographic breakdown of the world into north-south, core-periphery or First and Third worlds, while still significant, is diminishing in importance'. The politics of resistance should therefore focus on those international institutions that are said to represent the interests of transnational capital, such as the WTO. Workers throughout the world are said to have a mutual interest in upgrading standards. 'First World' workers would benefit from improved global standards, as these would increase the price of exports from the newly industrializing countries; and, on the other hand, workers in these countries would benefit from higher wages and better working conditions, and so employment would increase as a result of increased demand. In this way, the protests at Seattle in late 1999 were an unambiguously progressive example of the globalization of working class resistance. But were the conflicts and divisions at Seattle as clear-cut as this account makes out? One motivation for US labour protest was the assumption that US workers would lose their jobs as a result of competition from cheap labour overseas, and for this reason the AFL-CIO opposed China's entry into the World Trade Organization (AFL-CIO 2000). Even if we accept the argument concerning jobs for a moment, it is clear that in this case global solidarity does not automatically follow—more likely is a xenophobic reaction in which foreigners are accused of 'stealing our jobs'. Thus, Teamsters' Union President Jimmy Hoffa has argued that China's entry into the WTO would cost one million American jobs as '[t]here's always somebody that will work cheaper. There's always some guy in a loincloth' (cited in Brecher et al., 2000, p. 54). For all its claims to be promoting solidarity, such a strategy ultimately protects 'First World' workers at the expense of 'Third World' workers, thus undermining solidarity and—in the absence of wider social change—condemning the latter to even greater levels of poverty. The fact remains that while high levels of exploitation exist in 'Third World' sweatshops, these factories are often seen as desirable places of employment, when the alternatives may be even worse. The claim made by Union of Needletrades, Industrial and Textile Employees (UNITE) researcher Elinor Spielberg (1997, p. 113) that young girls in Bangladesh prefer prostitution to factory work is entirely without foundation, and betrays a 'malign universalism' dressed up as global solidarity (Kabeer, 2000, pp. 382–383; Tomlinson, 2001).

Related to these points, the collapse of the WTO talks at Seattle in 1999 was not simply because of the protests outside, but also because of conflicts between delegates inside the meeting. The United States advocated more free market reforms in agriculture and further liberalization of trade in services; Japan rejected further liberalization; the European Union wanted developing countries to open their markets further to agricultural goods; and many developing countries wanted to enforce Special and Differential Treatment clauses (such as preferential access for their exports as had been agreed at previous General Agreement on Tariffs and Trade (GATT) talks). The US administration also attempted to place labour standards on to the agenda, which was opposed by delegates from the developing world and the European Union. There was also much resentment at the setting up of special Green Room meetings where key issues were discussed among representatives from a select minority of countries. The collapse of the Cancun talks of the development round in 2003 also represented conflicts between the interests of different states, above all concerning agriculture (Islam, 2003).

Seattle was therefore more complex than the scenario outlined by theorists of transnational capitalism. This critique is made not to reject strategies of globalizing resistance, but to question the view that this will *automatically* promote a more progressive politics. This problem in turn can be linked to the broader weaknesses of the theories of transnational capitalism and Empire.

Critique 2: The State

In terms of the nation-state, the basic problem is the construction of a rigid dichotomy between global capital and the transnational state on the one hand, and the nation-state on the other. Robinson does accept the continued importance of the nation-state, a view also accepted by Negri (in Negri and Zolo, 2003), but they still tend to regard the nation-state as something that is being 'outgrown' by global capitalism. This is an 'outside-in' theory of the relationship between globalization and the state (Panitch, 2001, p. 11), which ignores the ways in which some states promote globalization (Burnham, 1997). Most of the institutions and summits that supposedly represent a nascent transnational state are actually created and authorized by nation-states, which implies the need for an 'inside-out' approach at least as much as an outside-in one (McMichael, 2001, p. 203). The creation of such institutions may involve the sharing of sovereignty—for instance through the European Union—but these are still promoted by, and allied with, nation-states.

Moreover, power within international institutions is unequally structured through the mechanisms and interests of nation-states, not transnational corporations. Similarly, disputes within organizations are structured by states, so that, for instance, trade disputes through the WTO are between nation-states and not transnational companies. The United States has lost in disputes through the WTO (Harris, 2003a, p. 73), but the fact remains that sanctions are implemented (or not, as the case may be) through nation-states. This entrenches hierarchical power, not only of capital against labour, but of some states against others. This hierarchy arises because of the time and cost of bringing trade disputes forward to the WTO's dispute settlement mechanism, and the fact that the only possible response is state-imposed trade sanctions. Clearly, sanctions brought by poor states against the US mean far less to the latter than sanctions by the US against the former (Toye, 2003, p. 117).

It is therefore too one-sided to argue that competition now takes place solely between transnational capitals, and not between states.

Critique 3: Capital Flows

These issues also have implications for how we understand the nature and direction of international capital flows. If we examine the transnational practices of leading transnational companies (TNCs), we see that they are not quite as global as one would expect. The transnationality index of the world's largest 100 companies measures the employment and assets held overseas by TNCs. For the year 2001, the average transnationality index was only 52.6 per cent. Only 57 of the 100 companies had an index measure greater than 50 per cent, and only 16 had an index of over 75 per cent (Dicken, 2003, pp. 221–222). One would expect these figures to be much higher, particularly as what is measured are assets and employment that compare home country to all other countries. Moreover, Harris (2003a, p. 69) makes much of the argument that the transnationality index tends to be greater for European than US companies, which supposedly shows that US hegemony is declining against the growing transnationalization of capital. But the reasons why transnationality is often greater for European companies is that their domestic markets are smaller. Moreover, the biggest TNCs tend to have relatively low transnationality measures: General Motors has an index rating of only 30.7 per cent and General Electric only 36.7 per cent (Dicken, 2003, pp. 221–224). Similarly, the boards of most major companies continue to be dominated by national representatives. Although there has been some movement towards internationalization, it remains limited, and usually means only small minority representation (Ruigrok & van Tulder, 1995, pp. 157–158).

But perhaps even more important is the fact that foreign investment is highly concentrated. Between 1993 and 1998, 'developed countries' received 61.2 per cent of world direct foreign investment (DFI), developing countries 35.3 per cent, and the former communist European countries 3.5 per cent (UNCTAD, 2002, p. 5). In 2001 developed countries received 68.4 per cent, developing countries 27.9 per cent, and the former communist European countries 3.7 per cent. This third of DFI going to developing countries in recent years was itself highly concentrated, with just five countries receiving 62 per cent and ten receiving 75 per cent of this proportion in 2001. The 49 least developed countries received just 2 per cent of the DFI inflows into developing countries and 0.5 per cent of total world FDI in 2001 (UNCTAD, 2002, p. 9). Moreover, China is the main recipient of FDI going to developing countries, accounting for as much as nearly 50 per cent of the total, but most of this investment is actually from within the East Asian region, and therefore does not mean a substantial relocation from the capital-rich West (Sutcliffe & Glyn, 1999, p. 119). DFI figures do not tell the whole story, as they do not distinguish between greenfield (new) investment and takeovers, nor the practice of subcontracting between TNCs and local suppliers. But the proportion of First World imports that originate from developing countries remains low, and in one respect the DFI figures actually *over-estimate* both the proportion of DFI that goes to the developing world, and total investment figures. This is because firstly the population of the developing world is much higher than the population of the developed world. If one looks at DFI inflows per capita, then the proportion is actually far more weighted towards the developed world. For the years 1995–99, developed countries received $474 on a per capita basis and for 2001 the figure was $583; for developing countries as a whole, for 1995–99 the figure was $37 and for 2001 just $41 (UNCTAD, 2002, p. 265). Secondly, FDI contributes only about 5.2 per cent of total world investment, and the stock of world inward FDI constituted only around 10.1 per cent of world GDP in 1995 (Hirst & Thompson, 1999). Thus FDI makes up a relatively small though growing amount of total world investment, and it is highly concentrated in relatively few countries. Clearly, these figures undermine any arguments concerning a straightforward transnationalization of capital. In the case of financial capital, despite an unprecedented increase in significance since the 1970s, there has not been a convergence between interest rates across the world, and there remains a close link between domestic saving and investment rates, all of which suggests that net international flows of long-term finance are not particularly great (Watson, 1999).

But even these arguments do not tell us enough about the current nature of the international system. Harris (2003a, pp. 69–70) argues that the fact that the US is the major recipient of foreign investment in the world today reflects its declining hegemony. In one respect this is perfectly correct, and the US' transition from the world's major creditor to the world's main debtor over the last twenty years reflects the fragile nature of such hegemony. But Harris misses the other side of the equation, *which is the fact that it is precisely because of this capital inflow that the US manages to maintain its hegemony* (Arrighi, 1994; 2003).

Critique 4: US Hegemony

It is certainly true that the undisputed hegemony of the post-1945 era is over. The United States accounted for around 50 per cent of world output in 1945, and this had declined to around 25 per cent by the 1980s (Harman, 2003, p. 38). Its global share of manufacturing stood at 40 per cent in 1963, but had declined to 24 per cent in 1987, and then slightly increased to 25 per cent in 1999. Japan's share over the same years went up from 6 per cent (1963), to 19 per cent (1987) and 20 per cent (1999). Germany's share was 10 per cent in 1963 and 1987, and post re-unification increased to 12 per cent (1997) (Dicken, 2003, p. 46). On the other hand, of the top 500 companies in 1998, 244 were US, compared to 46 for Japan, and 173 for Europe (Petras & Veltmeyer, 2001, p. 62). But to fully understand the continued hegemony of the US in the world order, we have to examine the relationship between the US state and international finance.

The end of the gold–dollar link and of fixed exchange rates from 1971–73 was part of a strategy designed to recover competitiveness in industrial production. In particular, the US governments of Nixon, Ford and (for a time) Carter pursued expansionary monetary policies and a relatively weak dollar, which were designed to increase production both at home and through cheaper exports abroad. However, the policy led to inflation and potentially undermined the international role of the dollar, and so a new tight monetary policy was adopted in 1979 under Carter, and especially under Ronald Reagan. In the early 1980s, the money supply came under tighter control, there were tax cuts for the wealthy, and increased deregulation of capital investment. From 1982 onwards, there was a big increase in military spending and a marked intensification of Cold War hostilities. The effect of these policies was a massive increase in the US' trade and budget deficits, and an increase in competition for capital investment to finance these deficits (Arrighi, 1994; 2003). This involved an increase in interest rates to attract financial capital to the US, which in turn led to a massive increase in interest payments for countries that had built up debt in the 1970s. The 1980s and 1990s therefore saw the promotion of continued US hegemony through the expansion of financial capital. US governments have therefore had some success in using the international role of the dollar to maintain hegemony since the 1980s, based on financing deficits through the selling of government debt securities (bonds), continued (but possibly declining) international demand for the dollar and the promotion of liberalized financial markets, as in the East Asian financial crisis of 1997–98, which aims to maintain financial hegemony (Wade, 2003). Moreover, its effective control of international financial institutions such as the IMF and World Bank, and the influence of the US Treasury and Federal Reserve Bank reinforces this hegemony (Peet, 2003). Thus, for all the hype about the 'new economy' boom of the 1990s, the United States became increasingly dependent on foreign purchase of debt securities, which itself helped to maintain a high value dollar in the absence of high interest rates as well as low inflation due to cheap imports (Gowan, 2001a, p. 363).

The US now possesses overwhelming military force in the world order, alongside the largest trade deficit in the world and, since the 'election' of Bush, a massively increasing budget deficit. In 2001 and 2002, military spending grew by 6 per cent and 10 per cent a year, which amounted to around 65 per cent and 80 per cent of total increases in Federal government spending in those years (Brenner, 2003, p. 21). Its military budget figures were already far higher than most of the combined spending of the next twelve or so powers, and at least 26 times greater than that of the seven main 'axis of evil' countries. At the same time, since early 2000, the Federal budget deficit has grown from 1.8 per cent of GDP to an estimated 3.7 per cent (2003) and 4.3 per cent for 2004 (Brenner, 2003, p. 21). In 2001, the trade deficit was a record $435 billion, which increased to an unprecedented $489 billion by 2003 (*Monthly Review*, 2003, p. 8). These deficits have been financed by foreigners speculating in the stock market, buying real estate, acquiring firms or setting up new sites, and buying US Treasury bonds. Equity purchases fell by 83 per cent from 2000 to 2002 as share prices fell, and so there has been a sustained movement into buying government bonds. In 2001, 97 per cent of the US current account deficit was financed by foreign purchases of these bonds. From 1992 to 2001, the foreign share of US national debt increased from 17 per cent to 31 per cent (*Monthly Review*, 2003, p. 10). None of this necessarily matters, so long as there is confidence in the US economy and the dollar, but there is a serious question mark as to whether a high trade deficit (5 per cent of GDP in 2002) is sustainable—it is more sustainable for the US than for other countries because of the international role of the dollar, but ongoing deficits are likely to further erode this role. Continued US hegemony therefore rests on quite weak foundations, but it nevertheless remains a reality. This was most nakedly demonstrated in the case of the so-called war on terror that followed the attacks on 11 September 2001, to which I now turn my attention.

Responses to September 11: US Imperialism Revisited

While the focus of protest at Seattle largely ignored nation-states, the wars against Afghanistan and particularly Iraq, and the ease with which the Bush administration simply by-passed international institutions such as the UN, showed clearly the continued, naked power of the nation-state, and of one state in particular. The notion that globalization had eroded state power, and made war less likely, was thus rendered problematic. The actions of the Bush administration therefore placed the concept of imperialism back on the agenda.

This focus on imperialism has led to a renewed focus on classical Marxist theories, and in particular the work of Lenin and Bukharin (Callinicos, 2002). These theories attempted to link the rivalry between imperialist powers before 1914 to what they perceived to be a new stage of capitalism. Thus, Lenin (1975) argued that imperialism had five characteristics: concentration of capital which led to monopoly; the merger of bank and industrial capital (financial capital); the export of capital; the formation of trusts and cartels; and the territorial division of the world. Monopoly was for Lenin a key characteristic and this was linked to the concentration of production, seizure of raw materials, the rise of national banks and colonial policy. This tendency toward monopoly did not mean the end of competition but rather its intensification. Bukharin (1972, pp. 108–109) further developed this contention, arguing that the world economy was dominated by competing blocs of nationally organized capital. Against Kautsky (2002), both Lenin and Bukharin argued that this intensified economic competition led to military conflict and the inevitability of war. There were serious problems with these theories even in 1914. For example, there was little evidence of a close correlation between monopoly and the export of capital, accumulation within the exporting countries increased in this period, and much of the capital that was exported was actually to other 'advanced' capitalist countries, and not to the colonies and semi-colonies (Emmanuel, 1972; Olle & Schoeller, 1982; Panitch & Gindin, 2003). These issues are not unrelated to attempts to update the theory for the current era, to which I now turn my attention.

Theorists of the new imperialism[1] argue that we are witnessing a repeat of the situation prior to the First World War. Talk of the war on terror or liberal humanitarianism is merely ideological cover for the latest imperialist phase of capitalist expansion, and the conflicts that arise between the imperialist powers as a result. According to this theory, since the collapse of Communism we have returned to the situation of inter-imperialist rivalry that characterized the pre-Cold War era. This does not mean that the confrontations are necessarily direct—'[m]ore typically they involve, as they have done throughout the history of imperialism, minor powers—"rogue states" in the modern parlance' (Rees, 2001, p. 23). Thus, the 1991 Gulf War upheld US prestige against Germany and Japan, the 1999 conflict over Kosovo/Serbia promoted US hegemony at the expense of the European Union, and the 2001 conflict in Afghanistan 'hemmed in' Russia, Iran and Europe (Rees, 2001). The 2003 conflict in Iraq was similarly a war exercised by the US for guaranteed long-term oil supplies, which involved the defeat of rivals like France and Germany, as well as potential long-term rivals such as Russia and China (Morgan, 2003). Thus, for theorists of the new imperialism, Lenin and Bukharin's approach, which focuses on the international expansion of capitalism and inter-imperial rivalry, remains indispensable for understanding contemporary politics.

There are important reasons for questioning the relevance of this approach to understanding the contemporary world. First, colonialism is largely dead, most territories have political independence, and many have developed strong indigenous classes—both exploiters and exploited—and states, with their own set of interests. The argument that the conflicts of the 1990s were simply arenas in which imperialist rivalries were played ignores the local dynamics that led to these conflicts in the first place. The Gulf War of 1991 was in part about US imperialism, but it was also about the invasion of Kuwait by Saddam Hussein. The war that followed was primarily concerned with commercial and strategic interests, and reflected double standards, but it was far more than simply 'functional' to the needs of imperialism. The small-power imperialism of the Iraqi regime in 1991 is barely mentioned in these accounts, as 'local' conflicts appear to be completely determined by global imperialist conflicts.

Following on from this first point, given the amount of competition between the major powers, it is difficult to argue that these wars were 'really' about inter-imperialist competition. Callinicos' (1994; 2003a) claim that the Gulf War of 1991 was about disciplining Japan and Germany ignores the fact that these powers actually financed the US-led intervention. Despite some disagreements, there was widespread cooperation over war in the former Yugoslavia and Afghanistan. Conflict was undoubtedly greater over Iraq in 2003, but it is mistaken to explain this away as purely a reflection of competing economic interests. All the main powers were agreed that Saddam had to be dealt with in some way, and it is highly unlikely that the aftermath of war will lead to a policy of colonial exclusiveness on the part of the United States, not least because the international oil industry is simply too complex for one country to have sole rights to the products of another state. Moreover, given the US' dependence on other countries for financing its twin deficits, such a policy would not be in the interests of the US anyway.

Moreover, what also stands out in the new imperialism analysis more generally, in terms of post-Cold War conflicts, is the relative silence on the nature of Milosevic's regime, and the role of al Qa'ida in these conflicts—these simply become functional to Great Power ambitions and rivalries. This reflects a neglect of the specific effects of imperialism on 'the periphery'. Since Lenin's day, this debate has been divided into the pessimists and optimists. Pessimistic accounts include the Third International under Stalin, and post-war dependency and underdevelopment theories. The basic argument of the pessimists is that imperialism leads to impoverishment, through the development of underdevelopment. Optimists (Warren, 1980; Harris, 2003) argue that imperialism will lead to capitalist development, which is progressive compared to non-capitalist modes of production. The problem with both of these views is that they are guilty of over-generalization, assuming uniform effects throughout the globe. Callinicos' (2003b, p. 13) argument that 'victory for US military power will weaken the struggle against poverty and hunger everywhere', clearly puts him in the pessimist camp, but to assume that imperialism alone can have such effects is nonsense. Poverty is not caused by imperialism in itself, but by a particular configuration of global and local, international and national factors. Neo-liberal policies have done little to address these issues, and in some cases have made things worse, but they are not the sole cause and nor can such policies be mechanically linked to military intervention. The victory of the US-led forces in Iraq may lead to foreign investment, but it is not at all clear that this alone will impoverish Iraqis. Indeed, impoverishment is more likely to be a result of lack of investment, a likely scenario in Afghanistan and the Balkans. This is not an endorsement of US war or investment, or the sanctions regime that preceded them, but it is a call for a more careful analysis of what is meant by imperialism and its likely effects.

The theory of the new imperialism has thus failed to recognize the significance of the political and economic changes that have taken place since Lenin's day. The problems of classical theories notwithstanding (see above), the main trend before World War I was the concentration of capital on a national level, with colonial annexation facilitating market access, investment and raw materials (Hilferding, 1981, p. 225). Today we have a far greater internationalization of capital, which flows mainly between First World countries, and the capital that is invested in developing countries originates from a number of nations. This does not mean that such capital is no longer tied to particular nation-states, but it does mean that the world cannot be divided into *exclusive* blocs. Economic competition has in many ways intensified, but in a free trade rather than colonial monopoly/territorial acquisition environment, power is exercised more by directly 'economic' rather than 'political' or military means (Green, 2002, pp. 58–59; Went, 2002/03, p. 490). Moreover, although economic competition between major powers continues to exist, it does not necessarily lead to war. A great deal of these changes are recognized by theorists of the new imperialism (Harman, 2000), but they have failed to draw the appropriate conclusions.

Accounts of the new imperialism correctly point to the continued importance of the nation-state, and of US hegemony, and in this respect they represent a useful corrective to theories of transnational capitalism. But it is one thing to recognize the continued importance of the nation-state, and quite another to suggest that little has changed since 1914. There are important reasons for suggesting that Lenin's and Bukharin's accounts were questionable for this period as well (see above). The new imperialism thesis simply exacerbates these weaknesses. Compared to 1914, there is a greater degree of interdependence of capitals throughout the world, and independent nation-states with their own interests. Competition exists between states and capitals, but this does not inevitably mean war, and the evidence of international cooperation, unequal and uneven as it is, is simply too great for the new imperialism thesis to be convincing.

Power, Agency and 'Centres of Globalization'

So far we have examined two approaches to globalization: first, the theory of transnational capitalism and, second, the theory of new imperialism. The first approach argues that as capital becomes transnational, nation-states become increasingly irrelevant or become increasingly transnationalized. US hegemony, at least in terms of the world economy, is said to be declining, and is regarded as being dysfunctional to the interests of transnational capitalists. Thus, Michael Hardt (2002b) claims that many transnational elites oppose war as it 'is bad for business because it sets up barriers that hinder capital flows'. Negri (in Negri & Zolo, 2003, p. 27) goes even further, arguing that 'the present *imperialist* ideology and practice of the Bush government are fast placing themselves on a collision path with other capitalist forces that, at the global level, work for empire'. The second approach argues that globalization has eroded the power of neither the nation-state nor US hegemony. While this approach agrees with the first view that nation-state regulation of capital has changed its character, there is strong disagreement concerning the character of US military hegemony, which is regarded as being functional to US capital, and which may be challenged by potential competitors, which in turn means that war between rivals remains a strong possibility or even an inevitability. Thus, in a brief tirade against the work of Hardt and Negri, Tariq Ali (2003a, p. 4) asserts that '[t]he politicians who impose neoliberal solutions at home are the same men and women who wage wars abroad, and it is done for the same reason. How could it be otherwise?'

These conflicting statements about the 'war on terror' reflect both the strengths and weaknesses of the two theories, and their respective understandings of contemporary globalization. The transnational capitalism/Empire approach recognizes the reality of significant cooperation between capitalist powers, and the fact that continued competition does not inevitably lead to war. But it tends to be at the expense of a convincing analysis of the continued importance of the nation-state, competition between capitals and states, and US hegemony. As a result, uneven development, and the continued hierarchies between states and capitals is downplayed. Given these oversimplifications, a smooth binary divide between transnational bourgeoisie and transnational proletariat, or of a revolutionary multitude within Empire, represents an unconvincing political alternative.

On the other hand, new imperialism theory focuses on imperialism through an analysis of US hegemony and inter-imperialist rivalry. Focusing on US hegemony usefully reminds us of the continued reality of US state and indeed economic power. But there is a tendency to exaggerate this power, at times reducing almost all world events to the malign practices of the United States. Focusing on inter-imperialist rivalries reminds us of continued competition between capitalist powers, but at the cost of the specific form that this competition takes. This theory also underestimates the significance of the rise of independent (but weak) power centres in the developing world, and it overestimates the degree to which competition between the most powerful imperialist states gives rise to war. Classical Marxist theory tended to assume the *necessity* of imperialism, and which included as a corollary the *inevitability* of war. Related to this argument, states were regarded as agents of imperialism because they were simply *functional to*, or *instruments of*, capital. The war drive of the Bush administration is therefore seen as a rational response to the crisis of US and world capitalism (Callinicos, 2003a). This leads to an analysis of imperialism that reduces imperialist war drives to the necessity of capitalist expansion, rather than a political project in its own right. The *Project for a New American Century* (1997; 1998) is therefore assumed to be an unproblematic expression of the logic of capital.[2] Moreover, imperialism is regarded as so all-pervasive that the politics of political movements in the former 'Third World' are either ignored, or regarded as objectively anti-imperialist.

In terms of a progressive politics of globalization, we are left with a potentially insurmountable dilemma. On the one hand there is the strategy of globalizing resistance to transnational capitalism and the transnational state, which leaves aside questions of nation-states, US imperialism, uneven development and war. On the other stands resistance to US/Western imperialism, which leaves aside analysis of weaker centres of global capitalism, political alternatives within imperialist states, and solidarity with people beyond nation-states, not least those that may suffer at the hands of anti-US dictatorships. One possible way out of this dilemma is to rethink the relationship between states and globalization, and by implication challenge one-dimensional views of power. Insofar as we can have a theory of the state, it must rest on a more contingent understanding of state–capital relations. Marx argued that the notion of separate economic and political spheres was a historical product of capitalist social relations. The political state is thus not derived from the capitalist economy, it is a constituent part of wider social relations. Economy or 'base' does not determine polity or 'superstructure'—this is not only empirically wrong, but actually a fetishization of capitalist social forms. Many Marxists pay lip-service to this analysis and then simply re-establish 'totality' by reasserting the agency of capitalist economy over state polity—through either instrumentalist or functionalist views of the state. But it needs stressing that contrary to these approaches, the state is a constituent part of capitalist social relations, which means that it too has agency. The relationship between state and capital accumulation is contingent, and varies in time and space and is not least dependent on social struggles within social formations. The very fact that the economic and the political are separated in capitalist societies means that securing such interests is problematic. Having said that, it would be mistaken to see such contingency as absolute, or to see the state as a neutral body, because this separation of different spheres also acts as a constraint on state capacity, as its reproduction ultimately rests on the continued accumulation of capital (Jessop, 2002, Chap. 1).

These comments on the state can also be applied to our understanding of contemporary globalization. Much of the mainstream globalization debate has implicitly focused on the relationship between power and contingency. Giddens (1999) and Held et al. (1999) have both argued that globalization is a process in which no single agency is in control. But the fact that globalization is a process in which no one has ultimate control does not preclude the fact that globalization relates to a set of processes in which some agents have far more power than others. Indeed, Negri (in Negri & Zolo 2003, p. 28) makes precisely this point when he argues that 'I do not doubt that the United States is a "global power", I only insist on another idea: that the power of the United States is subjected to (or in any case forced to dialogue with and/or contest) economic and political structures other than itself'.

The political implication of this discussion should be clear. Globalization is neither a process without any centres, nor one that is reducible to a particular centre. This means that it is a more complex process than the accounts that can be found in the theories of transnational capitalism or US imperialism.

The most convincing classical Marxist account of imperialism is therefore Kautsky's theory of ultra-imperialism, which recognizes the possibility of cooperation between nation-states even as capitalist economic competition persists. Kautsky failed to adequately theorize the ways in which this cooperation could be led by a dominant state, and paid insufficient attention to the reality of uneven development in this ultra-imperialist order. Nevertheless, his theory is more relevant to understanding the current world order than those of either Lenin or Bukharin. What is equally clear is that, since 1945 at least, the US has not acted as a colonial power, but has attempted to secure its hegemony through allied sovereign states. Insofar as this relates to the 'capitalist market', it is based on the recognition that sovereign states represent an important means of regulating capital. US hegemony is thus exercised through the (conditional) recognition of the state sovereignty of others, a strategy that carries all sorts of risks as dominant political actors in the developing world may at times challenge 'Americanism' within their own territories. These challenges have at times forced a variety of interventions based on the idea that what is good for the US state is also good for global capital, but which vary according to a number of political projects and policy proposals which cannot be reduced to the 'logic of imperialism'. Interventions have also taken place in contested areas of state formation where primitive accumulation has been particularly violent, factors which can be linked to the uneven development of capitalism and the relative marginalization of some areas of the globe. At the same time, there has been an increase in global integration and interdependence, particularly among the core capitalist states, but also in subordinate ways for the more marginalized states. The neo-liberal agenda has both intensified this interdependence and (relative) marginalization. For all these reasons, post-1945 imperialism has been ultra-imperialist and led by the US state at one and the same time. Equally, the record of these military interventions—despite the rhetoric of promoting human rights and freedom—is poor.

These points can be reiterated through explicitly relating them to 'the globalization debate' and, in doing so, drawing appropriate political conclusions. First, globalization must be understood in part as a political project that is closely linked, though not reducible to, the US state and the question of US hegemony. This does not mean that contemporary imperialism is simply a repeat of the nineteenth century, as we have witnessed both the universalization of the nation-state system and the increased transnationalization of capital. This globalization of capital has not led to dispersal of capital flows throughout the world, but instead has intensified the concentration of capital in some locations, and the relative marginalization of other places, which in turn has led to increased instability. Imperialist nations may enter wars in order to gain access to raw materials, but such interventions are as likely to be policing operations designed to increase stability in certain parts of the world. These operations are, even on their own terms, unlikely to succeed, first because they abstract from the specific social and historical conflicts that may (or may not) lead to successful capitalist development. Moreover, given neo-liberal dominance in the global order, the space for such development is undermined by the dominance of free trade, which generally ensures established producers will out-compete 'later developers'.[3] Thus, the very concentration of capital in the global order both sustains US hegemony and contributes to political instability within that order, particularly at the margins of global capitalism. This is a global order, then, in which the US state remains dominant, but also in which there is complex interdependence between the centres of capitalist power.[4]

But equally, it is a world order in which these centres have only limited control over events elsewhere. This provides considerable space for resistance to the current order, but the question of the progressiveness of such resistance needs to be addressed. It is not sufficient to simply repeat the anti-imperialist rhetoric of the past and assume that anti-imperialist movements automatically promote progressive alternatives.[5] At its worst, this can lead to the crudest anti-imperialist politics. Thus, Chitty (2002, p. 19) advocates 'a positive defence of the Taliban and Osama bin Laden, as the current representatives of Middle Eastern resistance to imperialist power, in their war against the USA and its proxies'. Far less crude, but still problematic is Harman's argument concerning national liberation. He rightly warns against taking calls for national liberation at face value, as this can be an excuse to maintain oppression. But he then argues that we should distinguish between the nationalism of the oppressor and oppressed, and that 'anti-capitalists in the West cannot simply sit back and say all rulers are equally bad. We have to throw our main efforts into seeking to thwart the imperialist ambitions of the already powerful' (Harman, 2003, p. 76). Such a perspective is as guilty of the double standards with which the 'West' is rightly condemned—Saddam Hussein is opposed when he has the support of the United States, but is supported when he is opposed by the United States. This is a purely reactive (and reactionary) anti-imperialism based on the politics of 'my enemy's enemy is my friend'. It is also one that logically follows from the new imperialism thesis, which reduces the actions of 'small powers' to an irrelevance, a theatre in which the big powers play out their rivalries. But this argument effectively endorses a political imperialism that denounces any agency—progressive or reactionary—in the developing world. These issues are taken up in the conclusion.

Conclusion: Critical Cosmopolitanism, Global Governance and Local and National Struggles

I want to conclude by making some tentative comments about the question of the relationship between anti-imperialism and progressive global solidarity. I have argued that the US does remain the hegemonic power in the world today, but that at the same time domination cannot be *reduced* to the power of the United States. It therefore follows that the principle of global solidarity means ongoing solidarity with oppressed people, irrespective of whether their governments have the support of Western governments. This principle should not be 'put on hold' when the United States chooses to undertake an unjustified war. Solidarity must be indivisible, linked to oppressed peoples throughout the world regardless of whether their government is supported or condemned by the United States or other Western powers (Halliday, 2002, p. 172). A principled anti-war position does not therefore mean that progressive global politics rejects *any* actions undertaken by imperialist powers—in the case of Iraq, there was a strong case for finding ways through the UN of putting pressure on the regime, such as continued arms inspections, human rights inspections, and better targeted sanctions. Anti-imperialist Marxists were perfectly correct that overthrowing Saddam was a job for the Iraqi people, but without any concrete proposals of solidarity, this was simply empty rhetoric—and one that played into the hands of the liberal pro-war lobby.

What is being advocated here, then, is a progressive global solidarity on a number of 'fronts'. Some social movements within 'global civil society' have adopted such a perspective. Thus, the Revolutionary Association of the Women of Afghanistan (RAWA, 2001a; 2001b) denounced the 2001 war while equally denouncing the attacks on the US, and al Qa'ida and the Taliban. Organizations such as the Labour Party of Pakistan, the Worker Communist Parties of Iraq and Iran, and the Afghan Revolutionary Labour Organization, among many others, condemned the US-led war, but equally condemned US enemies like the Taliban, Saddam Hussein and the Iranian regime. This principle of anti-imperialism together with global solidarity has also come to characterize some of the politics of anti-globalization movements. At the World Social Forum II at Porto Alegre in early 2002, a joint statement was made by social movements, which stated that 'we absolutely condemn [the terrorist attacks], as we condemn all other attacks on civilians in other parts of the world'. The statement went on to 'emphasise the need for the democratization of states and societies', and that we are 'against war and militarism . . . We choose to privilege negotiation and non-violent conflict resolution. We affirm the right of all the people to ask international mediation, with the participation [of] independent actors from the civil society' (World Social Forum 2002).

It is in this respect that there does need to be a more explicit globalization of resistance, which is not only *against* imperialism but *for* transnational solidarity. For Hardt and Negri (2004), such resistance will be led by the multitude against the institutions of Empire. This may at times be true, but they have a particularly underdeveloped conception of the multitude, and tend towards a rather uncritical acceptance of their spontaneous resistance. Moreover, they also betray a deeply problematic account of the question of domination by existing institutions. Indeed, in this respect their views are closer to the anti-imperialist Marxists. My discussion above suggested that nation-states are far from being neutral institutions, but at the same time they are sites of conflict, and concessions can be won from them. The same point can also be applied to international institutions, with the implication that globalizing resistance may some-times involve working through existing institutions such as the UN. This entails a critical engagement with the principles of cosmopolitanism. Associated with the cosmopolitan democracy school of Held, Archibugi and others (Held, 1996; Archibugi, 2003), this approach argues for the extension of democratic ideas to the institutions of 'global governance'. It has been rejected by Marxist anti-imperialists on the grounds that it undermines state sovereignty, and thus provides ideological justification for imperialist wars in the name of humanitarian intervention (Chandler, 2000). This anti-imperialist perspective argues that international institutions such as the United Nations and international norms such as the rule of law and human rights should be rejected as they advance imperialist rule (Anderson, 2002; Tariq Ali, 2003b). But a recognition of the one-sided ways in which imperialist powers may use these values and institutions is one thing, a wholesale rejection of such norms and organizations quite another.[6] For just as nation-states are sites of struggle, so too are institutions of global governance (Bartholomew & Breakspear, 2003). In the case of some of these institutions—particularly those relating to global economic governance such as the WTO—there may well be a case for abolition, but this cannot be assumed on the *a priori* grounds that such institutions are purely instruments of imperial rule. There is simply too much dissent at the UN for this to be the case, and an argument that blindly defends state sovereignty ignores difficult questions relating to the issue of genocide.[7] Indeed, given that a consistent and critical cosmopolitanism rules out unilateral enforcement of international norms, it can be used to *challenge* rather than reinforce imperialist rule.

Of course the UN is a far from perfect vehicle for addressing these issues, and it has at times been used by the US and other countries for its own ends. But it remains an important site of contestation within the global order. However, in keeping with the argument throughout this paper, and contrary to some interpretations of the cosmopolitan approach (see Kiely, 2004), it is also clear that globalizing resistance (either by working through or by rejecting institutions of global governance) is not on its own sufficient, and certainly no substitute for struggle within particular localities and within nation-states for a more progressive world order. Social struggles take place on many fronts, and a progressive politics that champions only local or national levels as opposed to global ones (anti-imperialism), or indeed which focus only on the global at the expense of local or national (Hardt & Negri (2000), liberal versions of cosmopolitanism), is bound to be limited.

Notes

1 My account of the 'new imperialism' is specifically applied to those, like Callinicos, who call for a relatively straightforward 'return to Lenin'. Recent attempts to rethink theories of imperialism, such as the essays in Panitch and Leys (2003), and Harvey (2003), are not explicitly addressed, although at times I draw on the arguments of the former (explicitly) to critique classical theories, and the latter (implicitly) to problematize state–capital relations.

2 Indeed, it is far from clear that the number of US military bases in the world is simply functional to capitalist expansion. There are too many cases of both high military commitments and low rates of US foreign investment, and low military commitments and high rates of US foreign investment, for a simplistic, unmediated relationship to be established (see the figures in Harris, 2003b, p. 5). This point is not made to completely sever the links between US capital and the US state (see the discussion of US deficits in section one above), but it is to problematize the use of simplistic assertions, such as the anti-imperialist left's use of right-winger Thomas Friedman's much cited, but very general, linking of the hidden hand of the global market and the hidden fist of the US military. This may be a useful rhetorical device, or even starting point for discussion, but is too often used to explain away particular wars such as those in Afghanistan and Iraq.

3 Indeed, earlier developers developed through state policies that protected domestic producers from foreign competition (Chang, 2002).

4 This is not to deny disagreements such as those over trade or even over the decision to go to war with Iraq in 2003. What I am questioning is the extent to which these reflect a repeat of nineteenth century inter-imperialist rivalry.

5 One anonymous reviewer for this article suggested that this point is so obvious one wonders why say it. Certainly one would hope it was obvious but it is not the position adopted by the Stop the War Coalition leadership in Britain. See also the brief discussion of Tariq Ali and Perry Anderson in the conclusion.

6 Indeed, this distinction is central to the cosmopolitan principle as employed even by 'soft' liberal democrats such as Held (2003), who opposed the wars in Afghanistan and Iraq (see also Archibugi, 2000).

7 Thus, the anti-imperialist left are fond of making the argument that 'the West' did not intervene in Rwanda because there was little economic interest in the country, as opposed to Iraq in 1990–91 and 2003. This may be true, but given the blanket non-intervention position of the anti-imperialist left, it is far from clear that it would have supported a campaign for a 'non-economic, non-self-interest based' intervention.

References

AFL-CIO (2000) Campaign for Global Fairness, www.aflcio.org/aboutaflcio.

Anderson, P. (2002) Force and consent, *New Left Review*, 17, pp. 5–30.

Archibugi, D. (2000) Cosmopolitical democracy, *New Left Review*, 4, pp. 137–150.

Archibugi, D., Ed. (2003) *Debating Cosmopolitics* (London: Verso).

Arrighi, G. (1994) *The Long Twentieth Century* (London: Verso).

Arrighi, G. (2003) The social and political economy of global turbulence, *New Left Review*, 20, pp. 5–71.

Bartholomew, A. & Breakspear, J. (2003) Human rights as swords of empire, pp. 125–145 in L. Panitch and C. Leys (Eds) *The Socialist Register 2004* (London: Merlin).

Becker, D., Frieden, J., Schatz, S. & Sklar R. (1987), *Postimperialism* (Boulder: Lynne Rienner).

Becker, D. & Sklar, R. (1987) Why postimperialism?, pp. 1–18 in Becker et al., *Postimperialism* (Boulder: Lynne Rienner).

Brecher, J., Costello, T. & Smith, B. (2000) *Globalization from Below* (Cambridge, MA: South End Press).

Brenner, R. (2003) Towards the precipice, *London Review of Books*, 25(3). Available at http://www.lrb.co.uk.

Bukharin, N. (1972) *Imperialism and World Economy* (London: Merlin).

Burbach, R. & Robinson, B. (1999) The fin de siecle debate: globalization as epochal shift, *Science and Society*, 63(1), pp. 10–39.

Burnham, (1997) Globalisation: states, markets and class relations, *Historical Materialism*, 1, pp. 150–160.

Callinicos, A. (2002) Marxism and global governance, pp. 249–266 in D. Held & A. McGrew (Eds) *Governing Globalization* (Cambridge: Polity).

Callinicos, A. (2003a) War under attack, *Socialist Review*, 273, pp. 12–13.

Callinicos, A. (2003b) The grand strategy of the American empire, *International Socialism*, 97, pp. 3–38.

Callinicos, A. et al. (1994) *Marxism and the New Imperialism* (London: Bookmarks).

Chandler, D. (2000) International justice, *New Left Review*, 6, pp. 55–66.

Chang, H.J. (2002) *Kicking Away the Ladder* (London: Anthem).

Chitty, A. (2002) Moralism, terrorism and war—response to Shaw, *Radical Philosophy*, 111, pp. 16–19.

Dicken, P. (2003) *Global Shift*, 4th edition (London: Sage).

Emmanuel, A. (1992) White settler colonialism and the myth of investment imperialism, *New Left Review*, 73, pp. 35–57.

Friedman, T. (1999) What the world needs now, *New York Times*, 28 March.

Giddens, A. (1999) *Runaway World* (Cambridge: Polity).

Gowan, P. (2001) Explaining the American boom: the roles of 'globalisation' and US global power, *New Political Economy*, 6(3), pp. 359–374.

Green, P. (2002) 'The passage from imperialism to empire': a commentary on *Empire* by Michael Hardt and Antonio Negri, *Historical Materialism*, 10(1), pp. 29–77.

Halliday, F. (2002) *Two Hours that Shook the World* (London: Saqi).

Halperin, S. & Laxer, G., Eds (2003) *Global Civil Society and its Limits* (London: Palgrave).

Hardt, M. (2002a) Today's Bandung, *New Left Review*, 14, pp. 112–118.

Hardt, M (2002b) Follies of our masters of the universe, *The Guardian*, December 18. Available at www.guardianunlimited.co.uk.

Hardt, M. & Negri, A. (2000) *Empire* (Cambridge, MA: Harvard University Press).

Hardt, M. & Negri, T. (2004) *Multitude* (Princeton: Princeton University Press).

Harman, C. (2000) Anti-capitalism: theory and practice, *International Socialism*, 88, pp. 3–59.

Harman, C. (2003) National liberation, in F. Reza (Ed) *Anti-Imperialism: A Guide for the Movement* (London: Bookmarks).

Harris, J. (2002) The US military in the era of globalisation, *Race and Class*, 44(2), pp. 1–22.

Harris, J. (2003a) Transnational competition and the end of US economic hegemony, *Science and Society*, 67(1), pp. 68–80.

Harris, J. (2003b) The military industrial complex in transnational class theory. Paper presented to GSA Conference, University of Surrey-Roehampton.

Harris, N. (2003) *The Rise of Cosmopolitan Capital* (London: I.B. Tauris).

Harvey, D. (2003) *The New Imperialism* (Oxford: Oxford University Press).

Held, D. (1996) *Democracy and the Global Order* (Cambridge: Polity).

Held, D. (2003) Violence, law and justice in a global age, pp. 184–202 in D. Archibugi (Ed) *Debating Cosmopolitics*, (London: Verso).

Held, D. & McGrew, T. (2002) *Globalization/Anti-Globalization* (Cambridge: Polity).

Held, D., McGrew, T., Goldblatt, D. & Perraton, J. (1999) *Global Transformations* (Cambridge: Polity).

Hilferding, R. (1981) *Finance Capital* (London: Routledge & Kegan Paul [first published 1910]).

Hirst, P. & Thompson, G. (1999) *Globalization in Question*, 2nd edition (Cambridge: Polity).

Islam, F. (2003) When two tribes go to war, *The Observer*, 22 June.

Jessop, B. (2002) *The Future of the Capitalist State* (Cambridge: Polity).

Kabeer, N. (2000) *The Power to Choose* (London: Verso).

Kautsky, K. (2002) Ultra-imperialism, *Workers Liberty*, 2(3), pp. 73–79 [first published 1914].

Kiely, R. (2004) Global civil society and spaces of resistance, pp. 138–153 in D. O'Byrne & J. Eade (Eds) *Global Ethics and Civil Society* (Aldershot: Ashgate).

Kiely, R. (2005) *The Clash of Globalisations: Neo-liberalism, the Third Way and Anti-Globalisation* (Leiden: Brill)

Klein, N. (2002) Reclaiming the commons, *New Left Review*, 9, pp. 81–89.

Lenin, V. (1975) *Imperialism: The Highest Stage of Capitalism* (Moscow: Progress [first published 1916]).

McMichael, P. (2001) Revisiting the question of the transnational state: a comment on William Robinson's 'Social theory and globalization', *Theory and Society*, 30, pp. 201–210.

Mertes, T. (2002) Grass-roots globalism, *New Left Review*, 17, pp. 101–110.

Monthly Review (2003), Editorial: what recovery?, 54(11), pp. 1–14

Morgan, P. (2003) Iraq, pp. 107–116 in F. Reza (Ed) *Anti-Imperialism: A Guide for the Movement* (London: Bookmarks).

Negri, T. & Zolo, D. (2003) Empire and the multitude, *Radical Philosophy*, 120, pp. 20–37.

Olle, W. & Schoeller, W. (1982) Direct investment and monopoly theories of imperialism, *Capital and Class*, 16, pp. 41–60.

Panitch, L. (2001) (with P. Gowan & M. Shaw) The state, globalization and the new imperialism: a roundtable discussion, *Historical Materialism*, 9, pp. 3–38.

Panitch, L. & Gindin, S. (2003) Global capitalism and American empire, pp. 1–42 in L. Panitch & C. Leys (Eds) *The Socialist Register 2004* (London: Merlin).

Panitch, L. & Leys, C., Eds (2003) *The Socialist Register 2004* (London: Merlin).

Peet, R. (2003) *Unholy Trinity: The IMF, World Bank and WTO* (London: Zed).

Petras, J. & Veltmeyer, H. (2001) *Globalization Unmasked* (London: Zed).

Project for the New American Century (1997) *Statement of Principles*. Available at http://www.newamericancentury.org.

Project for the New American Century (1998) *Letter to President Clinton on Iraq*. Available at http://www.newamericancentury.org.

RAWA (2001a) RAWA statement on the Terrorist Attacks in the US. Available at www.rawa.false.net.

RAWA (2001b) RAWA statement on the US strikes in Afghanistan. Available at www.rawa.false.net.

Rees, J. (2001) Imperialism: globalization, the state and war, *International Socialism*, 93, pp. 3–34.

Robinson, B. (2001a) Social theory and globalization: the rise of the transnational state, *Theory and Society*, 30, pp. 157–200.

Robinson, B. (2001b) Responses to McMichael, Block and Goldfrank, *Theory and Society*, 30, pp. 223–236.

Robinson, B. (2001/02) Global capitalism and nation-state-centric thinking—what we *don't* see when we *do* see nation-states: response to critics, *Science and Society*, 65(4), pp. 500–508.

Robinson, B. (2002) Capitalist globalization and the transnationalisation of the state, pp. 210–229 in M. Rupert & H. Smith (Eds) *Historical Materialism and Globalization* (London: Routledge).

Robinson, B. & Harris, J. (2000) Towards a global ruling class? Globalization and the transnational capitalist class, *Science and Society*, 64(1), pp. 11–54.

Ruigrok, W. & van Tulder, R. (1995) *The Logic of International Restructuring* (London: Routledge).

Sklair, L. (1991) *Sociology of the Global System* (London: Prentice Hall).

Sklair, L. (2001) *The Transnational Capitalist Class* (Oxford: Blackwell).

Spielberg, E. (1997) The myth of nimble fingers, pp. 113–122 in A. Ross (Ed) *No Sweat* (London: Verso).

Sutcliffe, B. & Glyn, A. (1999) Still underwhelmed: measures of globalization and their misinterpretation, *Review of Radical Political Economics*, 31(1), pp. 95–122.

Tariq Ali (2003a) Introduction, pp. 1–4 in F. Reza, *Anti-Imperialism: A Guide for the Movement* (London: Bookmarks).

Tariq Ali (2003b) Recolonising Iraq, *New Left Review*, 21, pp. 5–19.

Tomlinson, J. (2001) Vicious and benign universalism, pp. 45–59 in F. Schuurman (Ed) *Globalization and Development Studies* (London: Sage).

Toye, J. (2003) Order and justice in the international trade system, pp. 103–124 in M. Foot, J. Gaddis & A. Hurrell (Eds) *Order and Justice in International Relations* (Oxford: Oxford University Press).

UNCTAD (2002) *World Investment Report* (Geneva: UNCTAD).

Wade, R. (2003) The invisible hand of the American empire. Available at http://www.openDemocracy.net.

Warren, B. (1980) *Imperialism: Pioneer of Capitalism* (London: Verso).

Watson, M. (1999) Rethinking capital mobility, re-regulating financial markets, *New Political Economy*, 4(1), pp. 55–75.

Went, R. (2002/03) Globalization in the perspective of imperialism, *Science and Society*, 66(4), pp. 473–497.

World Social Forum (2001) Call of social movements. Available at http://www.forumsocialmundial.org.

Ray Kiely is Senior Lecturer in Development Studies at SOAS, University of London. His books include *The Clash of Globalisations* (Brill, 2005) and *Empire in the Age of Globalisation* (Pluto, forthcoming in 2005).

The Porto Alegre Consensus: Theorizing the Forum Movement

SCOTT C. BYRD

> One must speak for a struggle for a new culture, that is, for a new moral life that cannot but be intimately connected to a new intuition of life, until it becomes a new way of feeling and seeing reality.
>
> Antonio Gramsci (1985, p. 98)

Globalization describes what a number of people perceive as a fundamental change in the conditions of human life. Just what has changed and how it has changed, however, are matters of great contention—especially within the social movement community. From the vantage point of social movements, globalization offers contradictory possibilities. On the one hand, to the extent that globalization appears to reduce the ability of states to act within their own territories, social movements are dislocated from their usual position of petitioning states to redress grievances. The supposed weakness of states within the framework of globalization means that social movements must direct resources toward international institutional linkages, partnerships and coalitions that can diminish movement autonomy in the home country. On the other hand, globalization has provided social movements with new, possibly significant, opportunities and resources for influencing both state and non-state actors (Guidry et al., 2000). Globalization has in fact brought social movements together across borders in a 'transnational public sphere', a real as well as conceptual space in which movement actors interact, contest each other and their objectives, and learn from each other. Giddens (1994) describes this process as 'action at a distance', or the ability of actors in one place to influence events in other places through economic, political and media processes.

The World Social Forum (WSF), now in its fifth annual manifestation, represents such an opportunity for global, national and local movements to organize, network and struggle in solidarity under the banner 'another world is possible'.[1] The WSF first convened in January 2001 in Porto Alegre, Brazil at the same time as and in opposition to the World Economic Forum held in Davos, Switzerland.[2] The 'Forum movement' now encompasses many diverse thematic, regional and community gatherings throughout the Americas, Europe, Asia and Africa. The WSF's Charter of Principles states:

> The World Social Forum is an open meeting place for reflective thinking, democratic debate of ideas, formulation of proposals, free exchange of experiences and interlinking for effective action, by groups and movements of civil society that are opposed to neo-liberalism and to domination of the world by capital and any form of imperialism, and are committed to building a planetary society directed towards fruitful relationships among Humankind and between it and the Earth. (WSF, 2005a)

Houtart (2001) states that the WSF marks a turning point in social movement mobilization, a birth of a new political culture, in gestation for several years, manifesting as a search for alternatives to globalized capitalism and the neo-liberal model, as displayed at the World Economic Forum. The most recent 2005 WSF drew over 155,000 activists, Non-Governmental Organizations (NGO) campaigners, academics, journalists and trade unionists from more than 135 countries (WSF, 2005b). The WSF Charter of Principles goes on to claim that:

> The World Social Forum is a process that encourages its participant organizations and movements to situate their actions, from the local level to the national level and seeking active participation in international contexts, as issues of planetary citizenship, and to introduce onto the global agenda the change-inducing practices that they are experimenting in building a new world in solidarity. (WSF, 2005a)

The Forum's Charter of Principles creates a methodology or process for creating open gathering spaces for social movements from around the world to incubate projects and alternatives to economic globalization. Although many of the participants and activists refer to the Forum as if it were a new political agent, the authors[3] go out of their way to acknowledge that it is not a political agent.

> The World Social Forum is also characterized by plurality and diversity, is non-confessional, non-governmental and non-party. It proposes to facilitate decentralized coordination and networking among organizations engaged in concrete action towards building another world, at any level from the local to the international, but it does not intend to be a body representing world civil society. (WSF, 2005a)

The authors of the WSF have discouraged any interpretation of it as a deliberative body or institution. They have instead focused on the Forum as a pedagogical space for activists and organizers to learn what alternatives are being proposed and enacted around the globe. However, clearly the WSF has acted as a political space by giving activists an arena in which to network and develop common projects. The Forum was instrumental in organizing Brazilian social movements and NGOs to support and help elect Lula da Silva, a former radical union leader and member of Brazil's Workers Party, to that country's Presidency in October of 2002. During the third WSF, organizers from European peace groups used the opportunity to double the number of countries participating in their scheduled 15 February 2003 (F15) global rally for peace against the threat of war in Iraqi (Frankel, 2003). Many WSF themes, such as debt relief, socially responsible investment, and the idea of a more equitable globalization which have been discussed since the Forum's inception, are now gaining legitimacy with global economic powers, and have been taken up at the most recent World Economic Forum.

Debate between Forums[4] serving as political agent versus open space for exchange and movement building is one of the most contentious between more liberal interpreters of the Forum's Charter of Principles and its stricter adherents. This tension came to a head during the 2005 WSF when 19 'high-profile' intellectuals produced a 12-point 'Porto Alegre Manifesto'. The individuals (labeled the G-19) called on other participants at the Forum to sign-on to the list of proposals even though they had no participation in the creation of the document. The document outlined many of the main themes discussed at the 2005 WSF, including such items as debt cancellation, adoption of the Tobin tax on international financial transfers, promotion of equitable forms of trade, anti-discrimination policies for minorities and women, and democratization of international organizations (Anthony & Silva, 2005). For many at the Forum the list of policy statements signaled an attempt to produce a political platform for a gathering whose founding Charter of Principles disallows it. One of the original founders of the WSF Candido Grzybowski commented that: 'What kills this proposal is the method with which it was created and presented. It goes against the very spirit of the Forum. Here, all proposals are equally important and not only that of a group of intellectuals, even when they are very significant persons' (TerraViva, 2005, p. 1). The strength of the Forums seems to lie in the process by which decentralized coordination and networking among organizations is carried out, and not the policies advocated in the name of the Forum. Even though specific actions or policies are endorsed at the Forums they are proposed and promoted by organizations which are in attendance and not by individuals representing the Forums at large. This methodology produces a stabilizing framework where diverse organizations and issues may be discussed without the need to construct overarching policy platforms.

The WSF proved effective in bringing together all the different feelings and currents of thought that have come to comprise this rich and heterogeneous global justice movement now taking shape at the international level, and which has become highly visible since the mass protests against the World Trade Organization (WTO) in Seattle (Smith, 2004). The period beginning after 1999 was a new epoch in which worker's struggles, 'new social movements' of the north, and a new group of young activists (anarchists, anti-sweatshop, anti-biotech, peace and human rights movements) have come together via an interrelated set of efforts. The Zapitista uprising in Chiapas in 1994, protests in Seattle against the WTO in 1999, subsequent demonstrations against the perceived agents of corporate globalization in Washington DC, Melbourne, Prague, Gothenburg, Quebec City, and Genoa, and creation of the World Social Forum, coalesced to create a new diaspora of global contention (Fisher & Ponniah, 2003). Furthermore, the Forum movement has made clear its adversary all along to be the neo-liberal capitalist model

(WSF, 2005a) also known as the 'Washington Consensus' (Williamson, 1990) promoted by what Sklair (2002) and Robinson (2004) refer to as the transnational capitalist class. Thus, the intention of Forum authors from the beginning was to create a method of open, informal and decentralized organizing which countered the formal, top-down, closed-door characteristics of globalized capitalism adeptly displayed at the World Economic Forum.

Global Civil Society and the Porto Alegre Process

My intention in this article is to outline what I contend to be an emergent bottom-up model for reconstituting global civil society (GCS) that proves to be adaptive, decentralized and openly democratic. I also hope to continue the theoretical dialogue begun by many other authors in recent years.[5] This developing reflexive and mutually responsive process guiding the Forums' development through its many manifestations around the globe I describe here as the 'Porto Alegre Consensus'.[6] This consensus is not a list of policy issues or action plans but instead an agreed-upon set of methods by those attending the Forums serving to guide the process by which this 'globalization from below' expands and is reconstituted to meet the threat posed by the global neo-liberal capitalism. Whereas the Washington Consensus guides economic policies such as deregulation, privatization, liberalization, fiscal discipline, tax reform and property rights to encourage rapid economic growth of the global economy (Williamson, 1990), the Porto Alegre Consensus serves to thicken linkages between GCS actors, liberate communicative action, and horizontally integrate the struggle for global social justice.

More importantly, solidarity at the Forums is achieved through discursive frameworks with earnest respect for gender, cultural identity and diversity. Communicative openness originates from the desire to create a true transnational public sphere where ideas, resources and strategies are openly exchanged along self-transforming networks, and authority and power is diffused across movements and organizations establishing participatory decision-making structures. This new recipe for GCS did not originate by chance but is the outcome of careful planning by the Forum's original authors through adoption of the WSF Charter of Principles in 2001 and the willingness to host the Forums in Porto Alegre until the methodology matured and gained popular acceptance.

For an increasing number of theorists, GCS represents nothing less than the outline of a future world political and global governance framework. Keane (2003) describes GCS as a dynamic non-governmental system of interconnected socio-economic institutions that straddle the whole earth, and that have complex effects that are felt in its four corners. It is an unfinished project that consists of sometimes thick, sometimes thinly stretched networks, pyramids and hub-and-spoke clusters of organizations and actors who organize themselves across borders, with the deliberate aim of drawing the world together in new ways. Richard Falk (1995, p. 100) suggests that GCS recasts our understanding of sovereignty as 'the modernist stress on territorial sovereignty as the exclusive basis for political community and identity is displaced both by more local and distinct groupings and by association with the reality of a GCS without boundaries'. Lipschutz and Mayer (1996, p. 391) sees transnational political networks put in place by actors in civil society as 'challenging, from below, the nation-state system', and 'the growth of GCS representing and ongoing project of civil society to reconstruct, re-imagine, and re-map world politics'. Martinelli (2004) describes a similar model of global civil society that includes three basic principles of authority, exchange and solidarity alongside pluralistic and diverse strategies and methods acting as mechanisms for social integration. Taken together, representations of GCS portray a dynamic network of non-governmental organizations from the global to the grassroots, employing a diversity of methods and tactics, and that are in some cases intent on restructuring and in others reforming the mechanisms of global governance. In the following I hope to expand on these three basic principles of exchange, authority and solidarity in order to provide a framework for theoretical discourse regarding the Forums' methodology, development and popular engagement throughout the world.

Transnational Public Spheres and Open Exchange

This 'action at a distance', which Giddens (1994) refers to, does not actually occur from a distance. This action originates somewhere, proceeds through specific channels, does something, and has concrete effects in particular places (Guidry et al., 2000). That action is, however, mediated by discursive relationships that are forged through transnational public spheres. Transnational public spheres create the space for communicative action, tactical exchange, organizational networking, and resource conduits. Jurgen Habermas' ([1962], 1989) account of the bourgeois public sphere was meant to identify a new kind of space in which rational critical discussion by citizens, rather than sheer economic logic or the instrumentalities of state power, could assist in the formation of state policies and civil, political and social rights. Thirty years later, he still finds the public sphere very influential, noting that the bourgeois public sphere carried its own potential for self-transformation (Habermas, 1992). He also recognizes its transnational potential, invoking the 1989 demonstrations that brought down communism, although he admits that the demonstrations achieved their objectives only by being broadcast on global television networks that are themselves guided by principles other than those defining the democratic potentials of the public sphere. Regardless of its correspondence to communicative rationality with which Habermas is concerned, this notion of a potentially transnational public sphere has nonetheless become a critical element in the constitution of globalization and the role of social movements in it.

The consequence of this transnational public sphere is not simply its own development but, like globalization, it involves 'actions at a distance' that must be understood in terms of its consequences for real people and their struggles, all of whom occupy specific places and communities. That is, the transnational public sphere is realized in various localized applications and discourses, potentially quite distant from the original production of the discourse or practice in question. These transnational public spheres offer a place where forms of organizational networking and tactics for collective action can be transmitted across the globe. It is the medium through which various forms of collective action and social movement practices become 'modular' and transferable to distant locations and causes (Tarrow, 1994). It also provides the space where material resources can be developed and distributed across national boundaries in ways which limit the nation-state's capacity to sanctify and demonize the practices with claims of patriotism and alien influence. Noteworthy examples of this process are provided by Ball (2000) and Keck and Sikkink (1998) regarding the spread of human rights ideologies and movements throughout the global conduit created by the transnational public sphere. Keck and Sikkink (1998) also illustrate the potential for transnational mobilizing structures with their discussion of the 'boomerang effect', in which national and international human rights organizations bypass the target states and rely on international pressure from other states and the transnational human rights movement to help accomplish goals in a specific area. The WSF process provides a global mobilizing structure that serves to network organizations from the grassroots to the transnational providing an amplifying sphere to air grievances, gain access to power structures and resource pools.

The transnational public sphere has experienced rapid expansion due to the recent advances in technologies such as high-speed computers, information technologies, and open-source software (Castells, 2000; Bohman, 2004). The Internet has proved to be the global conduit where movement strategies and tactics may be shared and observed, mobilization alerts travel in real-time, and resources can be collected and dispersed to any point in the world (evident from 2004 Asian tsunami relief efforts). The 2005 WSF focused thematic discussions on the use and distribution of open source software and recycled computer systems for civil society organizations. All of the 1,000 computers used at the 2005 WSF employed open source software developed in open source language. A good part of the 2005 budget was also dedicated to helping manufactures of open communication systems (Milan, 2005). The 2005 edition also offered a new free translation system, and more than 400 panels and workshops were transmitted live online, permitting virtual participation around the world. The promotion of open source software such as Linux operating systems, open communication systems, and organizations like Creative Commons, which provides a flexible copyright framework, reflects the Forum's search for functional alternatives and models for a better, more open world. The idea of the transnational public sphere allows us to conceptualize these advances in terms of offering greater access to a global communication and mobilization framework that does not depend on corporations or developed countries for its future development and maintenance.

Discursive Frameworks and Opportunity Structures

The World Social Forums are attempting to create a discursive framework where collective decisions can be made inclusively alongside the heterogeneous concerns of various cultures and identities as well as local, national, and international interests. At the 2005 Forum one could find a vibrant assortment of workshops and panels from participatory budget planning introduced by the Workers' Party in Porto Alegre, to resistance of inequitable free trade agreements, and lectures on sustainable agriculture and genetically altered crops. Some of the 11 thematic spaces at WSF 2005 were: defending Earth and the people's common goods—as an alternative to mercantilism and control by transnational corporations; defending diversity, plurality and identities; communication; anti-hegemonic practices, rights and alternatives; social struggles and democratic alternatives—against neo-liberal domination, and towards construction of international democratic order and integration of peoples (WSF, 2005a). These themes were selected by open consultation through participation of 1,863 organizations posting what they planned to discuss during the forum on a website (WSF, 2005c). This process was promoted as a way to make the thematic decisions more democratic while maintaining the events diversity and transforming it into a space that is increasingly capable of facilitating linkages and common actions among participants.

While meetings at the World Economic Forum, UN, WTO and other global institutions are often closed and maintain top-down hierarchies, the WSF promotes a transparent organizing structure for its events. All workshops, seminars, round tables, panel discussions and testimonials are openly posted and participants are free to attend whichever event they want. There is no separate entrance for different delegates, no excessive scrutiny as one enters a certain venue. The WSF does not have a draft agreement text to be negotiated. Instead, different groups can come up with different statements on different issues, thus respecting diversity and pluralism. An enormous number of workshops and working groups organized by the participating social movements and organizations are used as opportunities for encounters and exchanges, to spread information on the different national experiences of resistance to neoliberal policies, and for coordination of efforts and activities with an eye on the future. Chico Whitaker, one of the original authors of the Forums describes this process:

> The Forum opens from time to time in different parts of the world—in the events where it takes place—with one specific objective: to allow as many individuals, organizations, and movements as possible that oppose neoliberalism to get together freely, listen to each other, learn from experiences and struggles of others, and discuss proposals for action; to become linked in new nets and organizations aiming at overcoming the present process of globalization dominated be large international corporations and their financial interests. (Whitaker, 2003, p. 1)

The openness of the discourse during the sessions produces a framework that is very inviting and non-threatening to individuals and organizations with different backgrounds, tactics and cultures.

Fisher and Ponniah's (2003) analysis of the documents from the 2002 WSF reveal these differences among the various networks within the participants as well as areas of convergence. They draw attention to five significant debates: revolution vs. reform; environment vs. economy; human rights or protectionism; the universality of values; and the debate between the local, national and global issues and positions. Despite the differences, several areas of agreement including the perception of a common adversity unify the movements. The perception is that corporate domination has been organized across global space by the most powerful northern states in the world in collaboration with economic and political elites from the southern states. Simultaneously, this expansion is occurring in conjunction with the suppression of political, economic, cultural, racial, gendered, sexual, ecological and epistemological differences. The documents acknowledge the striking aspect of the current form of globalization is its capacity to reproduce, rearticulate, and compound traditionally oppressive social hierarchies. Many of the participants and facilitators view neo-liberal globalization as not simply economic domination of the world but also the imposition of monolithic thought constructs, that consolidate vertical forms of difference and prohibit the public from imagining diversity in egalitarian, horizontal terms. Capitalism, imperialism, mono-culturalism, patriarchy, white supremacy and the domination of biodiversity have coalesced under the current form of globalization and constitute the primary challenge of the movements represented in the WSF conference documents. Thus, the discursive frameworks and public spheres created by the WSF authors and organizers have allowed participants to find commonality in their grievances as well as discover differences in their epistemologies and tactics in order to ultimately build larger networks of contention, which are culturally and conceptually diverse.

Conceiving globalization as producing new opportunity structures for social movements such as with the World Social Forums allows us to examine movements within important frameworks that are already highly developed in social movement theory. A 'political opportunity structure' is the way in which present allocations of resources and power privilege some alternatives for collective action while raising the cost of others. The political opportunity model allows us to conceptualize both social movements within globalization and vice versa, since we can conceptualize the latter either as an independent or dependent variable in movement analysis (McAdam, 1996). Thus, movements can both be affected by and transform political opportunity structures. The flexibility afforded by such a perspective opens up the possibility for analysis of the discursive, mutually transforming relationships between states and societies (Migdal et al., 1994). Both the developing idea of the Forums as transnational public sphere as well as a structure from greater political opportunity brings us to the analysis of the Forums' organizational structure and democratic systems.

Authority, Power and the Forums' Organization

Regarding global democratization and the building of a global civil society, the World Social Forums can be looked at from two angles. On the one hand, it can be analyzed as an example of an emerging institution that may embody seeds of global democracy. From this perspective, it is particularly important to look at organizational design and the way decision-making structures function. From another angle, it provides a space for actors who may construct democratic projects in different contexts, both local and global, to transfer those modular templates anywhere on the planet. Among its organizers and participants there have been different approaches towards emphasizing these different identities of the WSF that are by no means incompatible (Teivainen, 2002). The formal decision-making power of the Forum process has been mainly in the hands of the Organizing Committee, consisting since its beginning of the Central Trade Union Confederation (Central Única dos Trabalhadores—CUT), the Movement of Landless Rural Workers (Movimento dos Trabalhadores Rurais Sem Terra—MST) and six smaller Brazilian social movement organizations (SMOs). In response to what many claimed was a lack of transparency and democracy, repetition of dialogue, and political disparities between large and small organizations and feedback received from the Mumbai Organizing Committee, the 2005 WSF bought changes in its methodology and decision-making structures. Forum authors and organizers took the risk of allowing the Forums' methodology to be self-managed by its participants by asking them how they wanted the Forums to progress and develop (WSF, 2005c; Caramel, 2005). Furthermore, the WSF has claimed all along to have no centralized leadership, no position of power. There is no hierarchy or reporting structure within the WSF. All participants, as long as they neither advocate nor use violence, can take part in discussions about finding alternatives to the capitalist model for globalization. The World Social Forums also do not make decisions on courses of action that are binding on those who attend its meetings (Fisher & Ponniah, 2003). The underlying assumption in this method is that the Forums do not represent a deliberative body or actor that would take political stands and thereby need rigorous decision-making procedures.

The media has tended to look at the WSF as a political actor in itself, though many of the organizers have wanted to downplay this role and argue that they simply provide a space for different groups to interact (Solomon, 2001). These different conceptions of the event have clashed, for example, when the media has asked for 'final declarations' and considered the lack of any such final document a proof of weakness in the organizational structure. The unwillingness to formulate political statements, beyond the Charter of Principles drafted in 2001, is occasionally questioned among some organizers and related actors who would like to see the WSF as an organization expressing opinions on certain issues, such as the war in Iraq, and crises in the Palestinian Territories, Haiti and Darfur.

Even if it is not clear whether the WSF will become a more active political entity with more explicit internal will-formation mechanisms, it is obvious that until now the most important impact of the Forums on democratic projects has consisted of the myriad encounters between different groups and activists within its confines (Teivainen, 2002). In the final assessment, the Forums' informal organizational frameworks and decentralized forms of authority serve to make it one of the most promising civil society processes that may both contribute significantly to global democratization initiatives and work to constitute such an initiative in itself. The enthusiasm it has generated around the world will also bring it various dilemmas. Conceived as a civil society initiative, the Forum movement has had NGOs, grassroots organizations, party structures and trade unions proposing different forms of cooperation. Such was the dispute at the

2004 European Social Forum between the 'horizontals' and the 'verticals' (Osterweil, 2004). Some organizers may emphasize the importance of clinging to strictly defined civil society partners, others are likely to have more pragmatic positions on obtaining material and political support. These decisions will work to shape the future of the Forums and may have significant effects on the organizational and leadership structures. On the other hand, many have questioned formal and organizational problems they believe make it an undemocratic space:

> These problems include a lack of transparency in decision making, hierarchical organization, as well as special treatment of celebrities and the creation of elitist tiers that privilege the more well known and consolidated components of the movement over many of the smaller and more grassroots and perhaps more radical organizations. A number of people have also criticized what they consider to be the privileging and co-optation of the forum by institutionalized political structures like political parties, trade unions, and mainstream NGOs that, in addition to being hierarchical organizations themselves, tend to be reformist or social democrat in their philosophy. This is seen as integrally related to the lack of transparency and democracy within the Forum Structure. (Osterweil, 2003, p.184)

There has also been concern over sponsoring organizations at the Forums such as the Ford Foundation, and PetroBras, Brazil's state-owned petroleum company. Many of the organizers understand that to make the Forums sustainable and actionable they must risk partnering with strange bedfellows, but is not always easy to see the differences between 'alternative' globalization proposals with the idea of many business leaders being involved in the process, and the prospect of another, better world without their influence. This is an inherent difficulty that cosmopolitan theorists have faced in developing their mechanisms for civil society organizations and grassroots movements to influence policy and achieve agency within this hierarchy of transnational corporations and state institutions.

In perhaps the best known of such models from David Held (1995), GCS organizations provide the space for transnational public spheres which, taken together, operate as a basis for dispersed sovereignty in a system of global governance, generate critical resources directed towards the institutional power required by such governance and provide opportunities for voluntary association at the 'local' level. Nevertheless, civil society is by no means self-governing in Held's model, being constrained within a wider framework of cosmopolitan democratic law that 'delimits the form and scope of individual and collective action within the organizations of state and civil society. Certain standards are specified, which no political regime or civil association can legitimately violate' (Held, 1993, p. 43). Of course, for this cosmopolitan democratic law to have any authority, transnational sovereign institutions are required, though Held imagines these also being constrained by such a law, particularly by the principle of subsidiarity or the dispersal of sovereignty, but also through ensuring that these are representative global institutions (Baker, 2002). Held summarizes his model as involving the call for a double-sided process of democratization in both political and civil society. Thus, although Held sees civil society as one of the agents of democratic global governance, it is as much acted upon as actor, object as well as subject of his cosmopolitan democracy. This feature is mirrored in the theory of other cosmopolitan democrats. Archibugi (1998, p. 219), for instance, wants GCS to participate 'in political decision making through new permanent institutions', but then states that such institutions 'would supplement but not replace existing intergovernmental organizations. Their function would be essentially advisory and not executive', which points to agency as a crucial element missing from cosmopolitan democrats' theories of GCS.

Falk illustrates this hope in the agency of GCS with his call for 'globalization from below' through the activities of transnational social movements. 'Globalization from below', such as displayed at the Forums, is seen as an alternative to the hegemonic 'globalization from above' imposed by transnational capitalist elites through a worldwide normative network premised not on human rights but on the rights of capital flow, multinational corporations, and 'liberalized' markets. For Falk there can be a democratic global normative framework or 'law of humanity'. Yet unlike Held, with his weak notion of agency, Falk sees GCS as the only means to this humane law—'as the hopeful source of political agency needed to free the minds of persons from an acceptance of state/sovereign identity' (Falk, 1995, p.101). Furthermore, such global governance, contrary to Held who seeks to achieve it 'from above' from 'cosmopolitan law', must be built 'from the ground up' and continue to be anchored in GCS itself (Baker, 2002). This universality 'from below' is also sought by Paul Ghils, who wonders whether the 'universality of action in association' makes 'civil society and its transnational networks of associations the *universam* which competing nations have never succeeded in creating' (Ghils, 1992, p. 429). Thus, from this perspective, the Forum movement could represent nothing less than the outline of a future world political and global governance framework. There is this continuing 'framework of rights' involved in instances where WSF process is invoked from the 'bottom-up' and the cosmopolitan perspective informs our understanding of these mechanisms, and indicates that this facet of the Forums process is essential to the future evolution of global democratic structures.

Methodology, Consensus and Movement Solidarity

I describe the Porto Alegre consensus as a set of agreed-upon methodologies serving to guide the process by which the World Social Forums and the Forum movement thickens the linkages between GCS actors, liberates communicative action, and horizontally integrates the struggle for global social justice. This consensus is not a list of policy demands or actions plans, but a self-adapting process partly laid out in the Forums' Charter of Principles, but, more importantly, interpreted and renegotiated by the many participants engaged in the process and the many different manifestations of the Forum all over the world. The discursive frameworks, communicative openness, and participatory decision-making structures established by the process not only allow organizations and activists to share strategies and projects, amplify political frames, and build solidarity, it also serves to stabilize the global social justice movements and GCS (Chesters, 2003). Chesters describes the Forum gatherings as 'Plateaus' or moments of intensive network stabilization where formulation and shaping of political projects, strategic and tactical reflection, construction of alternative means of communication and information exchange, and development of mechanisms for the expression of solidarity and mutual aid may be achieved. This stabilizing process may help explain the Forums' success in drawing large audiences and the motivation behind its continuance, but can methodology actually drive a global movement? If so, then it will certainly influence the way in which we conceive of global transnational movements.

Though my theoretical dialogue covered the landscape of transnational public spheres, political opportunity structures and cosmopolitan democracies, there are other theories that may inform activist and scholarly understanding of the Forum movement. More importantly, there is the question of praxis. What does the Forums' process mean for the over a quarter of the planet's population who struggle daily in abject poverty, and will the Forums' panels, workshops, and cultural gatherings actually produce an alternative globalization that is better than the one we have now? If the Forums prove to be a powerful mechanism for struggle that works to improve the livelihood of oppressed peoples, and creates practical alternatives to global capitalism that begin to balance geopolitical power relations then the process will be legitimated. Unfortunately, there is no concrete framework for evaluating such questions. The Forums seem to operate on more of a qualitative system of relationships and encounters rather than a procedure that gives rise to clear empirical data points. Consequently, this questions the Forums' ability to self-manage its own evolution without established reflexive systems built into the process.

Although the World Social Forum may be the most promising embodiment of GCS to emerge in the modern world, the challenges and tasks before it are daunting.[7] The plethora of critiques leveled against the Forum process include: the lack of transparency and democratic decision-making; the gatherings are too big and chaotic; lack of direction or final declarations; too centralized and commodified (Sen, 2003). In North America, home of the Washington Consensus, the Forum process has had a rather tough go of it. The Boston Social Forum held in August 2004 drew about 5,000 participants and, although a success by the organizers' standards, was also perceived as being a gathering of the usual white, affluent activists (Berkshire, 2004) poised to protest the Democratic National Convention occurring the next week. The Northwest Forum that was to be held in Seattle during the autumn of 2004 fell apart due to a breakdown of the planning process which left the Indigenous Programming Committee and Youth Planning Committee pulling out at the last minute (NWSF, 2005). Though a setback, the organizers of the Northwest Forum admit that their experience was an opportunity that may ultimately bring the organizations together to work out their differences and commit to greater coordination in the future. In the final calculus, the Forum process requires activists and organizations to be introspective and assess their own biases towards power and control, movement strategies and tactics, and intra-movement networking and collaboration. This may be one of the most overlooked characteristics of the Forums, its ability to provide movements and organizations the opportunity to become more open, equitable and democratic.

The 2006 Forums will be 'spread out' across the globe, in Asia, Africa, Europe and the Americas, providing yet another concrete possibility to give the process a better geographical and cultural balance while integrating transnational networks of contention. This will also give scholars, organizers and activists an opportunity to refine their assessments and critiques of the Forums. The reflexive process between Forum incarnations and the participatory assessment and corresponding revisions of Forum methodology is at the heart of the Porto Alegre Consensus. This dance between theory and practice is crucial to the role that the Forums play in reconstituting global civil society and within the possibility that exists of constructing future alternative globalizations which are more just, equitable and sustainable.

Acknowledgements

This article was adapted from a paper presented at the North America Global Studies Association Conference, 22 April 2004 at Brandeis University, Waltham, MA, USA. During revision I added content regarding the 2004 and 2005 WSF process.

Notes

1   The World Social Forum 'slogan' from the first World Social Forum in 2001. I interpret the phrase to represent the hope and possibility of building other more just and equitable forms of globalization.

2   The World Economic Forum is generally accepted to be a meeting of global business, industry, and governmental leaders whose aim is to define global economic strategies and policies. From the World Economic Forum's website

(www.weforum.org): The World Economic Forum is an independent international organization committed to improving the state of the world. The Forum provides a collaborative framework for the world's leaders to address global issues, engaging particularly its corporate members in global citizenship.

3   I use the term 'author' to refer to those activists responsible for 'authoring' the Forum's original Charter of Principles. This term is separate from Forum organizer, which I use to describe someone who interprets and facilitates the Forum process.

4   I use 'Forums' to describe the many thematic and regional manifestations of the Forum movement since its inception from Europe to Africa and the community Forums in Italy. I use Forum to represent the annual World Social Forum or the original 2001 Forum held in Porto Alegre, Brazil.

5   Literature on the Forums both popular and academic has grown exponentially in recent years. The breadth of ideas and critiques represented in these pieces is well beyond the scope of this article. I would at least like to recommend the online text *Challenging Empires* located at: http://www.choike.org/nuevo_eng/informes/1557.html, and the special issue of the *International Social Science Journal*, 56(182) on 'cultures of politics' and the Forums.

6   Bernard Cassen, one of the original founders of the Forum, first put forth the hope of a Porto Alegre Consensus challenging and if not eventually replacing the Washington Consensus.

7   Again, to summarize all of the critiques of the Forums in limited space would not do them justice. Please see texts from note 5 above as well as Sen (2003) and Smith (2004).

References

Anthony, D. & Silva, J. A. (2005) World Social Forum: the consensus of Porto Alegre?, 30 January. Available at http://www.ipsterraviva.net/TV/WSF2005/viewstory.asp?idnews=153.

Archibugi, D. (1998) Principles of cosmopolitan democracy, in D. Archibugi, D. Held & M. Köhler (Eds) *Reimagining Political Community* (Cambridge: Polity).

Baker, G. (2002) Problems in the theorisation of global civil society, *Political Studies*, 50, pp. 928–943.

Ball, P. (2000) State terror, constitutional traditions, and national human rights movements: a cross-national quantitative comparison, in J. Guidry, M. Kennedy & M. Zald (Eds) *Globalizations and Social Movements: Culture, Power, and the Transnational Public Sphere* (Ann Arbor: University of Michigan Press).

Berkshire, J. C. (2004) A social occasion, *The Nation Online*, 29 July. Available at http://www.thenation.com/doc.mhtml?i=20040816&s=berkshire.

Bohman, J. (2004) Expanding dialogue: the Internet, the public sphere and prospects for global democracy, in: N. Crossley & J. M. Roberts (Eds) *After Habermas: New Perspectives on the Public Sphere* (Malden, MA: Blackwell).

Caramel, L. (2005) World Social Forum activists reorganize to face critics, *Le Monde*, 25 January. Available at http://www.truthout.org/docs_05/printer_012605H.shtml.

Castells, M. (2000) *The Network Society* (Malden, MA: Blackwell).

Chesters, G. (2003) Shape shifting: civil society, complexity and social movements, *Anarchist Studies*, 11(1), pp. 42–65.

Falk, R. (1995) *On Humane Governance: Towards a New Global Politics* (Pennsylvania, PA: Pennsylvania University Press).

Fisher, W. F. & Ponniah, T., Eds (2003) *Another World is Possible: Popular Alternatives to Globalization at the World Social Forum* (London: Zed Books).

Frankel, G. (2003) Organizers of antiwar movement plan to go beyond protests, *Washington Post*, 3 March.

Ghils, P. (1992) International civil society: international non-governmental organizations in the international system, *International Social Science Journal*, 133, pp. 417–431.

Giddens, A. (1994). *Beyond Left and Right: The Future of Radical Politics* (Cambridge: Polity Press).

Gramsci, A. (1985) *Selections from Cultural Writings*, David Forgacs and Geaffrey Nowell-Smith (Eds) (Cambridge, MA: Harvard University Press).

Guidry, J.A., Kennedy, M.D. & Zald, M.N. (2000) Globalizations and social movements, in: J. Guidry, M. Kennedy & M. Zald (Eds) *Globalizations and Social Movements: Culture, Power, and the Transnational Public Sphere* (Ann Arbor: University of Michigan Press).

Habermas, J. ([1962]1989) *The Structural Transformation of the Public Sphere: And Inquiry into a Category of Bourgeois Society* (Cambridge, MA: MIT Press).

Habermas, J. (1992) Further reflections on the public sphere, in C. Calhoun (Ed) *Habermas and the Public Sphere* (Cambridge, MA: MIT Press).

Held, D. (1993) Democracy: from city-states to a cosmopolitan order?, in D. Held (Ed) *Prospects for Democracy* (Cambridge: Polity Press).

Held, D. (1995) *Democracy and the Global Order: From the Modern State to Cosmopolitan Governance* (Cambridge: Polity).

Houtart, F. & Polet, F., Eds. (2001) *The Other Davos: The Globalization of Resistance to the World Economic System* (London: Zed Books).

Keane, J. (2003) *Global Civil Society?* (Cambridge: Cambridge University Press).

Keck, M. & Sikkink, K. (1998) *Activists beyond Borders: Advocacy Networks in International Politics* (Ithaca, NY: Cornell University Press).

Lipshutz, R. & Mayer, J. (1996) *Global Civil Society and Global Environmental Governance. The Politics of Nature from Place to Planet* (Albany, NY: State University of New York Press).

Martinelli, A. (2004) *From World System to World Society*. Available at http://www.sociologistswithoutborders.org/documents/FROMWORLDSYSTEM_TOWORLDSOCIETY_000.PDF.

McAdam, D. (1996) Conceptual origins, current problems, future directions, in D. McAdam, J. McCarthy & M. Zald (Eds) *Comparative Perspectives on Social Movements: Political Opportunities, Mobilizing Structures and Cultural Framings* (Cambridge: Cambridge University Press).

Migdal, J. S., Kohli, A. & Shue, V. (1994) *State Power and Social Forces* (Cambridge: Cambridge University Press).

Milan, S. (2005) World Social Forum: open systems for open politics, 26 January. Available at http://www.ipsnews.net/interna.asp?idnews=27175.

Northwest Social Forum, NWSF (2005) Statement of the Planning Committee of the Northwest Social Forum. Available at: http://www.nwsocialforum.org/.

Osterweil, M. (2003) De-centering the Forum: is another critique of the Forum possible?, in J. Sen, A. Anand, A. Escobar & P. Waterman (Eds) *The World Social Forum: Challenging Empires*. Available at http://www.choike.org/nuevo_eng/informes/1557.html.

Osterweil, M. (2004) A cultural-political approach to reinventing the political, *International Social Science Journal*, 56(182), pp. 495–507.

Robinson, W. I. (2004) *A Theory of Global Capitalism: Production, Class, and State in a Transnational World* (Baltimore, MD: Johns Hopkins University Press).

Sen, J. (2003) How open? The challenge of dogma, the forum as logo, the forum as religion: skepticism of the intellect, optimism of the will. Available at http://www.choike.org/documentos/how_open.pdf.

Sklair, L. (2002) *Globalization, Capitalism and its Alternatives* (Oxford: Oxford University Press).

Smith, J. (2004) The World Social Forum and the challenges of global democracy, *Global Networks*, 4(4), pp. 413–421.

Solomon, N. (2001) A different world is possible: Porto Alegre vs. the corporate media, *Socialism and Democracy*, 15(2), pp. 25–39.

Tarrow, S. (1994) *Power in Movement: Social Movements, Collective Action, and Politics* (New York: Cambridge University Press).

Teivainen, T. (2002) *The World Social Forum and global democratization: learning from Porto Alegre, Third World Quarterly*, 23(4), pp. 621–632.

TerraViva (2005) A divisive consensus, 31 January. Available at http://www.ipsterraviva.net/tv/wsf2005/viewstory.asp?idnews = 179.

Williamson, J., Ed (1990) *Latin American Adjustment: How Much Has Happened?* (Washington, DC: Institute for International Economics).

Whitaker, C. (2003) Notes about the World Social Forum, 14 April. Available at http://www.forumsocialmundial.org.br/dinamic.php?pagina=bal_whitaker_ing.

World Social Forum (2005a) Charter of Principles. Available at http://www.forumsocialmundial.org.br/main.php?id_menu=4&cd_language=2.

World Social Forum (2005b) The fifth WSF in the balance. Available at http://www.forumsocialmundial.org.br/noticias_01.php?cd_news=1709&cd_language=2.

World Social Forum (2005c) Methodology of 2005. Available at http://www.forumsocialmundial.org.br/main.php?id_menu=5_4&cd_language=2.

Scott Byrd is a graduate student in the department of Sociology at the University of California, Irvine in the United States. He researches and writes on issues of global governance, international development, alternative globalization movements, and self-organizing activist networks. His thesis research was conducted throughout Brazil interviewing authors, organizers and activists involved in the World Social Forums' process.

The New Imperial Conjuncture and Alternative Futures for Twenty-first Century Global Political Economy

GANESH K. TRICHUR

This paper investigates the new imperial conjuncture, by engaging with four recent interventions on the US war on terror and its impact on the global political economy. I review the works of the historical sociologist Michael Mann, the political scientist Chalmers Johnson, the historical anthropologist Emmanuel Todd, and the Marxist geographer David Harvey (Mann, 2003; Johnson, 2004; Todd, 2003; Harvey, 2003). The common terrain of these four interventions is the global disorder at the end of the twentieth century, marked by social breakdown rather than revolutionary crisis (Hobsbawm, 1994, p. 459), resembling in many ways the system-wide chaos that followed the collapse of the nineteenth century liberal world order. In 1944, Karl Polanyi linked the ruins of nineteenth century civilization to the 'torrent of events' unleashed on humankind in the twentieth century.

> A social transformation of planetary range is being topped by wars of an unprecedented type in which a score of states crashed, and the contours of new empires are emerging out of a sea of blood. But this fact of demoniac violence is merely superimposed on a swift, silent current of change which swallows up the past often without so much as a ripple on the surface. (Polanyi, 1957, p. 4)

A half-century later, Eric Hobsbawm traced the global turmoil at the end of the 'short' twentieth century to the effects of the collapse of the Soviet Empire and the absence of any effective mechanism for keeping control over the world economy.[1] If self-regulating markets brought about the catastrophic end of the nineteenth century liberal world order, neo-liberal market states under the globalization project of the 1980s (McMichael, 1996)[2] accelerated the end of the post-1945 Bretton Woods world order. Charles Tilly argues that although in 1989 it appeared 'as though the aging century might be contemplating retirement from the business of mass destruction', during the 1990s wars 'burrowed inside regimes' with a shift from interstate to intrastate violence, facilitated by a vibrant arms trade and the 'democratization' of the means of destruction (Hobsbawm, 1994, p. 561).[3] Civil wars and widespread violence undermined the power and function of nation-states in relation to supranational global governance institutions.

Accompanying this growing (but uneven) disempowerment of all states were three closely related developments. The first was the financial expansion of the 1980s, which Giovanni Arrighi argues is integral to the globalization project. Arrighi suggests that the current financial expansion marks the 'autumnal' moment of the US systemic cycle of accumulation, the last of four systemic cycles that organized the evolution of historical capitalism. Each cycle comprises a material expansion phase—in which capital accumulates primarily through investment in production and trade—and a financial expansion phase—in which 'over-accumulated' capital switches from investments in production and trade, to investments in finance, property titles, and other claims on future income. Arrighi points to an exceptional bifurcation defining the current conjuncture, in which East Asia emerges as the epicenter of world liquidity even as the US retains the most concentrated coercive power (Arrighi, 1994, pp. 352–353).

The second development was the celebration of the disintegration of the Soviet Empire represented by Fukuyama's (1992) thesis of 'the end of history' and the triumph of liberal democracies. Fukuyama invoked Michael Doyle's Law that liberal democracies do not wage war against each other, to argue that the end of the twentieth century inaugurated an era of perpetual peace. By contrast, Samuel Huntington's (1996) clash of civilizations thesis forecast irreconcilable conflicts between Western civilization (comprising the US and Europe), and the rest of the non-Western world—comprising, in particular, the Muslim countries, 'Confucian' China and 'orthodox' Russia. As a response to both Fukuyama and Huntington, Hardt and Negri maintain that the emergence of a smooth space of global control by a new postmodern form of imperial sovereignty ('Empire'), now replaces the declining power of modern sovereign states, and marks the end of geopolitics as we know it (Hardt & Negri, 2000; 2004). The third development of the late twentieth century, 'following the exhaustion of the tradition of social revolution in the mode of October 1917' (Hobsbawm, 1994, p. 449), is the sudden and exhilarating convergence of global social justice movements against financial globalization represented in Seattle 1999 and its aftermath (Mertes, 2004). These movements emphatically claim that another world is possible.

The four approaches to the new imperialism by Johnson, Todd, Mann and Harvey, stake rather different positions. None, apart from Harvey, addresses the implications of the new anti-globalization movements in shaping the imperial conjuncture. Johnson focuses on the long-term effects of fixed military capital (Johnson, 2004, p. 257). Johnson argues that its far-flung network of bases makes US military expansion a permanent political goal, locking the US into an irreversible imperialist course of endless war, intensification of domestic surveillance and disinformation, the decline of American democracy, and ineluctable bankruptcy and blowback. Harvey relates Hannah Arendt's insight that the endless accumulation of political power is the necessary accompaniment to the endless accumulation of capital, with Arrighi's demonstration that historical capitalism is a 'history of hegemonies expressive of ever larger and continuously more expansive power'. Harvey sees the outlines of an emergent Eurasian power bloc (Germany, France, Russia, and China) in response to the US imperial project, as possibly 'the next step' in that cycle (Harvey, 2003, pp. 34, 140, 84–85, 200). Mann's vision, in contrast, outlines the effects of the new militarism on the dialectic between terrorism and state terrorism. Mann sees US imperialism as incongruous in an age dominated by nation-states and nationalism, and incoherent in its political and ideological pursuit of territorial imperialism and war on Muslim terrorism. Finance capital may carry an American passport, but its fragile domination over productive capital accentuates the vulnerabilities of the military giant, transforming the new imperialism into a 'simple militarism'. Mann's pragmatic realism emphasizes asymmetries between US military, economic, ideological, and political power to suggest that US decline is reversible conditional on its abandonment of unilateralism. In contrast, Johnson, Todd, and Harvey all argue that US decline is irreversible. Johnson and Todd note analogies between the US Empire and the Roman Empire of antiquity, while Harvey sees stronger similarities between the US and British imperialisms. Harvey deploys Giovanni Arrighi's theoretical apparatus (Arrighi, 1994; Arrighi & Silver, 1999) to explain capitalist imperialism as a recurring resort to 'accumulation by dispossession' (Arrighi's financial expansion) in the context of over-accumulation crises. The recurring failure to deal with the surplus capital problem through internal reforms led not only to the global depression of the 1930s and the world wars of 1939–45; it also produced the context for a twenty-first century imperialism. Harvey is cognizant of East Asia's regional resurgence, and his analysis is close to Todd's in affirming Europe's potential. Todd highlights the parasitical dependence of the US on its productive Eurasian protectorates that emerged during the 1950–90 period of a globalized US hegemony. One of the first to predict the breakdown of the Soviet Empire using data on anthropological and demographic changes, Todd now optimistically predicts a Eurasian regional resurgence based on a Franco-German rapprochement in alliance with Russian military power that not only counterbalances US military presence in the region, but also signals an imminent breakdown of the American order (Todd, 2003, pp. xvii, 144).[4] Todd's compelling insights into growing democratic dynamics (emerging out of structural demographic and educational transformations) in peripheral spaces of the world system contradict the media-saturated portrayals of ethno-religious violence. The new militarism emerges as a US attempt to disguise the extent of its dependence on productive Eurasian peripheries as well as an accelerating internal decay.

Empire, Militarism, and the New Imperialism

All four authors see the emergence, in the aftermath of the Cold War, of a new set of US military managers (neo-conservative hawks) intent on global military domination through a unilateralist and militarist vision of how to overcome world disorder as the hallmark of the new imperialism. Mann points to the military temptation underlying the shift toward unilateralism—the technological revolution in military affairs suggested that military wizardry could achieve victory followed by moral good without risk to Americans. Todd and Mann see the Anglo-Saxon attack on weak Muslim states as a virtual clash of civilizations, and Harvey notes how the Christian right's impact on US support for Israel's violent repression of Palestinians converts Huntington's clash of civilizations thesis into a geopolitical fact (Mann, 2003, p. 83; Todd, 2003, p. xxii; Harvey, 2003, pp. 191, 207).[5] Todd argues that imperial unilateralism is not the result of a strongly willed plan. Adopted in anticipation of the final collapse of Russia during a time (1990–97) of accelerating capital inflows into a US economy floating into deeper trade deficits, the new militarist path is really half-imperial and half-liberal.[6] Harvey agrees that neo-conservatism overlaps neo-liberalism in its support for the myth that free markets deliver freedom and well-being to all, merely transforming an earlier low-intensity warfare into an open aggression as a putatively final solution to global chaos. In the shift from consent to coercive unilateralism, Harvey sees the accuracy of Arrighi's observation that the US is really converting its declining hegemony into exploitative domination, even as the new militarists seek to follow in the footsteps of the British Empire.[7] Johnson, by contrast, argues that the world-view of the new militarists is different from liberal military humanism and low-intensity warfare deployed during the Clinton years.[8] If the 1990 National Security Strategy projected US power into strategic energy spaces like the Middle East where the US does not have permanent presence, its 2002 counterpart declared 'preventive war' as imperial policy. Clinton's foreign policy, cloaked in euphemisms (indispensable nation, humanitarian intervention, and globalization), gave way to the Bush administration's assertions of the second coming of the Roman Empire. Todd interprets both the Clinton euphemisms and the uncloaked new militarism (war making on military midgets) as revealing deep-seated US insecurities. A 'militaristic, agitated, uncertain, anxious country projecting its own disorder around the globe' is hardly the 'indispensable nation' it claims to be (Todd, 2003, pp. xviii). Harvey points to the abstract universalism of the US Project for the New American Century (Harvey, 2003, pp. 50–51)[9]—Todd insightfully argues that such abstractions conceal the real decline of US universalism[10]—that coincided with the rejection of the 1997 Kyoto Protocol on global warming and the Ottawa treaty banning land mines. The US walked out of the 2001 UN Durban Conference on racism, and withdrew from the 1972 Anti-Ballistic Missile Treaty. It unilaterally declared an 'axis of evil', denied rights to Afghan prisoners and, despite documented abuse of Iraqi prisoners, consistently demands immunity for US citizens from the International Court of Justice.

A second synchronous development related to the new unilateralism transforms US foreign policy into a political culture of military Empire.[11] Though Mann sees in the new territorial imperialism only an indirect and informal Empire (Mann, 2003, p. 13), for Johnson the militarized planetary geography built during and after the Second World War is a new Empire, not of colonies, but of 'permanent naval bases, military airfields, army garrisons, espionage listening posts, and strategic enclaves on every continent of the globe'. Taking or leasing exclusive Eurasian military zones legitimized through alliances and mutual security pacts for containing communism, this militarized geography of bases constitutes the institutional form of the new imperialism. US Department of Defense publications suggest an expanding investment in militarized fixed capital: the plant replacement value of 725 overseas US bases is approximately $118 billion.[12] Regional commanders in chief (CINCs) rule these bases, report directly to the President and the secretary of defense,[13] and hire private military contractors to supply the logistics of operating the military empire.[14] Elaborate networks of planetary surveillance connect these bases through advanced forms of telecommunication networks.[15] Johnson notes the deep-seated contradictions that afflict the new militarism. The media and Hollywood films distort military life by presenting it as romantic, patriotic, and fun (Johnson, 2004, p. 25).[16] Embedded reporters in the Iraq war transmit 'antiseptic wars into the nation's living rooms' (Johnson, 2004, pp. 115–116).

Observing such 'spectator-sport militarism', Mann argues that the US loses the more important ideological war played abroad, where mass communication weapons level the visibility of the playing field. With no historical precedent in previous Empires, the Qatar-based Arab TV network Al-Jazeera broadcasts voices of victims (Mann, 2003, pp. 101, 118–120). Its depiction of wanton killing of civilians and abuse of Iraqi prisoners scorns the moral pretensions of the US military. The expansion of bases into the southern Eurasian region between 1999 and 2003 in conjunction with its occupation of Iraq secures the US a vital strategic bridgehead on the Eurasian land mass separating Western Europe from Russia and China. For Harvey, this strategic presence in the center of world energy supplies may ensure US global dominance for the next fifty years, forestalling consolidation of a Eurasian bloc and controlling access to the energy needs of expanded reproduction in China (Johnson, 2004, p. 189; Harvey, 2003, pp. 198–199).

If Johnson and Harvey portray the overwhelming global reach of US military might, Mann and Todd are much more skeptical. Todd sees a necessary relation between the increased economic dependence of the US and its remilitarization. In fact, the US downsized its military spending during 1990–95. Its remilitarization during 1999–2001 came after an exponential increase in the US trade deficit between 1997 and 1999. Nevertheless, military expansionism masks a decline in US power. Japan, South Korea, Germany, Saudi Arabia, and its allies largely financed the first Gulf War.[17] US unilateralism left it almost alone in financing the second Iraq war. The US Eurasian bases are a mere show of empire: 'Attacking the weak is hardly a convincing proof of one's own strength'. Much of the world really remains off-limits for the new imperialism, turning it into what Mann calls 'simple militarism', marked by 'power but not authority, ruthless arrogance leading to overconfidence, eventually leading to hubris and disaster' (Mann, 2003, p. 245).[18] In its wars against Islamic terrorism, Mann points out the naïve faith—that Muslim spaces can always be simplified and mastered—that seduces the new imperialists, and produces incoherence between US military, economic, political, and ideological powers. In an 'age of nation states' whose hallmark is multiple ethnicities and plural nationalisms, the US has the military power to invade, not the political power to securely rebuild. It lacks ideological power—Al-Jazeera's portrayal devastates the US image of itself as liberator—to counter regional blow-backs; it uses its money power to bribe autocratic regimes that have no interest in democracy; and it aids in the oppression of Palestinians. In its simplistic reduction of Arab identities to terrorism or fundamentalism[19] the US ignores the emergence of Islamist movements out of the 1970s populist struggles (its core constituencies were young dissident intellectuals and the poor) against repressive and corrupt Arab states, as a response to the developmental failures of Arab socialism, Western Marxism, and secular nationalism. Arab regimes showered with US military aid exercise state terrorism on nationalist freedom fighters. 'Terrorism begets state terrorism, and vice versa.' In this endless dialectic, the new imperialism's bias in favor of state terrorism creates more, and newer, terrorists, more determined rogue states, and it weakens US global leadership. Freedom fighters are too deep-rooted to eradicate by mere state repression. The more the Israeli state terrorizes Palestinians with US support, the more international the Palestinian appeal becomes.

Mann points out that despite the decline of radical Islamism and international terrorism during the mid-1990s (Mann, 2003, pp. 179–180),[20] US foreign policy revived them by consistently confusing Muslim national liberation struggles with international terrorism, and attacking them both together. Mann sees a bleak future for present international terrorist networks as long they are unable to 'make the two connections forged in Afghanistan in the 1980s and 1990s—with Muslim liberation struggles, and with a resonant anti-American struggle, comparable to the anti-Soviet struggle' (Mann, 2003, 187). Al-Qaeda's influence—with active CIA and US support (Mamdani, 2004)—in the Afghan nationalist war against Soviet occupation, led to a surge in radical Islamism across the Middle East that ended by the new millennium. Its call for all Muslims to unite against the US resonates little with Arab regimes and mass Muslim movements. Mann argues that an undifferentiated US war on Islamic terrorism not only converts national into international terrorists, it may also 'end one thousand years of Muslim disunity'. The new militarists

> strengthen the connections between Islamists, pan-Arabists and nationalists, and specifically between international (Al-Qaeda type) terrorists and the purely national freedom fighters/terrorists like Hamas or Hezbollah, creating more enemies for the United States. In Iraq, it ... convert[s] terrorists into legitimate guerillas ... [and] will intensify the state terrorism necessary for a military regime to counter them.

Against an international Muslim resistance, the new militarism only fights a losing war (Mann, 2003, pp. 178–179, 185–190, 259).

The contradictions of this losing war emerge differently in Harvey's analysis of the new imperialism. Responding to Arrighi's concepts,[21] Harvey argues that the new militarism pursues a territorialism sharply at variance with the capitalist logic of power.

> [Capitalist imperialism is] a contradictory fusion of 'the politics of state and empire' (imperialism as a distinctively political project on the part of actors whose power is based in command of a territory and a capacity to mobilize its human and natural resources towards political, economic, and military ends) and 'the molecular processes of capital accumulation in space and time' (imperialism as a diffuse political-economic process in space and time in which command over and use of capital takes primacy).

Harvey argues that these two logics are internal relations. Shifts in the capitalist logic necessitate shifts in the territorial logic, and vice versa. Capitalist imperialism continually seeks spatio-temporal fixes to recurring problems of over-accumulation of capital. In the wake of the 1973–75 over-accumulation crisis, the post-World War II US-dominated regime of expanded reproduction succumbed to the domination of finance capital which secured adaptive transformation of state structures everywhere into neo-liberal apparatuses of 'accumulation by dispossession', backed by the coercive powers of the US state. Class struggles within the US ruled out internal reform as an option. The late twentieth century US response to over-accumulation crisis parallels the late nineteenth century British response to the crisis of over-accumulation. In both cases, declining opportunities for profitable expansion along the trajectory of an earlier expanded reproduction path gave way to a financial expansion. The volatility inherent in neo-liberal imperialism abroad—e.g. IMF-imposed shock therapies savagely devalued capital in Russia and Eastern Europe while privatization enabled acquisition of state assets at rock-bottom prices; speculative capital movements unleashed the Asian financial crisis in 1997–98—also produced chronic insecurity within the US. The 1999 collapse of the hi-tech dot.com economy revealed finance capital as 'unredeemable fictitious capital supported by scandalous accounting practices'. 'The result was a ferment of local, dispersed, and highly differentiated social movements battling either to confront or to hold off the neo-liberal practices of imperialism orchestrated by finance capital and neo-liberal states' (see Harvey, 2003, pp. 26–34).

In response to this ferment of unrest, political control shifted from neo-liberal to neo-conservative rule, thus ending thirty years of neo-liberal hegemony in a newly emerging relation between the territorial and capitalist logics of power. In capitalist imperialism, the capitalist logic generally dominates the territorial logic; in the current conjuncture—one in which the US has given up hegemony (leadership through consent) for domination through coercion— the new imperialism[22] registers outright contradiction between the two logics. Harvey points out how both the US–Iraq War at the start of the twenty-first century and the British–Boer War at the onset of the twentieth century occurred at the end of their world hegemony, alongside a contradiction between the two logics of global power. The contemporary capitalistic logic 'points to the draining away of economic power' from the US, faced with a territorialism that seeks to preserve US global dominance at all costs; it seeks 'regime change in Washington', faced with the contemporary 'surge towards militarism' (Harvey, 2003, pp. 33, 201–207).

Deepening Imperial Contradictions

However, the surge towards a new militarism, Mann (2003, p. 83) argues, 'appears at a moment when most of the world felt it did not need the American Empire'. For Mann, the explanation lies in the incongruity of imperialism in the contemporary age of nationalism. Todd, however, furnishes a more compelling explanation for this paradox in the context of two large-scale socio-historical reversals. The first reversal emerged out of the effects of the adoption of US free enterprise capitalism in Europe and Japan during the 1950 to 1990 period of globalization.[23] The adoption of free market principles by development states profoundly transformed and regionalized the world economy, even as it profoundly weakened and deformed the US economy and society, creating a 'mutual vassalage' (Arrighi, 1994) between the US and its protectorates registered by two indicators that during the course of neoliberal hegemony became structural elements of the world system. On the one hand, its accelerating trade deficits signal the decline of US productive power[24] and its dependence on the rest of the world; the early 1970s trade deficit with Japan has since spread to the entire globe.[25] On the other hand, growing capital flows into the US since the 1970s are a sign of its financial power and world preference for investing in US financial markets. The collapse of the Soviet sphere only accelerated these trends. Between 1990 and 2000, US trade deficits went up from $100 billion to $450 billion, while the volume of balancing capital inflows to the US over the same period increased from $88 billion to $865 billion. Imperial tribute—in the form of a regular flow of foreign capital to balance US trade deficits—is really the investment of global profits in US Empire. Liberal deregulated financial mechanisms employ 'accumulation by dispossession'[26] to channel global profits into US stock and bond markets because the US (and Wall Street) offers maximum security for financial investments.[27] The low wages in the productive peripheries and accelerating income inequalities, within and between, North and South, and a consequent global stagnation in demand during neo-liberal hegemony (1970–2000) transformed the US economy into a consumer state maintaining high effective demand for world production.[28] The continuity of these financial inflows, however, depends on the confidence of global oligarchs in the dollar's ability to represent itself as world money.[29]

Todd points to a second reversal, the redistribution of democratic and oligarchic energies in the global economy, in the context of a largely unnoticed cultural revolution. If the intensification of income inequalities during the period of financial globalization strengthened forces in the global North promoting oligarchical dynamics, the cultural revolution between 1980 and 2000 (marked by the generalized decrease in birth rates and an equally generalized increase in literacy rates) is strengthening forces in the global South that promote democratic dynamics.

> The developing world is heading toward democracy—pushed by the movement toward full literacy that tends to create culturally more homogeneous societies. As for the industrialized world, it is being encroached on to varying degrees by a tendency toward oligarchy—a phenomenon that has emerged with the development of educational stratification that has divided societies into layers of 'higher', 'lower', and various kinds of 'middle' classes. (Todd, 2003, 196)

Todd estimates that younger generations in the global South will achieve universal literacy by 2030; and the world's population will achieve a stable equilibrium between births and deaths by 2050.[30] The Cultural Revolution explains the paradox of growing intellectual equality (the educational revolution) amidst growing economic inequality (financial globalization); it also explains how intense cultural disorientation springing from educational and demographic changes contributes to increasing ethno-nationalist violence—a mark not of regression, but of a crisis of transition to modernization (Todd, 2003, pp. 20–46).

The global trend towards democratization, however, renders the US role as protector of democratic principles at best redundant. At worst, the growth of US oligarchical tendencies makes it aggressively receptive to global democratic tendencies. US economic dependence paradoxically requires a minimum level of global disorder. US energy-dependence is no rational explanation for its imperialism; Todd (2003, 57, 116–118, 139-142) argues that the generalized decline in US economic performance explains its obsession with Arab oil.

> The American fixation on the oil of the Muslim world has more to do with fears of being kicked out of the region than with designs to expand an empire. It says more about the worries of the US than about its power—first, a worry over the all too real prospect of overall economic dependence for which the energy deficit is only a fitting symbol; and second, a worry over the prospect of losing control over its two productive protectorates, Europe and Japan.

Mann underlines a mix of motives—Iraq's switch from dollars to euros as reserve currency, Hussein's affront to the *pax Americana*, as well as a genuine desire to bring democracy to the region—behind the Iraq attack. The fact that it did not have weapons of mass destruction (WMD) made it easy target. North Korea has WMD but no oil, though, like Iran, its switch to the euro makes it part of the axis of evil. 'The war is about oil, but filtered through the over-confidence of the new imperialists' and 'the very success of American hegemony over the previous period'. He cites Raghda Dirgham to argue that the war is really 'for the sake of American greatness via the window of Iraq' (Mann, 2003, pp. 207–10; 218).

Johnson attaches 'crucial roles' to 'oil,[31] Israel, and domestic politics'.[32] Contra Harvey, who argues the Iraq invasion, is 'all about oil' (Harvey, 2003, pp. 8–12, 18–25), Johnson points out how the US project for 'democracy' alienates Saudi Arabia (Johnson, 2004, pp. 257, 281, 306–307, 25, 307–308).[33] 'It is more than possible that a truly popular government in Saudi Arabia would be hostile to the US. A serious interruption of Saudi oil supplies would produce an economic catastrophe for the US, even if it had exclusive control of Iraq's oil production'. A more encompassing explanation underlies the new militarism. 'Whatever the original reason the US entered a country and set up a base, it remains there for imperial reasons—regional and global hegemony, denial of the territory to rivals, providing access for American companies, maintenance of "stability" or "credibility" as a military force, and simple inertia.' Johnson subsumes all these interests under the post-Cold War US awareness of its military power—'because we have it we deserve it'—as the 'explanation' for US militarism. The inseparable and inexorable pressures of imperialism and militarism[34] make it inconceivable that the US give up its military bases that ensure its global dominance (Johnson, 2004, pp. 234–36, 26, 152, 3).[35] Militarism becomes, in short, the fetishization of power to the point where it overflows into imperialism.

Alternative Twenty-first Century Futures

What global futures emerge out of the imperial conjuncture? Although the US elevation of terrorism into a universal force institutionalizes a long-term state of perpetual war, Todd argues that its ebbing universalism, and its lack of a tradition of military might on the ground, makes empire-building and imperial peace impossible missions (Todd, 2003, pp. xxiii, xvi, 98, 3, 79, 118, 80–82). Mann persuasively argues that nation-building in Iraq is not comparable to the reconstruction of Germany and Japan after 1945, because the US lacks expertise on ethno-national conflicts that dominate an age of nationalism. Its proliferation of WMD[36] frustrates democratic impulses in the Middle East while provoking reliance on WMD by smaller nations, as protection against US unilateralism (Johnson, 2004, p. 285; Mann, 2003, p. 255). In the future, mutual deterrence will mediate relations between the US and North Korea. In Iraq, low-intensity urban guerilla warfare, which other Arabs join to resist the US occupation, is an 'enduring cancer' though not 'another Vietnam'. Mann, however, does not think American power is in decline, though he predicts US unilateralism will end the new militarism by accentuating extremely uneven power resources that lead to 'imperial incoherence and foreign policy failure', while 'puny Arabs and Muslims expose the soft underbelly of American military'. Mann does not see the demise of the new imperialism coming from the rise of another power or from 'imperial overstretch'. He dismisses Europe's powers of military intervention, and argues that 'voluntary abandonment of the imperial project' would 'preserve most of the US hegemony'. If we accept his argument, the reinstatement of the militarist conservatives in the November 2004 elections should further erode US power, because over-employment of hard power (compelling others to do as the US wishes) not only destroys the effectiveness of consent (persuading people to want what the US wants), it also rapidly deflates it. US unilateralism deepens fractures in the Northern Alliance, increases the proliferation of WMD, both of which accelerate systemic chaos (Mann, 2003, pp. 243–244, 261, 13, 261, 264–265). Mann's vision is correct, but he misleadingly associates the strength of US financial power with US hegemony during the 1990s. Financial expansions historically register the decline of world hegemonies. The US is no exception to this historical rule. Todd is correct to see the new militarists as gravediggers of an American empire that will probably end by 2050, with a financial meltdown preceding an inevitable reduction in US power and standard of living.

> The most likely scenario is a stock market crash larger than any we have experienced thus far that will be followed by the meltdown of the dollar . . . that would put an end to any further delusions of "empire" . . . [However], the breakdown of the machine will be just as surprising as was its emergence. (Todd, 2003, p. 98)

Similarly, Harvey argues that the unbalanced reliance of the US on finance capital makes it brazenly inconsistent of the IMF not to impose structural adjustment procedures on the US considering the astonishing volume of global capital needed to support the growing the US deficit ($2.3 billion a day at the beginning of 2003). Even though 'the IMF is the United States', there are real limits to the willingness of East Asia to finance the spiraling US trade deficits (currently at 6 per cent of US GDP) or to continue holding foreign exchange reserves in dollars (China's accumulated foreign exchange reserves in November 2004 amounted to $515 billion). The compelling contradiction between the capitalist and territorial logics of power will tear the latter to shreds.

Harvey points out that just as speculative movements of capital into and out of Thailand, Indonesia, and Argentina fueled booms that soon after collapsed with capital flights and social disasters, the flight of speculative capital into Wall Street in the 1990s that generated a boom may well be reversed. '[If regime change in Washington does not happen] the vast drain imposed by an even stronger turn to a permanent war economy may amount to a form of economic suicide for the United States' (Harvey, 2003, p. 76; also pp. 206–207). There are already some signs that indicate the accuracy of this assessment. In an interview with the Financial Times (23 November 2004), Li Ruogu (deputy governor of the People's Bank of China) insists that China will not adopt any appreciation (revaluation) of the renminbi in the near-term to 'solve the US's structural problems'. It would also 'take into account the conditions and wishes of neighboring Asian economies on any moves towards a flexible exchange rate policy in the future'.

Johnson argues that if the globalization project delayed the beginning of US decline, then the cumulative impact of the shift to militarism and imperialism only accelerates it further (Johnson, 2004, p. 13).[37] Johnson's critique of militarism nevertheless overestimates US military power in neglecting to relate twentieth century military transformations with the current crisis of the interstate system of sovereign states. As Arrighi (1994, p. 79) observes: 'It is as if the modern system of rule, having expanded spatially and functionally as far as it could, has nowhere to go but "forward" towards an entirely new system of rule or "backwards" towards early modern or even pre-modern forms of state- and war-making'. I relate Arrighi's observation to an emerging global pattern of reliance by different agencies on the non-sovereign private market supply of military services in the context of a more general privatization revolution. This privatization of power emerged out of the 'security gap' and the relative demilitarization of states at the end of the Cold War. The contemporary 'scope, location, and criticality' of the role of privatized military firms (PMFs) in the prosecution of warfare after their first appearance in the African civil wars of the 1990s, makes Peter Singer observe: 'Not within the last two centuries, at least, has there been such a reliance on private soldiers to accomplish tasks directly affecting the tactical and strategic success of [military] engagement' (Singer, 2003, p. 18). David Barstow (*New York Times*, 19 April 2004) reports how the Pentagon's privatization of the Iraq war enables 'dozens of private security companies [to] set up shop in Baghdad'. 'Privatized Military Firms unblushingly charge $500–1500 a day for their most skilled operators, and security costs in the Iraqi war could claim up to 25% of the $18 billion budgeted for reconstruction, a huge and mostly unanticipated expense'.

Each surge of scattered violence from the Iraqi resistance highlights not only the criticality of the role of the new private suppliers of 'force protection'; the upward trend in US war-casualties also highlights the inevitably escalating US costs of protection. Rising protection costs combine with increasingly ineffective protection to stultify the US imperial project. I suggest that the historical resemblance between the contemporary growth of PMFs and an earlier era of mercenary soldiers central in the war-making and state-making pursuits of medieval Europe pushes the new militarism 'backwards' into an essentially pre-modern pursuit of a territorial logic of power.[38] The contemporary expansion in the role of PMFs also relates to a qualitative transformation in the role of the traditional soldier because of changing Northern perceptions of challenges to its security from those spaces in the South experiencing state collapse, humanitarian disasters, and terrorist threats. In response, the North invests increasingly in a new type of 'flexible soldier' skilled in non-traditional roles whose work blurs boundaries between policing, intelligence, and military agencies (Dandeker, 2003). Since the 1990s, the North utilizes 'armed global street workers' to police conflict-ridden Southern spaces, for 'peacekeeping, peace enforcement, peace support operations and humanitarian intervention'. These armed services serve as flexible forces 'equipped with the appropriate hardware, force structures, and people policies that will enable states to respond swiftly, in collaboration with allies and/or friends bonded in "coalitions of the willing", to a wide variety of crises whose precise nature is quite difficult to predict in advance' (Kummel, 2003, pp. 417–433). The new soldier-type, the re-problematization of Northern security, and the radicalization of the politics of development are closely related outcomes. As Mark Duffield (2001, p. 42) argues: 'Development and security have increasingly merged. Representing underdevelopment as dangerous not only demands a remedial process of social transformation, it also creates urgency and belief ensuring that this process is no longer trusted to chance.' The new imperialism in its undifferentiated war on terrorism continues, in short, the mid-1990s Northern policy of incorporating conflict into mainstream aid policy. The need for 'regime change' along with commitments to 'restructure' Southern societies represents a more general Euro-US response to perceptions of threats to Northern security.

In the light of these Northern propensities, it is difficult to agree with Harvey's vision of a benevolent Euro-US combination as an alternative to the violence of the new militarism.

Harvey's 'special debt' (Preface to Harvey, 2003) to Arrighi, nevertheless produces a vision sharply at odds with Arrighi's vision of the future. Although the coercive power of the US faces no serious external challenge:

> [The US] has even greater capabilities than Britain did a century ago to convert its declining hegemony into exploitative domination. If the system eventually breaks down, it will be primarily because of US resistance to adjustment and accommodation. And conversely, US adjustment and accommodation to the rising economic power of the East Asian region is an essential condition for a non-catastrophic transition to a new world order. (Arrighi and Silver, 1999, cited in Harvey, 2003, p. 75)

Moreover, Harvey does not mention another essential condition that Arrighi and Silver consider necessary for a non-catastrophic transition to a new world order:

> An equally essential condition is the emergence of a new global leadership from the main centers of the East Asian economic expansion. This leadership must be willing and able to rise up to the task of providing system-level solutions to the system-level problems left behind by U.S. hegemony. The most severe among these problems is the seemingly unbridgeable gulf between the life-chances of a small minority of world population (between 10 and 20 percent) and the vast majority. In order to provide a viable and sustainable solution to this problem, the track laying vehicles of East Asia must open up to a new path of development for themselves and for the world that departs radically from the one that is now at a dead end. (Arrighi and Silver, 1999, p. 289)

Harvey surprisingly does not even consider East Asian leadership of the world system as a possibility 'worth fighting for', soliciting instead political commitments to a Euro-US combination that would create 'a more benevolent "New Deal" imperialism' (Harvey, 2003, pp. 209–211). The US, however, as Todd argues, has rejected such 'hard options' that entail 'rebuilding an industrial base; paying the price of the true loyalty of one's allies by treating their interests with respect; confronting forcefully the true strategic adversary, Russia, rather than simply toying with it; and imposing an equitable peace on the Israeli-Palestinian conflict' (Todd, 2003, p. 144). Moreover, as Todd points out, powerful centrifugal forces work against the Euro–US combination that Harvey advocates. The attraction of the US imperial integration option for Europe's oligarchs lies in the US role as 'the global champion of a revolution in inequality' and in the US project during the financial expansion of the 1980s, of 'more money and power for those who are already the wealthiest and the most powerful'. Nevertheless, the deep divergence of European and American worldviews, Todd argues, is nothing short of a 'clash of civilizations'. The violence and religious fervor in the US contrasts sharply with a less violent and agnostic Europe, and American differentialism towards Blacks, Hispanics, and Muslims operates to the detriment of Europe's pluralistic interests.[39] More importantly, the long history of generations of peasant suffering inscribed in European and Japanese societies (their 'genetic code') and their belated experience of peace and prosperity, makes them place a high premium on social equilibrium and social security (Todd, 2003, pp. 172–178).[40] The US export of ultra-liberal unregulated capitalism constitutes grave dangers for the state-centered societies of Europe and Japan.[41]

Harvey and Todd correctly point out the growing regional restructuring of the world economy. Harvey makes insightful comments on the ways in which molecular processes of capital accumulation lead to 'passive revolutions' that congeal into regional spaces with a structured coherence (Harvey, 2003, pp. 101–104). Todd goes a step further, to argue that globalization is really the name for the production of such regions based on geographical contiguity. He predicts that Eurasian demographic dynamics tend towards an intra-regional rapprochement (especially closer ties between France and Germany) and closer economic and military collaboration between Europe and Russia—made necessary by the unsettling militaristic behavior of the US (Todd, 2003, pp. xx, xxiii, 58, 182–185). Unlike Todd, Harvey is much more cognizant of the relative importance of East Asian regional developments.

> [T]he challenge to US dominance posed by East and South-East Asia seems far more serious. Financial and productive power has continued to accumulate in the region, draining power away from North America as well as, to a lesser degree, from Europe. Unlike Europe, the region shows little sign of any attempt to create a formal structure of political-military power, and the relationships between states are networked rather than formal, capitalistic rather than territorial ... While it seems unlikely ... that any coherent territorial logic of power will develop in the region, the power of the capitalistic logic looks more and more overwhelming and prospectively hegemonic in the global economy, particularly as the huge weight of China, and to a lesser degree, India increasingly enter into the balance. (Harvey, 2003, pp. 83–84)

Harvey sees the violently disruptive primitive accumulation processes in China as sparking both economic growth and infrastructural investments by absorbing the world's capital surplus, though such surplus-absorption in China will be calamitous for the US economy (Harvey, 2003, pp. 208–209).[42] The link between expanded reproduction and accumulation by dispossession, Harvey argues, is an organic and dialectical process, with implications for the movements struggling for a better world.

> If the current period has seen a shift in emphasis from accumulation through expanded reproduction to accumulation by dispossession and if the latter lies at the heart of imperialist practices, then it follows that the balance of interest within the anti- and alternative globalization movements must acknowledge accumulation by dispossession as the primary contradiction to be confronted. But it ought never to do so by ignoring the dialectical relation to struggles in the field of expanded reproduction. (Harvey, 2003, pp. 176–177)

This is surely a correct assessment. Nevertheless, I want to argue that keeping in mind the dialectical relation between these two forms of struggle entails investing as much primacy to contradictions generating workers' struggles in the field of expanded reproduction in China as the primacy accorded to the contradictions generating the forms of resistance to dispossession through the neo-liberal project of privatization of the global commons. How to keep in the fore the connectivity between these two forms of struggle is a question of politics. It does entail expressing solidarity with the labor struggles in China as much as it entails expressing solidarity with the contemporary 'movement of movements' in their struggles against accumulation by dispossession. It may also entail recognizing the inevitability of switching processes, which, Arrighi (1994) argues, are a recurring feature in all world hegemonic transitions. The capitalist logic in the current and in previous world hegemonic crises not only switches from continuing its investments in material developmental paths that have exhausted their profitability to new and more profitable material developmental paths as in China and East Asia; it also holds back from doing so during the relatively indeterminate duration of the over-accumulation crisis, by speculating and gambling. The different financial crises in different states and regions that marked the unfolding of the globalization project through accumulation by dispossession as well as the multiplying financial scandals and frauds within the US (referred to as 'imaginative accounting practices' in the media), are testimony to the effects of this 'holding back'. However, the speed and pace of the gales of 'creative destruction' sweeping through China are equally testimony to the effects of a definitive switch from holding back surplus capital to investing it in the material expansion of the 'Greater China Circle'. If the connectivity between the different forms of struggle must not be lost, as Harvey correctly maintains, it does not follow that a new trajectory of Euro-US leadership will be more benevolent than 'the raw militaristic imperialism' currently pursued. There is no historical evidence to support the putative benevolence of a joint Euro-US global leadership. As Todd argues, the democratizing tendencies in the global South, powered by advancements in literacy and falling birth rates, contrast sharply with the tendency within both Europe and the US toward oligarchical systems of power. If we accept the implications of this 'reversal', then an East Asian and Chinese 'civilizational' leadership may well have much more 'benevolence' to offer. One of the benefits of such an outcome is the possibility of subverting the perdurable global hierarchy in the distribution of wealth and income (with Europe and the US at the top of the hierarchy, along with Japan), and thereby increasing the life-chances of the global majority (most of whom are located in the Asian region). Why Harvey does not find this a welcome possibility is not clear. Be that as it may, the 'pressure from below' from the social movements that Arrighi and Silver (1999) talk about, has widened and deepened from transition to transition, leading to larger and larger social blocs with each new world hegemony. In the last analysis, the strength and struggles of these deepening pressures from below in ordering the systemic chaos in conjunction with a resilient East Asian network power, will determine the possible contours of a more egalitarian and democratic future for the twenty-first century world system.

Notes

1   See Hobsbawm (1994, pp. 4, 449, 459 and 562–3) Hobsbawm (1994, p. 368) argues that the communist revolution was 'an engine of conservation', one that worked to preserve the global order during the twentieth century. While it transformed 'state power, property relations, economic structure and the like', at the same time it froze other aspects of social life 'in their pre-revolutionary shapes', protecting them 'against the universal continuous subversion of change in capitalist societies'.

2   The concept of a 'globalization project' is a central organizing theme in McMichael (1996): it is related to the collapse of the US-sponsored 'development project' in the transitional decade of the 1970s and the emergence of financial deregulation and a debt regime that led to the demise of the Third World in the 1980s.

3   Civilian casualties over the twentieth century as a whole rose disconcertingly, from 5% in WW1, 50% in WW2, up to 90% in wars of the 1990s. See Chesterman (2001), cited in Tilly (2003, pp. 68, 56).

4   In 1979, Todd published *The Final Fall*, which predicted the decomposition of the Soviet sphere, at the very moment of the start of the Second Cold War.

5   Todd argues forcefully and insightfully that 'universal terrorism'—the concept used by the US to redefine itself as the leader of a global crusade to justify preemptive interventions—has no historical or sociological justification. It is simply 'absurd from the standpoint of the Muslim world, which will eventually work its way through its transitional crisis without outside intervention. It could only be useful to the US if it somehow needs to have an Old World embroiled in a state of permanent war' (Todd, 2003, p. 44). Johnson argues that the US acceptance of a 'clash of civilizations' and wars to establish a moral truth allegedly the same in every culture, 'sounds remarkably like a jihad, especially given the Bush administration's ties to Christian fundamentalism'. Such a moral crusade will alienate Saudi Arabia, which by 'turning off its oil supply could transform the United States into a huge junkyard' (Johnson, 2004, p. 287).

6   Todd claims that the direction of US foreign policy resembles the 'current of a river' that chooses 'the path of least resistance' (Todd, 2003, p. 143). Between 1990 and 1997—precisely during the accelerating implosion of the Soviet bloc—the balance of capital movements between the US and the rest of the world increased from $60 billion to $271 billion, enabling the US 'to indulge in large amounts of conspicuous consumption without worrying about paying for it out of its own production' (see Todd, 2003, pp. 125–132).

7   Harvey argues that the new imperialism 'will continue a political economy that rests on accumulation by dispossession' (the dispossession of Iraqi oil being the most flagrant beginning point) 'and do absolutely nothing to counter the spiraling inequalities that contemporary forms of capitalism are producing. Continuation of neo-liberal politics at the economic level entails a continuation if not escalation of accumulation by dispossession' (Harvey, 2003, pp. 201–202, 208). Harvey notes how Empire's apologists relate benefits to the world from a Pax Americana with the Pax Britannica in the last half of the nineteenth century. For him, both the early twentieth century British Boer War and the early twenty-first century US–Iraq War emerged after the

rejection of 'internal reform' as an option (see Harvey, 2003, pp. 75, 4, 181–182). Johnson and Todd use Roman precedents as referent for the new imperialism. Mann doubts the utility of this comparison. The US has 'more uneven imperial powers than any of its historic predecessors', though the Roman and the European Empires were 'far more powerful' than the US can be. The Roman analogy is incorrect primarily because in the contemporary 'age of nationalism'—in which 'peoples of the world are held responsible for their own destinies'—the world's dominant ideologies pedaled through the mass media, 'contradict any imperialism'. Outside intervention requires for its justification, 'a much higher standard than the Roman, British or Belgian empires could ever have met'. Only extreme conditions today justify such intervention, and they need to be 'quick and beneficent'. Second, unlike the US, which destroys everything around it and invests little in Empire, the Romans built up the places they conquered and assimilated the locals in the conquered lands. 'The Europeans could not do that, let alone the US' (see Mann, 2003, pp. 13, 120, 97).

8   Mann points to an 'embryo version' of the new imperialism under the Clinton years—using US military power for 'purely humanitarian reasons'—that is not reducible to 'using militarism offensively to remake the world into a better place'. Mann sees affinities in 'the mindset' of the new militarists—'achieving morally desirable goals through violence'—and older 'imperialists, fascists and ethnic cleansers' (Mann, 2003, pp. 7–8).

9   Todd points out three features of US theatrical micro-militarism. First, never resolve a problem decisively, to justify endless rounds of military action by the one and only superpower. Second, concentrate on third-rate powers like Iraq, Iran, North Korea, Cuba, etc. Third, develop new arms systems that can be advertised as putting the US far ahead of the field in an endless arms race (Todd, 2003, p. 21).

10   Todd sees universalism as 'a fundamental resource for any state' that seeks to rule over a nation or over a vaster, multiethnic, and 'imperial domain'. This 'ebbing of a universalist sentiment' in the US prevents 'an egalitarian, just, and responsible vision of the planet' (see Todd, 2003, p. 125).

11   Johnson argues that by 2002, the US no longer had a 'foreign policy' (Johnson, 2004, p. 22). Mann points out that in contrast to the term 'imperialism', the new militarists invest 'Empire' and 'imperial' with 'noble, civilizing, even humanitarian sentiments'. Empire brings 'peace, freedom and democracy', and saves oppressed peoples from their own 'rogue' leaders (Mann, 2003, p. 9). Johnson notes that the sense of separation between 'homeland' and 'empire' is in crisis (Johnson, 2004, p. 5). Harvey similarly remarks about the new imperialist mind-set: 'Military activity abroad requires military-like discipline at home' (Harvey, 2003, p. 193).

12   The *Base Structure Report* (BSR) details 'the physical property owned by the Pentagon'. The *Worldwide Manpower Distribution by Geographical Area* (Manpower Report) provides numbers for military personnel (army, navy, marines, air force) at each base, plus Department of Defense civilians, locally hired civilians, and dependents of military personnel (Johnson, 2004, pp. 153–154). In conjunction the two reports reveal an arresting picture of the extent and dimensions of the US military empire, despite discrepancies. The PRV is 'the reported cost of replacing the facility and its supporting infrastructure using today's costs (labor and material) and standards (methods and codes)'. The 725 US military bases (small, medium, and large installations) in 38 countries, along with installations listed as 'other' (sites with a PRV < $10 million), are valued at $118 billion.

13   CINCs work like Roman proconsuls, enforcing extraterritorial 'status of forces agreements' (SOFA) on host governments to ensure immunity to American troops for crimes committed against local residents They oversee intelligence, special operations, space assets, nuclear forces, arms sales, and military bases. They produce mini-foreign policy statements for each region ('theater engagement operations'), by deploying thousands of Special Forces that train local militaries in state terrorism ('foreign internal defense'), through military programs like the International Military Education and Training Program (IMET). IMET (founded in 1976 in the wake of the Nixon doctrine that 'Asian boys should pay for Asian wars') pays foreign officers and soldiers to take courses in the School of the Americas (SOA) now renamed WHISC (the Western Hemisphere Institute for Security Cooperation) (see Johnson, 2004, pp. 121–122, 124–126, 132, 135–140).

14   All US military bases in the Persian Gulf region depend on private contractors for their defenses, amenities, and operations. Complex weapons systems today 'are heavily contractor-dependent'. The top PMCs—like Vinnell, Military Professional Resources, Inc. (MPRI), Kellog, Brown & Root (B&R), Dyncorp, Science Applications International Corporation, and others, 'are among the most profitable business' in the US today (Johnson, 2004, pp. 140–148). Camp Bondsteel in the Balkans is a base camp for the 'military-petroleum complex', built by B&R in 1999 for $36.6m (annual operating costs of $180m), as part of a US strategy to secure and control Middle Eastern and Central Asian oil supplies. The oil-drilling and construction company Halliburton acquired B&R in 1962 (see Johnson, 2004, pp. 140–148).

15   Started in 1964, by 1999 Intelsat had 19 satellites in geostationary orbit. Antennas, trained from base listening posts on an Intelsat or other communications satellite, easily eavesdrop on messages. Bases for tapping into telecom

copper cables include Diego Garcia's submarine pens (Indian Ocean), White Beach (Okinawa), La Maddalena Island (Italy), Holy Loch (Scotland), and Rota (Spain) (see Johnson, 2004, pp. 161–163). Since 1981, the English-speaking global North (UK, US, Canada, Australia, and New Zealand) formalized 'informal covert intelligence-sharing arrangements' under the code-name 'Echelon'. The Echelon program for satellites and computers designs interception of nonmilitary communications for the 'UKUSA signals intelligence alliance', and monitors and operates some 120 satellites worldwide. Johnson sees it as a form of 'state-sponsored information piracy' (Johnson, 2004, pp. 165–166).

16   US soldiers appear as liberators of Afghan women, helpers of natural disaster victims in the Philippines, or protectors of Bosnians, Kosovars, or Iraqi Kurds (but not Rwandans, Turkish Kurds, or Palestinians) from ethnic cleansing campaigns (Johnson, 2004, pp. 112–113).

17   They contributed $54 billion of the estimated $64 billion in war expenses during the First Gulf War of the 1990s.

18   Todd points out that US soldiers stationed in Central Asian bases in Uzbekistan are isolated and numerically insignificant. 'A strike force today, they could find themselves hostages tomorrow' (Todd, 2003, p. 160). These ground forces 'cannot directly control the geographic area that produces the vital merchandise and amasses the financial sums necessary for America's day-to-day existence'. The threat of US aerial bombardments is constrained by Russian power. 'So long as the latter exists, America does not have the total power that could sustain long-term economic security in the new role it must play as the world's dependent rentier' (Todd, 2003, pp. 124–125).

19   Mann points out that 'Arabs' may be nationalists, pan-Arabists, or Pan-Islamists, in short a multiplicity of identities that are impossibly subsumed under 'Muslim or Islamic fundamentalists' (Mann, 2003, p. 179). Todd's demographic analysis of fertility rates shows that 'the Muslim world, at least as a demographic block, does not exist. Among Muslim countries, one notices the greatest divergence of birth rates from 2.0 births per woman in Azerbaijan to 7.5 in Niger. The Islamic world is a microcosm of the transitions of so-called Third World countries around the globe' (Todd, 2003, pp. 30–43).

20   Radical Islamism mobilized behind 'theodemocracy', a sovereignty resting not on the state but in the *umma*, the entire religious community, conforming to the Koran (Mann, 2003, p. 116). See Kepel (2003) for an account of the decline of radical Islamism and international terrorism during the mid-1990s.

21   Arrighi's theoretical and historical apparatus demonstrates the role played by successive world hegemonies in making and remaking the modern world system in order to 'resolve the recurrent contradiction between an "endless" accumulation of capital and a comparatively stable organization of political space'. To do this, Arrighi differentiates between two opposing logics of power by paraphrasing Marx's general formula of capitalist production M-C-M' (M' > M) into the territorial logic of power T-M-T' (T' > T) and the capitalist logic of power M-T-M' (M' > M). In the first formula, 'abstract economic command or money (M) is a means or intermediate link in a process aimed at the acquisition of additional territories (T')'. In the second formula, 'territory (T) is a means or an intermediate link in a process aimed at the acquisition of additional means of payment (M')'. Arrighi draws upon Anthony Giddens' concept of states as 'containers of power' to differentiate between the two logics. 'Territorialist rulers tend to increase their power by expanding the size of their container. Capitalist rulers, in contrast, tend to increase their power by piling up wealth within a small container and increase the size of the container only if it is justified by the requirements of the accumulation of capital' (Arrighi, 1994, p. 33).

22   The new militarism makes military preparedness the highest priority of the US state. Global military spending rose to $798 billion in 2000, with the US accounting for 37% of that amount, by far the largest proportion. The US 'was also the world's largest arms salesman, responsible for 47% of all munitions transfers between 1996 and 2000' (Johnson, 2004, pp. 52–63).

23   Todd sees the Marshall Plan and the US-led global market system of 1950–75 as a period of 'positive imperialism' (see Todd, 2003, pp. 67, 14–15). In the long US twentieth century, Arrighi argues, 'the US regime became dominant through an inflation of the "consumption norm" of the US labor force and an internalization of world purchasing power within the organizational domains of US governmental and business organizations. It promoted a world trade expansion through the redistribution of this purchasing power to a select group of allied and client states and through the adoption by these same states of the inflated US consumption norm. It sustained the expansion through a speed-up of the transfer of primary inputs (oil in particular) from Third to First World countries by multinational corporations. And it attained its limits in the great inflation of protection and production costs of the late 1960s and early 1970s' (Arrighi, 1994, p. 348).

24   Oil, the US strategic obsession, accounts for only $80 billion within the 2001 trade deficit, manufactured goods (the rest) represent $366 billion. The US industrial deficit has doubled in a little over five years since it stood at 5% in 1995. Further, swollen by fraudulent practices of private companies, the US financial sector (financial services,

insurers, and the real estate market) from 1994 to 2000 grew twice as fast as industry, 'with a "value" equal to 123 per cent of industry'. GNP figures for the US reveal less and less the real value of the economy. Todd argues that an imperial model of the Roman type does allow one to understand this process, namely as the economic consequences of a specific political and economic organization (Todd, 2003, pp. 66–67). He points out that the economic domination of a particular sphere has political and military origins, and asymmetrical principles of exchange organize the processes of globalization (Todd, 2003, p. 63). The end of the Roman republic led to the collapse of the middle classes and the beginning of the political form known as 'empire'.

25 The collapse of communism not only permitted new countries to enter into this asymmetrical system of exchange; it dramatically accelerated this dependence between 1990 and 2000 as the US trade deficit went from $100 billion to $450 billion. Today it is China that has the largest trade surplus with the US. Todd calls the US trade deficit 'an imperial levy' (see Todd, 2003, pp. 14–15, 63–71). In 2001, the US trade deficit with China was $83 billion, with Japan $68 billion, with South Korea $13 billion, to add up to a total trade deficit with these East Asian spaces of $164 billion. The US trade deficit in 2001 was $60 billion with the combined EU ($29 billion with Germany, $10 billion with France, and $13 billion with Italy). The US trade deficit with Mexico in 2001 was $30 billion! America has trade deficits with Israel ($4.5 billion), Russia ($3.5 billion), and Ukraine ($0.5 billion).

26 Harvey sees accumulation by dispossession as the ruling class alternative to internal reforms. It is the contemporary version of Marx's 'primitive accumulation', in which the ruling bourgeois classes resort to spatio-temporal fixes (backed by coercive state power) to the exhaustion of profits from accumulation along particular geographical trajectories of expanded reproduction.

27 Wall Street is the endpoint of this security seeking mechanism—$3,059 billion invested in US markets in 1990, $13,451 billion in 1998 (see Todd, 2003, pp. 79–99). The increase in stock market capitalization is grossly out of proportion to the real growth of the US economy; it represents 'a sort of inflation of the [global] rich'. 'The extraction of profits swells incomes that are then poured into the market where the relative scarcity of the "goods" (stocks) to be bought, produces increases in their nominal value' (Todd, 2003, p. 96). However, 'if Americans consume too much and the influx of capital ceases, the dollar will crash' (Todd, 2003, p. 89).

28 Todd makes illuminating analogies between imperial Rome and the imperial US. Just as imperial Rome integrated and 'globalized' the entire Mediterranean economy (from which it siphoned tribute) through its political domination of the region, the globalizing (or imperializing) American society first integrated all of the 'free world' and then, after the fall of communism, virtually the totality of the planet, from which it siphons off flows of capital. 'Increasingly the rest of the world is producing so that the US can consume'. Todd argues that the US experience of social polarization during 1970–2000 is of the Roman type; it combines the development of a plutocracy and the expansion of a plebeian class in the sense that it had during the Roman Empire. During 1994–2000 America reached the stage of 'bread and circuses', when it accelerated in the imperial direction (Todd, 2003, pp. 74, 76).

29 Mann observes that the willingness of foreign investors (including OPEC oil producers) to hold US liquid assets actually finances the military strike-power of the US (see Mann, 2003, pp. 50–51, 74–75).

30 Fukuyama's vision of the triumph of liberal democracies is partially correct, it is verified in the multiplication of democracies in Eastern Europe, the former Soviet republics, Latin America, Turkey, Iran, Indonesia, Taiwan and South Korea. Fukuyama's vision, however, does not see that the trend *progression* of democratic dynamics in 'those (poorer) places where it was weak' is accompanied by the trend *regression* of democratic dynamics in those (wealthier) places where it was formerly strong'. In 2001, the average worldwide birth rate had fallen to 2.8 children per woman, a rate that is approaching the 2.1 rate of 'zero population growth'. Todd points to the correlation between lower birth rates and political modernization by relating 'the microcosm of the family' to the 'world of politics' (Todd, 2003, p. 35). The progress in basic literacy and the increasing control over birth rates 'show humanity winning the struggle to extract itself from chronic underdevelopment' (Todd, 2003, p. 32).

31 Johnson is skeptical that control of Iraqi oil enables US domination of Europe and China, even as he notes China's negotiations for an oil pipeline from Kazakhstan to Shanghai, and its attempts to obtain oil from Russia an Angarsk (Siberia) to Daqing (Manchuria) pipeline (Johnson, 2004, p. 170). Oil interests and support for Israel dictated US expansion in the Middle East at least since 1953, and the US actively seeks oil and bases in West Africa and Central Asia. The US has plans to build a naval base in Sao Tome (Gulf of Guinea). Nigeria, Angola, and Equatorial Guinea supply 15% of US oil imports (projected to grow to 25% by 2015). In Colombia, the US protects the Occidental Petroleum's oil and gas interests (Johnson, 2004, pp. 308–311). US military bases in Central Asia (Kazakhstan, Kyrgyzstan, Uzbekistan, and Georgia), facilitate its plans to tap Turkmenistan's vast gas reserves. The Caspian Sea Basin contains 6% of global oil reserves and 40% of its natural gas reserves. Azerbaijan, Kazakhstan, and Turkmenistan have low labor costs and non-existent environmental standards. The US has plans for a 1091-mile-long oil pipeline from Baku (capital of Azerbaijan)

to Ceyhan (deep-water Turkish port)—via Azerbaijan (just north of the rebellious Armenian enclave of Nagorno-Karabakh) to Georgia's (Black Sea) port of Batumi, and then south-west through volatile Turkish Kurdistan, to Ceyhan (Johnson, 2004, pp. 168–185). For Harvey's interpretation (2003, pp.123–124).

32   Johnson notes 'the looting of workers' pension funds by CEOs, the tax cuts that favored the rich, and the crisis of civil liberties', during the 1990s (Johnson, 2004, p. 236). For Harvey this is crucially explanatory (Harvey, 2003, pp. 181–182).

33   Iraqi oil accounts for only 10% of world reserves while Saudi Arabia and the other Gulf States account for some 45% of world oil reserves.

34   As the US Empire grows, it goes to war significantly more often, wars provoke diversification of military bases, and displays of advanced weaponry become a powerful advertising medium for arms sales (cf. Johnson, 2004, pp. 236, 253, 214). US arms sales make up 44% of world arms trade (Greider: cited on p. 214). From 1997 to 2001, US arms exports were $44.82b. Russia (next largest arms exporter), sold $17.35 b. (Johnson, 2004, p. 133). New bases require more new bases to protect the ones already established, producing 'ever-tighter cycles of militarism, wars, arms sales, and base expansions'.

35   Tilly's 'ratchet-effect' explains why inflated wartime budgets fail to return to pre-war levels. In states that have not suffered great war-losses, the ratchet appears for three reasons. The growth in state power during wartime gives officials 'new capacity to extract resources, take on new activities, and defend themselves against budget cuts'. Second, 'wars either cause or reveal new problems that call for state attention'. Finally, wartime debt accumulation creates new burdens on the state (Tilly, 1992, p. 89). The US expansion of anti-terror war to incorporate a loosely defined 'axis of evil' intensified investments in homeland defense and surveillance mechanisms that largely parallel monstrously expanding balance of trade deficits.

36   Bahrain, Kuwait, and the United Arab Emirates (UAE) received advanced military equipment (missiles, helicopters, fighter planes, and bombs). Kuwait and Qatar provided the US with bases without restrictions. Turkey refused to provide bases for the Iraq attack, despite the US offer of between $16 billion and $32 billion in 2003; 90% of Turks opposed the war (see Mann, 2003, pp. 21, 219–220, 243, 245–247).

37   Johnson points to dangers arising out of the conflation of the work of the armed forces in defense of the nation, and the work of law enforcement under penal codes of the different states. The 1878 Posse Comitatus Act prevents the military from policing US citizens. 'By expanding the meaning of national security to include counterterrorism and controlling immigration, areas in which it now actively participates, the Pentagon has moved into the domestic policy businesses. The new Department of Homeland Security, created in 2003, combines many formerly civilian agencies and works closely with the Pentagon and the Northern Command' (Johnson, 2004, pp. 120–122, 285–294).

38   Further, as Frederic Lane points out, key innovating enterprises during the fifteenth and sixteenth centuries of Western European oceanic expansion 'usually combined characteristics of government with characteristics of business', in that they were simultaneously "force-using" and "profit-seeking". It was only in and through colonial exploitation that there emerged a long-run tendency toward increasing separation of the pursuit of power from the pursuit of profit (Lane, 1979, pp. 30–43). By contrast, the new militarism tends to resemble the early medieval fusion of pursuit of power with pursuit of profit, and the position of the UN itself, as Singer observes, increasingly resembles that of the medieval papacy. 'While the UN still has moral authority ... it has been forced to swerve from one financial crisis to the next and is forever negotiating with constituents who refuse to pay debts ... Like the papacy, it [the UN] too will look to contract out to private military agents' (Singer, 2003, pp. 59–60).

39   Europe needs to maintain peaceful relations with the Muslim world—which supplies it with a large percentage of its immigrants (Pakistanis, North Africans, and Turks)—in order to insure its own internal peace. The US causes destabilizing 'internal as well as international turmoil for Europe' (Todd, 2003, pp. 186–187).

40   The US experience by contrast, stems from 'a process of one-sided exploitation and expenditure of wealth it did not create'. American society is 'the recent outcome of a highly successful colonial experience' that evolved over 300 years, thanks to the importation of literate workers to a resource-rich world'. American success involved 'playing out its soils, wasting its oil, and by looking abroad for the people it needed to do its work' (Todd, 2003, p. 177).

41   For the effects of 'Anglo-Saxon capitalism' on Japanese society, see Dore's (2000) insightful study. The regular gains of the far right in a number of recent European elections (in Denmark, the Netherlands, Belgium, France, Switzerland, Italy, and Austria) testify to the strains and stresses on Europe's social fabric. It is certain that 'American-style deregulation' within the socially cohesive German and Japanese societies 'will trigger a rise of the far right'; it threatens German social cohesiveness more than 'the French republican model that combines individualism and state guarantees. In terms of social values the conflict between the US and France

is partial while the opposition between the German and American social conceptions is absolute'. The anti-Bush demonstrations in Europe drew much larger crowds in Germany than in France. European emancipation 'will owe as much to this German movement as to any French action' (Todd, 2003, pp. 180–181).

42   Harvey also notes that 'primitive accumulation that opens up a path to expanded reproduction is one thing, and accumulation by dispossession that disrupts and destroys a path already opened up is quite another'. He sees accumulation by dispossession as the 'primary contradiction'; it is also more damaging to 'long-term hopes, aspirations, and possibilities of the mass of the impoverished' compared to 'primitive accumulation' processes (see Harvey, 2003, 164). The relevance of the distinction that Harvey draws between primitive accumulation and accumulation by dispossession is somewhat unclear. Harvey argues that Marx's primitive accumulation is a recurring process, hence he substitutes Marx's concept with his accumulation by dispossession. Yet in other places it seems that, these are two different if concurrent processes in terms of their effects.

References

Arrighi, G. (1994) *The Long Twentieth Century* (New York: Verso).

Arrighi, G. & Silver, B. (1999) *Chaos and Governance in the Modern World System* (Minneapolis: University of Minnesota Press).

Chesterman, S., Ed (2001) *Civilians in War* (Boulder, CO: Lynne Rienner).

Dandeker, C. (2003) Building flexible forces for the 21st century: key challenges for the contemporary armed services, pp. 405–416 in G. Caforio (Ed) *Handbook of the Sociology of the Military* (New York: Kluwer Academic & Plenum Publishers).

Dore, R. P. (2000) *Stock Market Capitalism: Welfare Capitalism: Japan and Germany versus the Anglo-Saxons* (Oxford, & New York: Oxford University Press).

Duffield, M. (2001) *Global Governance and the New Wars: The Merging of Development and Security* (New York: Zed Books).

Fukuyama, F. (1992) *The End of History and the Last Man* (New York: Avon Books).

Hardt, M. & Negri, A. (2000) *Empire* (Cambridge, MA: Harvard University Press).

Hardt, M. & Negri, A. (2004) *Multitude* (New York: Penguin).

Harvey, D. (2003) *The New Imperialism* (New York & Oxford: Oxford University Press).

Hobsbawm, E. (1994) *The Age of Extremes* (New York: Pantheon Books).

Huntington, S. (1996) *The Clash of Civilizations and the Remaking of World Order* (New York: Touchstone Books).

Johnson, C. (2004), *The Sorrows of Empire* (New York & London: Metropolitan).

Kepel, G. (2003) *Jihad: The Trail of Political Islam* (Cambridge, MA: Harvard University Press).

Kummel, G. (2003) A soldier is a soldier is a soldier!? The military and its soldiers in an era of globalization, pp. 417–433 in G. Caforio (Ed) *Handbook of the Sociology of the Military* (New York: Kluwer Academic & Plenum Publishers).

Lane, F. C. (1979) *Profits from Power* (New York: SUNY Albany Press).

McMichael, P. (1996) *Development and Social Change* (New York: Pine Forge Press).

Mamdani, M. (2004) *Good Muslim Bad Muslim* (New York: Pantheon Books).

Mann, M. (2003) *Incoherent Empire* (New York & London: Verso).

Mertes, T., Ed (2004) *A Movement of Movements* (New York: Verso).

Polanyi, K. (1957) *The Great Transformation* (New York: Beacon Press).

Singer, P. (2003) *Corporate Warriors* (Ithaca, NY: Cornell University Press).

Tilly, C. (1992) *Coercion, Capital and European States, AD 990–1992* (Oxford: Blackwell).

Tilly, C. (2003) *Politics of Collective Violence* (New York: Cambridge University Press).

Todd, E. (1979) *The Final Fall* (New York: Karz Publishers).

Todd, E. (2003) *After the Empire: The Breakdown of the American Order*, Trans. C. J. Delogu (New York: Columbia University Press).

Index

For Product Safety Concerns and Information please contact our EU
representative GPSR@taylorandfrancis.com
Taylor & Francis Verlag GmbH, Kaufingerstraße 24, 80331 München, Germany